# The FILMS of ANTHONY QUINN

1937 publicity photo

In *Blood and Sand* (1941)

In *Ride, Vaquero!* (1953)    In *China Sky* (1945)

In *Attila* (1954)

In *Wild Is the Wind* (1957)

# The FILMS of
## ANTHONY QUINN

### ALVIN H. MARILL

The Citadel Press   Secaucus, N. J.

*To* Morris *and* Rose
— *who always cared*

First Edition
Copyright © 1975 by Alvin H. Marill
All rights reserved
Published by Citadel Press
A division of Lyle Stuart, Inc.
120 Enterprise Ave., Secaucus, N.J. 07094
In Canada: George J. McLeod Limited
73 Bathurst St., Toronto, Ont.
Manufactured in the United States of America by
Halliday Lithograph Corp., West Hanover, Mass.
Designed by William R. Meinhardt
Library of Congress catalog card number: 74-29542
ISBN 0-8095-0470-6

# Acknowledgments

Grateful acknowledgement is extended to the following supporting players (in alphabetical order):

| | |
|---|---|
| LEWIS ARCHIBALD | JUDY MARILL |
| ALAN G. BARBOUR | DOUG MCCLELLAND |
| DENNIS BELAFONTE | FRANK MCFADDEN |
| MIKE BERMAN | DAVID MCGILLIVRAY |
| GUY GIAMPAPA | LEO PACHTER |
| PIERRE GUINLE | JAMES ROBERT PARISH |
| MARALEE HASTINGS | CHARLES PHILLIPS REILLY |
| RUSS JAMISON | BOB SMITH |
| STEPHEN KLAIN | CHARLES SMITH |
| LEONARD MALTIN | MRS. PETER SMITH |

and

for the extraordinary participation of
JOHN COCCHI
as the Credit Watcher

also to the Academy of Motion Picture Arts and Sciences, the British Film Institute, Apco-Apeda, Bruco Enterprises, Movie Star News, ABC, CBS, NBC, Universal Pictures, Paramount Pictures, Warner Bros., 20th Century-Fox, RKO Pictures, Metro-Goldwyn-Mayer, United Artists, Columbia Pictures, Cinerama Releasing Corporation, National General Pictures, American-International Pictures, and Richard Feiner & Company, Inc.

and to the Staff of the Theatre Collection at The Lincoln Center Library of the Performing Arts.

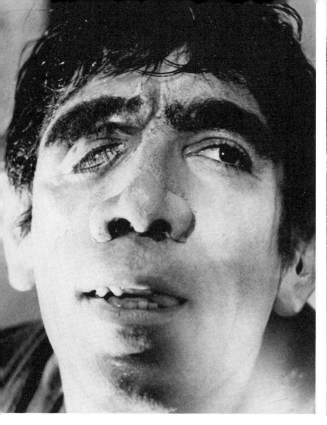

In *The Hunchback of Notre Dame* (1957)

In *Lust for Life* (1956)

# Contents

In *Barabbas* (1962)

In *The Shoes of the Fisherman* (1968)

In *Lawrence of Arabia* (1962)

In *Requiem for a Heavyweight* (1962)

In *The Visit* (1964)

In *Deaf Smith and Johnny Ears* (1973)

# Arthur Kennedy on ANTHONY QUINN

There are some people in the world who have a unique gift—a gift for creating excitement under almost any conditions. Tony Quinn is one such person. I've had the privilege of knowing Tony for more than thirty years, since we worked together in Hollywood for the first time in *City for Conquest*. I still see many of the people there —some of course have passed on because thirty years is a substantial chunk out of a man's life. You work with people, you adore them, and then you drift apart. Tony has this remarkable faculty of remaining in touch, and you know when you see him that you're still his friend. For with Tony there's an endearing quality, a fierce loyalty to his friends. Not that Tony's a paragon of virtue. He is quick-tempered, sometimes thoughtless, but I think when he discovers that, he tends to overcompensate. He has that quality. He is terribly generous although I think that the most remarkable facet of Tony Quinn is his extraordinary capacity of fulfilling every moment of every day. I doubt very much whether in his entire life he has ever been bored.

I remember when we were making *Lawrence of Arabia*. Tony was sculpting in stone or playing tennis with a pro or painting. One afternoon we were in the foothills of the Atlas Mountains in Berber country and we stopped in a little town. No one knew Tony; I don't imagine they even had a radio in this community. Then we wandered into the souk, the marketplace, and there is something about Tony that always seems to draw a crowd. I remember that there was an old blind musician playing an ancient, one-stringed instrument, and Tony began to bargain for it with him. Almost at once, nearly everybody in the marketplace had gathered around us, and Tony ended up paying fifty times what the instrument was worth. Of course, everything is for sale in that part of Morocco, and he wound up buying, I'll always remember, ancient doors, sand-blasted with traces of paint, plus brass, rugs and other things. "What the hell are you going to do with all this junk?" I asked him. Well, I found out years later that he had turned those doors into coffee tables and they were just exquisite. Tony always has been a genuine artist, in and out of acting. He has what the collector calls "the eye" and he loves to pick young artists and help them along financially or in whatever way he can.

Another time Tony and I were in Almeira in Spain, and I was thumbing through a magazine and spotted a marvelous bronze statue of a fighting bull. "Tony," I said, "now that's really a bull," and he said, "Jesus, let's find out who did it." So he called Madrid and a half hour later we were in a car headed for the artist's studio. Mind you, we were something like three or four hundred miles from Madrid. Thankfully, I wound up with the bull, but Tony came away with twenty or thirty magnificent pieces of the artist's work.

Jimmy Cagney once told me, when we were all working on *City for Conquest,* that acting styles change every seven years or so. I found it interesting because of course a particular style is probably created by some individual—outstanding or offbeat. The thing about Tony, though, is that he has gone on year after year and has probably worked more than any other actor of his generation. In the years since we first met, I've never known Tony not looking forward to something or other in the way of a characterization—and this spans a period of three decades. Now the picture business is a strange business, and we have all gone through the various upheavals, but Tony is always there. This is one of those qualities I admire enormously in him—he will never let up; he is always in there creating.

Sometimes things, I suspect, might have been a little down for him. The only period of his life when, I think, things were rather difficult was in the late forties. Tony replaced Marlon Brando as Stanley Kowalski on Broadway and, I'll never forget, he had come into this place he had rented in Westport—he had been acting with Uta Hagen and the show had taken a one-week break for Christmas. Well, he came in and told us he'd just been given a bonus of a thousand dollars. He was so delighted and pleased by the fact he had a thousand-dollar bonus, I'll never forget, but whether he's enormously successful financially or not he's still the same Tony. We had a marvelous Christmas—it was one of several I spent with Tony—and it brought home the fact to me that he is the kind of person who could enjoy himself immensely under virtually any set of circumstances. It's back once again to that capacity for living, for never being bored.

The best thing I can say to describe Tony Quinn is that he is one man who lives life to the fullest.

---

Arthur Kennedy has acted with Anthony Quinn in five films and succeeded him in the Broadway production of *Becket.*

In *The Secret of Santa Vittoria* (1969)

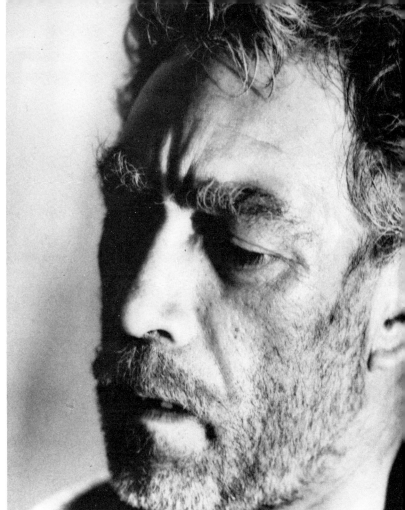

In *Zorba the Greek* (1964)

# ANTHONY QUINN:
## The Man From Chihuahua

In *The 25th Hour* (1967)

Anthony Quinn at age seventeen

# QUINN: The Man From Chihuahua

"I'll tell you something," Anthony Rudolph Oaxaca Quinn once confessed. "There is no thrill in acting that can compare with the thrill of getting up in a pulpit and preaching. You're so involved personally, to such a high point. There's *never* anything else to equal it." Quinn experienced this thrill when he was preaching for Aimee Semple McPherson at her Angelus Temple and playing the saxophone at her street-corner rallies. He was fourteen at the time. When he was sixteen, he was sparring with Primo Carnera, and at seventeen, he engaged in an

occasional duet with the legendary Chaliapin. Three years later, he was acting for Mae West and drinking with John Barrymore. These were some of the early highs for Anthony Quinn.

There also were the days picking walnuts in El Paso as a youngster, working as a farm laborer beside his parents in San Jose, running with the gangs of the Mexican slums of Los Angeles. The study of his career is the story of a man's rise from utter poverty as a disadvantaged minority youngster to international fame as

With fiancée Katherine DeMille in 1937

one of the screen's larger-than-life figures. The route was the classic Hollywood story—learning his craft by accepting even the smallest of roles while making certain the audience saw him. And it is to his credit that, in Hollywood's caste system of the thirties, he overcame his initial typecasting after grunting and glowering through dozens of villain and Indian roles, working in second-rate potboilers with a bit in an occasional "class production" thrown his way.

He was born in Chihuahua, Mexico, on April 15, 1915. His father Frank was twenty at the time; his mother Manuela, a Mexican girl with Indian blood, was seventeen. Quinn's paternal grandfather had come to America from County Cork and managed to find work on the Southern Pacific Railroad as a laborer, despite the "Men wanted—no Irish need apply" warnings. He drifted to Mexico and married a girl named Sabina, who came from a middle-class family. She grew to be an indomitable woman and a strong influence on the grandson she at first refused to accept. Their son Francisco first met Manuela when the latter turned up one day at the Quinn house to offer her services as a launderess.

Of his parents Quinn says, "My father was a dreamer who thought that Pancho Villa and his revolution had the answers. He and my mother both fought in the revolution." His mother's revolutionary activities were fairly short-lived. She became pregnant and was shipped back to Chihuahua from the front. Sabina

Quinn wanted nothing to do with Manuela and her child and moved away. Manuela tried following her, first to Juarez where she once again saw her husband and lived with him briefly, becoming pregnant again, and then to El Paso, where she gave birth to Stella Quinn (now married to Martin Goldsmith, a screenwriter).

In El Paso, she again caught up with Frank, now a railroad laborer as his father had been, living in a boxcar with his mother. Grudgingly, Sabina Quinn accepted her daughter-in-law, and the family hired out as cheap labor with the other wetbacks in the local walnut groves. They moved with the crops, as migrant workers do even today, and eventually arrived in San Jose, where five-year-old Anthony bent his back beside his grandmother picking tomatoes and melons at ten cents an hour. Not long thereafter, the Quinns found themselves in the slum section of Los Angeles, the City of Opportunity. Frank Quinn found work tending the animals at the zoo of the old Selig Studios, and later became an assistant prop man, making thirty dollars a week. In January 1936, Frank was killed in a freak auto accident, and young Tony was on his own. "You didn't live in those days," he later said, "you just tried to exist. Before I was eighteen, I had worked as a shoeshine boy, newsboy, carpenter, electrician, butcher in a slaughter house, taxi driver, cement mixer, trucker, clothes cutter, boxer, laborer. I was foreman of an apricot ranch with the Camarillo Apricot Growers Association when I was fourteen, with 150 people under me. The best job I had was foreman in a mattress factory. But the truant officer was never far behind."

For a teen-ager from the slums, Tony lived a full life. "I was fourteen when I met the most magnetic personality I was ever to encounter. Years later, when I saw the great actresses at work, I would compare them to her. As magnificent as I could find Anna Magnani, Ingrid Bergman, Laurette Taylor and Ethel Barrymore, they all fell short of that first electric shock Aimee Semple McPherson produced in me." Quinn became rather deeply involved with the Foursquare Gospel Church, popularly known as the "Holy Rollers," preaching on corners, mostly in Spanish, on the East Side of Los Angeles.

At sixteen, Tony earned some extra money—five or ten dollars per fight—as a sparring partner for Primo Carnera. The youngster was in the welterweight class and was taken on by a promoter named Pop Foster, whose stable of teen-aged boxers fought at "smokers." Quinn himself lasted through sixteen amateur bouts, but quit after being floored in the seventeenth.

Dancing provided another way of making money, because the winning cup could always be pawned or sold back to the management for five dollars. Samples of the smooth Quinn footwork can be glimpsed in his roles in *Swing High, Swing Low,* dancing with Carole

With six-month-old Christopher Anthony, who drowned two years later in W. C. Fields' swimming pool

Lombard, and with Rita Hayworth in *Blood and Sand* and Ann Sheridan in *City for Conquest,* not to mention Alan Bates in *Zorba the Greek.*

Manuela Quinn married a man named Frank Bowles when Tony was a teen-ager, and the two never warmed to each other. Tony and Stella moved in with their grandmother, while Mr. and Mrs. Bowles began a new life in another section of Los Angeles. Quinn has admitted in his autobiography, *The Original Sin,* that he has never forgiven his mother, but says "I understand why she did it. She was only twenty-six when my father died. Frank [Bowles] offered her security, and maybe she deluded herself that eventually he and I would work things out, but I never could swallow the fact that he bore the same name as my father. I swear that if his name had been George or Harry, I might have been able to accept him."

Anthony Quinn did not speak English until he was twelve—he really hadn't needed to until he went to Belvedere Junior High and later to Polytechnic High School in Los Angeles—and when he did, he discovered that he had a speech defect. "I was tongue-tied. Anyway, I had an operation on my tongue and paid for it on the installment plan. I was about eighteen, I guess, and worked in a drama school as a janitor. The teacher, Mrs. Katherine Hamill, gave me speech lessons. Then I was in a couple of plays while I was at the school. Once I did Noel Coward's *Hay Fever.* I got the part because the leading man took sick, and I was so nervous, I played the whole scene with my fly open."

Until Mrs. Hamill fired Quinn with the idea of becoming an actor, he had leaned toward a career in architecture. "The only one who gave me any hope had been Frank Lloyd Wright," Quinn recalls. "I had drawn plans for a supermarket and won first prize at school during the eleventh grade. I called up Wright's office and was able to obtain an interview." According to Quinn, the talk he had with the noted architect helped make the decision to become an actor, but not for the reason that the Quinn drawings were bad. Wright brought up the subject of Quinn's speech diffiiculties and gave the teen-ager the advice that "being a good draftsman is not enough if you want to be a great architect. You will be meeting people and influencing their lives, and you have to be able to enunciate your ideas and philosophy. They are not going to listen to you if you don't sound clipped and decisive."

Quinn therefore stayed on at Mrs. Hamill's school and joined a group called the Gateway Players, acting in things like Gorky's *The Lower Depths.* While with the group, he learned that Mae West was in the market for Latin types to play gigolos in *Clean Beds,* a new play she was producing. Quinn auditioned for (and, according to his autobiography, with) Mae West and won the role of an eccentric sixty-five-year-old ex-Shakespearean ham! The character, named Worth, allegedly was patterned after John Barrymore in the George S. George (Yovacca G. Satovsky) play about boarders in a transient roominghouse.

"We opened at the Hollytown Theater in Hollywood in early 1936 and I got ten dollars a week playing a part that was obviously a takeoff on Barrymore." Later Quinn noted, "My relationship with John Barrymore [who apparently had seen Quinn in *Clean Beds* and loved the caricature] was that of neophyte actor and his idol. He, Gene Fowler and John Decker took me under their wing, and I feel very fortunate to have been part of their original 'clan.'" Quinn's first professional notice was in Katherine T. Von Blon's *Los Angeles Times* review of *Clean Beds:* "Anthony Quinn played the actor with fine bravado and emotion." (*Clean Beds,* incidentally, finally reached Broadway, in a completely different production, in May 1939, and closed after four performances.)

While appearing in *Clean Beds,* Quinn was asked to go for an interview at Universal Pictures. He had been seen by director Lew Landers (then Louis Friedlander), who offered him a small role in the film *Paroles for Sale.*\* "I saw your play," Quinn says Landers told him, "and I thought you were wonderful. I'd love to use you in this picture. This afternoon, we're doing a sequence. It's not very much—you don't talk at all—but if you don't mind doing it, I'll tell them to give

---

\*Quinn subsequently disclosed for the first time, in a 1974 magazine interview: "I started as an extra in a picture called *The Milky Way* with Harold Lloyd and got three dollars and twenty cents a day for that."

you seventy-five dollars for it." Quinn's scene, lasting about forty-five seconds on the screen, has him in the center of a group of prisoners watching a show at the very opening of the film. "I was laughing in the middle of the show when suddenly somebody shoved a knife into my back. In the middle of the laugh, I fell and died. That's all I had to do. The director was very sweet to me and shot it as a big close-up." Quinn received fifteenth billing in a cast of less-than-box-office names (in fact, most of the minor players were better known than the two leads, Henry Hunter and Ann Preston), and the film premiered at New York's Roxy Theater in June 1936. It was the first of more than 110 Quinn screen performances in the next thirty-eight years.

Two gangster bits followed, and are usually uncredited in Anthony Quinn filmographies since he was unbilled in both: he was one of villainous Joseph Calleia's hoods in MGM's *Sworn Enemy,* a minor item starring Robert Young and Florence Rice (sportscaster Grantland's niece); and he was a torpedo for gangster Arthur Loft in RKO's *Night Waitress,* a waterfront melodrama with Margot Grahame, the English girl who had starred in *The Informer,* and Gordon Jones, former UCLA halfback. Then Quinn again was on the bum. He and a friend hopped a freight train for Texas and dug ditches on a road gang for thirty-five cents a day. The two found themselves in Ensenada, Mexico, waiting for a job on one of the fishing ships that pulled into port. "I picked up a discarded Los Angeles paper," Quinn remembered. "I read an article that said that Cecil B. DeMille was having difficulty casting a picture called *The Plainsman.* He couldn't find enough authentic Indians to play some important parts called for by the script."

The drifters hitchhiked back to Glendale where Quinn attempted to pass himself off as a full-blooded Indian who spoke Cheyenne fluently. He managed to con his way onto the lot and bluff through an audition with DeMille personally. The role, Quinn had been led to believe, was that of a young warrior inciting the Indian nation to go to war against the frontiersmen with an impassioned speech against the white man. The actor noted, "I could already see the scene—thousands of Indians on the plain, ready for the charge. I saw myself climbing very slowly up on top of a huge rock looking over my people, then beginning the speech. I saw myself slowly building, getting the rhythm of the speech—inciting the crowd, exciting them—until I finally cried, 'W-A-R-R-R!' And they would shout, 'War! War!'" What Quinn finally got was a lengthy speech in Indian gibberish after being captured by Buffalo Bill (James Ellison) and Wild Bill Hickok (Gary Cooper).

Eclipsing his on-screen performance as "a Cheyenne Indian" in *The Plainsman* was Quinn's on-the-set per-

In the early 1940s as a 20th Century-Fox contract player

formance which he suggested that DeMille was directing the scene entirely wrong. Shockwaves reverberated throughout the Paramount lot and the tale of the novice actor, doing a bit in a DeMille picture, telling the Old Man his business made Quinn an overnight legend at the studio—and undoubtedly throughout Hollywood. Here is the way Quinn tells it: "During the filming, I objected to the way I was supposed to deliver this monologue. I spoke up and said I thought I should address my remarks to Gary Cooper. The various assistants around DeMille said he should fire me, but he said, 'The boy is right,' and he let me do the part the way I thought it should be done, and then he tried to place me under personal contract to him. I turned him down."

Among those on the set during Quinn's big (and only) scene was Katherine DeMille. "I saw a girl talking to DeMille," Quinn has said. "She was dark-haired, with beautiful skin and the most piercing eyes I've ever seen. She looked part Indian, and I thought it was a good omen that I had another Indian there; I thought perhaps she was also in the picture. Apparently DeMille had been talking to her about me. She looked over my way, and I realized she was the great man's daughter."

She is one of Cecil B. DeMille's four adopted children. Born in Vancouver, British Columbia, she was the only child of artist Edward Gabriel Lester and his wife Cecile. Katherine was orphaned when her father was killed during the war and her mother died a few months later, and was seven when she came into the DeMille household. She made her screen debut in her father's production *Madam Satan* in 1930, and also appeared in his *The Crusades* in 1935 and *Unconquered* in 1947, among her nearly two dozen credits.

The word had already spread by the time Anthony Quinn had gotten his four-page Indian speech on film and DeMille had paid him for three days' work. Rapidly becoming a cause célèbre, Quinn found himself being sought out by Carole Lombard, among others. Famous herself for her outspoken ways, Lombard readily identified with the young actor who had told off DeMille. In the course of their conversation, she told Quinn that she was to start a new film the following week, that there was a marvelous part open, and that she'd call director Mitchell Leisen to get it for him. Leisen was impressed with the Lombard buildup and offered Quinn the small role of the Panamanian lothario who makes a play for Carole in *Swing High, Swing Low*—before Fred MacMurray floors him. The dialogue was in Spanish, he'd be paid $200 a day, and he'd get five or six days' work. The director then phoned Frank Tuttle, who was about to start a Crosby movie called *Waikiki Wedding*. "Sure enough," Quinn recalled, "Tuttle had heard the story of the young boy who had dared tell DeMille where to put his camera." And Tuttle gave Quinn the role of a bogus native at $200 a week for ten weeks—which was $50 a week more than DeMille had offered. In one week, the actor ended up with three roles.

While working on *Waikiki Wedding,* he again got Carole Lombard's assistance. She told him that Henry Hathaway was preparing a sea picture, *Souls at Sea,* and that George Raft had turned down the key role of Powdah, refusing to take second billing to Gary Cooper. The front office decided then to replace Raft with Lloyd Nolan, but reconsidered when Nolan's resemblance to Raft was pointed out. Quinn then tested for the role and was told he had it, so he sent his agent to discuss salary with studio head Adolph Zukor. The prolonged haggling, however, allowed enough time for Raft to withdraw his initial refusal and accept the part. Instead, Quinn was given a standard players' contract and joined Paramount's already legendary roster of outstanding character actors, which, in retrospect, gave him the seasoning needed for the long haul in films. Ironically, Quinn not only survived the Paramount "stock company" but became a bigger star than any of his fellow actors in the group.

Quinn was given a good-sized role in *The Last Train from Madrid* and at least was well cast along with Gilbert Roland in parts for Spaniards. Consider, for instance, that Dorothy Lamour and Robert Cummings also portrayed Spanish characters. *Partners in Crime,* which followed, was the first real "B" Quinn made with the well-remembered roster of players whose performances made Paramount's tightly knit, hour-long crime melodramas such delights.

The actor rapidly established himself, because of his long face, thick brow, firm jaw and menacing scowl, as one of the chief screen villains on the lot, although he later found himself boxed in by this typecasting. *Daughter of Shanghai,* his first of five films with director Robert Florey, gave Quinn his initial role in an Anna May Wong film, and the two became great friends, with Miss Wong, toward the end of her career in the 1960s, making appearances in films with Quinn, who was now a star.

Cecil B. DeMille once again used Anthony Quinn—in *The Buccaneer.* As before, Quinn hoped to get the leading role, but his youthful appearance was against him. And it was Katherine DeMille who pointed out that fact to her father. The actor instead was given the role of Beluche, a member of Jean Lafitte's crew. Two decades later, when DeMille was planning to remake the film (as a musical!), Quinn was given the director's chair after DeMille himself became too ill to make, as it turned out, the final Cecil B. DeMille production.

Anthony Quinn married Katherine DeMille on October 21, 1937. Each was twenty-two. Both had been working on separate films until six, and got together two hours later at All Saints Episcopal Church in Hollywood. Writer Jerry Asher was best man and Natalie Visart, one of DeMille's designers, was bridesmaid. DeMille himself gave the bride away, but he never really warmed to Quinn as a son-in-law. In fact, in his autobiography, DeMille makes only this single reference to Quinn: "The actor in *The Plainsman* whose association with me was to be most constant and most intimate was a young man whose part is listed in the cast only as 'Northern Cheyenne Indian.' His name is Anthony Quinn, and, as well as being a highly talented and popular star today, he is also my son-in-law, the husband of my daughter Katherine."

Quinn himself has said this of his relationship with DeMille: "I would rather not comment on it except to say that I am glad to have met him and am grateful that he was foresighted enough to adopt Katherine." Another time, this: "I think DeMille kind of thought I was an Indian from some reservation and was always terrified that the tribe would gather around his house one night for a war dance." As Quinn's angular appearance, high cheekbones and black hair prevented him from getting anything but ethnic roles for many years, so his wife's deep olive skin and straight dark hair limited her screen career, especially in the area of the all-American types so popular in the late thirties and wartime forties.

During the years immediately following his mar-

With director Robert Rossen, Dolores Del Rio and Dr. Alfonso Gaona, impresario of the Plaza Mexico, at a 1950 premiere

riage, Quinn took a fierce pride in his determination to establish himself outside of the DeMille family, and he continued his professional villainy on the screen in 1938 and 1939 in countless action-packed, well-paced gangster melodramas, primarily under the direction of Robert Florey, Louis King and Edward Dmytryk, in Harold Hurley's efficiently run "B" unit, one of Adolph Zukor's artistic prides and monetary joys. The unit, with actors like Lloyd Nolan, Anna May Wong, J. Carrol Naish, Akim Tamiroff, Lynne Overman, Larry "Buster" Crabbe, Gail Patrick, Richard Denning, and (for a short time) Robert Preston, among others, long had been noted as one of the most versatile in films. Noted "B" movie authority, Don Miller, has pointed out that Paramount, in the late 1930s, had some of the finest character players in movies on its payroll and juggled them with dexterity, casting the villains in one as heroes in the next, winning the girl in one and playing her father in the next. "Quinn," Miller thought, "was less of a utility man because of his sinister looks and would usually be the hood." Most of the films Quinn made during this time told their stories in the titles: *Tip-Off Girls, Hunted Men, Bulldog Drummond in Africa, King of Alcatraz, King of Chinatown, Island of Lost Men, Television Spy, Emergency Squad.* Usually he was a hood in J. Carrol Naish's gang, or Akim Tamiroff's, or

Lloyd Nolan's, and consistently he would be bumped off just before the boss got his.

Occasionally Paramount gave Quinn a featured spot in one of its more expensive productions. He worked for the third time with DeMille in the railroading epic, *Union Pacific,* playing a sartorially splendid henchman of gambler Brian Donlevy, and he menaced Crosby and Hope in *Road to Singapore,* the first in that comedy series, and later in *The Road to Morocco.* He also was a meanie in Hope's version of *The Ghost Breakers.*

Quinn's relationship with DeMille may or may not have been an influence on the front office at Paramount. Years later, the actor commented in an interview: "I didn't want anyone to think I was getting anything out of it [marriage to Katherine DeMille]. I didn't want them to think I was marrying into the Royal Family of Hollywood." One DeMille-associated incident points up the entire problem, as Quinn saw it. During the filming of *Union Pacific,* picnic-style lunches had been prepared for location breaks. At one of them, DeMille asked his son-in-law to join him and his associates in a reserved area of the outdoor commissary. The next day, one columnist wrote: "Now that Tony Quinn is the boss's son-in-law, he feels it beneath him to break bread with the common people on location." The item so upset Quinn that he refused to work in any further DeMille films, and he would not even consider negotiating a renewal of his player contract when it ended in 1940. The professional and social breach between Anthony Quinn and the DeMilles widened through the years, until Academy Award night in 1953, when Katherine DeMille became the only woman in motion picture history to see her husband and her father receive Oscars in a single ceremony.

Early in 1939 the Quinns had their first child, Christopher, while Tony himself continued in the Paramount stock company at a reasonably respectable weekly salary in excess of $250. The following year, Quinn's agent signed him with Warner Bros., where he took tenth billing in the Cagney film, *City for Conquest,* playing the sharpie dancer who entices Ann Sheridan into becoming his professional partner. The role was not dissimilar to the one he had portrayed shortly before in *Road to Singapore* when he was Dorothy Lamour's dancing partner. *City for Conquest* featured Elia Kazan as a gangster and introduced a young Arthur Kennedy, both of whom would have a closer association with Quinn in later years. Warners also had Anthony Quinn do his stock gangster bit in several B's and allowed him to play Chief Crazy Horse to Errol Flynn's Custer in Raoul Walsh's exciting *They Died With Their Boots On.** Quinn's Warner Bros. salary was three times as great as at Paramount.

On March 15, 1941, Anthony and Katherine Quinn were observing the social amenities with the DeMilles. Young Christopher wandered away from the gathering, crossed the street, fell into a lily pond on the estate of neighbor W. C. Fields, and drowned. Later that year, the Quinn's second child, Christina, was born, and Katherine gave birth in 1942 to another daughter, Kathleen. (Son Duncan was born in 1945 and daughter Valentina in 1952.)

Quinn was loaned to 20th Century-Fox for the Rouben Mamoulian remake of *Blood and Sand,* in which Tyrone Power played the old Rudolph Valentino role. As Power's boyhood friend and rival matador, Quinn has little to do for much of the film, until Rita Hayworth invites him to dance with her. Then Quinn, in a few, deft scenes, demonstrates why many in Hollywood were suggesting that he should consider remaking many of the Valentino films. When the subject had

come up several years earlier, recalled Quinn, "I asked Jack [Barrymore] and he told me that the critics and the old Valentino fans would tear me to pieces, and those who didn't know the famous silent film lover couldn't care less."

Returning to the Paramount lot briefly, Quinn donned his best sneers and scowls along with the studio's Arab robes and burnooses to once again menace Messrs. Crosby and Hope and leer at Mlle. Lamour in *Road to Morocco.* The Paramount stop was a side trip on his way to 20th Century-Fox, where he had signed a three-year contract. First assignment: the lavish Technicolor version of Sabatini's *The Black Swan,* Quinn's second swashbuckler and his second with Tyrone Power. Decked out this time in a curly red wig and black eye-patch, and decorated with a jagged cheek scar, Quinn looked evil enough as the blackguard Wogan, henchman to the villainous pirate Billy Leech, played to the hilt by George Sanders. Quinn's next role, though, was in the film classic, *The Ox-Bow Incident,* William Wellman's masterful psychological Western which made a topical plea for the dignity of the law. In the role of the hapless Mexican who has trouble understanding English, Quinn was superb as one of the three doomed men about to be lynched by an enraged mob.

He was next cast, again as a Mexican, in the Marine saga, *Guadalcanal Diary,* playing the fearless, lone survivor of a wartime patrol. Then, he donned Indian feathers and loincloth (again) to play Yellow Hand opposite Joel McCrea's William Cody in *Buffalo Bill,* also under William Wellman's direction. Quinn's remaining films at 20th Century-Fox were simply programmers, although *Roger Touhy, Gangster* had potential in its topical subject matter (Touhy, serving ninety-nine years in Joliet State Prison for kidnaping, had engineered a mass escape in late 1942 and had recently been recaptured). In it, Quinn again played a convict. *Ladies in Washington,* curiously billed as a comedy, dealt with foreign spies, attempted suicides, unfaithful husbands and a murder. Quinn was an enemy agent with the exotic name, Michael Romanescue, and had what could loosely be called "a romantic lead"—at least, as the publicity blurbs for the picture pointed out, Quinn received his first screen kiss! Then came two mediocre musicals, both directed by Gregory Ratoff and both starring June Haver: *Irish Eyes Are Smiling,* a Runyonesque thing produced, naturally, by Damon Runyon; and *Where Do We Go from Here?,* a "fantasy" in which Quinn turned up as the Indian chief who sold Manhattan Island to the Dutch for twenty-four dollars and change.

"I began to go from studio to studio," Quinn later said. "I have always been in the process of discovering.

---

*The film *Manpower* was not among these, although it has been included erroneously among Quinn's credits for years and is even perpetuated in *The Warner Bros. Golden Anniversary Book,* a complete filmography based on studio files. Apparently Quinn had been announced for the role of "Smiley Quinn," which subsequently was played by Barton MacLane. Curiously, *three* New York newspaper reviews credit Anthony Quinn in their cast listings for the film.

Quinn (third from right in top row) and wife Katherine (third from right in front) at a Screen Producers' Guild party for Cecil B. DeMille. Top row: Rod La Rocque, Fredric March. Ben Alexander, Richard Cromwell, Ricardo Cortez, Paul Kelly, Yul Brynner, Laraine Day, Charlton Heston, William Boyd, Lon Chaney Jr., Gary Cooper, Ward Bond, Quinn, Henry Wil-coxon and James Stewart. Front row: Jesse Lasky, Virginia Grey, Loretta Young, Julia Faye, Walter Brennan, Jane Darwell, Shannon Day, DeMille, Barbara Stanwyck, Reginald Denny, Jetta Goudal, Claudette Colbert, Raymond Hatton, Susan Hayward, Katherine DeMille, Beulah Bondi and Eddie Quillan.

That's the way it was for me then. I didn't mind playing Indians, but a lot of the other parts I was in made me unhappy. I was frequently the leading man's friend [*The Perfect Snob,* for one] or a gangster [*Irish Eyes Are Smiling,* et al]." After his stint with 20th, he signed on with RKO Pictures and did a handful of action films—the second lead with John Wayne, Randolph Scott and Douglas Fairbanks, Jr. In *China Sky,* Quinn was a Chinese guerrilla leader, and in *Back To Bataan,* a Filipino guerrilla leader. In *Sinbad the Sailor,* he popped up as an evil emir, and in *Tycoon,* a good-bad Latin type. "I felt useless," he has said. "I felt, Christ, nothing is happening to me. How long can I go on, being at one studio after another and not making it at any studio?"

The final film in what can be classified as the first phase of Anthony Quinn's movie career was the interesting, unpretentious little story entitled *Black Gold,* said to be his favorite Quinn movie and the only one in which he ever appeared with his wife. He played Charley Eagle, a gentle, friendly, uneducated Indian with an understanding, well-educated wife and an adopted Chinese son. The story is based loosely on the exploits of an American Indian who became a millionaire from oil on his lands and who endeavored to enter the white man's world by breeding and training race-horses, one of which (the film's title) won the 1924 Kentucky Derby. The independently made film was the second to be released under the Allied Artists banner when that company grew from the ashes of the old Monogram Pictures. It was not favorably received by the few critics who managed to catch up with it through poor distribution, although it stands in screen history as the first "Anthony Quinn movie."

Late in 1947 Quinn left Hollywood for a try at the Broadway stage. "Sam Wanamaker asked me to play in the production he was staging of Emmet Lavery's *The Gentleman from Athens,*" said Quinn. (Actually, the title role had been written with John Garfield in mind.) "I grabbed it. In Boston, Elliot Norton, the leading critic there, called me the greatest actor he had ever seen.* The play folded after seven performances in New York, however, and I was stuck. But I had tasted the theater. With Norton's review, I felt that all was not over. I had no money left, though. I was broke." He himself had put up $25,000 for the play in which he starred as an aggressive Greek-American from Athens, California, who gets himself elected to Congress by dubious means. Quinn's old friend from the days at

---

*Norton, writing in *The Boston Post,* said: "Mr. Quinn, who was a blanketed Injun, and sometimes a Maharajah in the movies, until he became the gentleman from Athens, California, is a wow in this show. His stage experience is very slight, but he apparently needs none. He

Warner Bros., Elia Kazan, then offered him the role of Stanley Kowalski in the national company of *A Streetcar Named Desire,* opposite Uta Hagen. Quinn and Miss Hagen began rehearsals on June 15, 1948, and then went in to sub for Jessica Tandy and Marlon Brando while the latter two took brief vacations. The national company then began its tour in Pittsburgh before settling down in Chicago for six months. Quinn continued playing Stanley on the road opposite Judith Evelyn, while Uta Hagen replaced Jessica Tandy on Broadway. Then, Quinn was brought in to swap roles with Ralph Meeker (who had replaced Brando) in August 1949.

Shortly before assuming the Stanley Kowalski role on Broadway, Quinn made his television acting debut on the Philco Playhouse in a production of *Pride's Castle,* based on Frank Yerby's best seller. Catherine McLeod and Louise Allbritton were his two leading ladies, and playing a small role in the live production was a young actor named Jack Lemmon. The remainder of Quinn's television acting during this period was three productions in 1951 and three in 1955. (Ironically, in one on CBS' *Danger* series, he was directed by Yul Brynner, whom Quinn later would direct in *The Buccaneer.*) Quinn subsequently shunned television until convinced to star as Thomas Jefferson Alcala in the series *The City* during the 1971-72 season.

Quinn continued with the *Streetcar* company, again going on the road when the Broadway run ended in December, 1949. The brief tour began in Philadelphia on the day after Christmas and concluded in Boston in March. He and Uta Hagen then recreated their starring roles in a new production of the Tennessee Williams play which was brought back to Broadway for a limited engagement in May. Unfortunately, it had been booked into the cavernous New York City Center where the actors were forced to perform at full shout. The reviews were in agreement about the high quality of the acting, not too surprising considering that all members of the company had been performing their roles, either on the road or on Broadway, for nearly two years. Robert Coleman, critic for the New York *Daily Mirror,* for one, thought that "Anthony Quinn's Stanley is the equal or superior of that created by Marlon Brando."

In August, Quinn opened off-Broadway in a second Sam Wanamaker production, *Borned in Texas,* a revival of Lynn Riggs's 1930 play, *Roadside.* In this venture, which lasted a mere five performances, Quinn (playing opposite Marsha Hunt) starred as a swaggering, earthy figure named Texas—sort of a contemporary Southwestern Zorba. Then, continuing his stage work, Quinn did a brief stock tour of *Born Yesterday* in the role of Harry Brock, the crass junk dealer tycoon.

In the spring of 1950, after concluding his *Streetcar* run, the actor resumed filmmaking following a three-year absence. "When I returned to Hollywood, my salary was way down, and I played in *The Brave Bulls* for peanuts." In the Robert Rossen film, still considered the definitive fictional screen study of bullfighting, Quinn co-starred as the manager of the brilliant matador (Mel Ferrer) who has turned coward. The role, though, was too undefined for Quinn, known for often creating something out of a nothing part, to mold a solid characterization.

Back on the East Coast, Quinn's final appearance on the stage for many years was not even seen in New York. He opened in March 1951, in Wilmington, Delaware, in S. N. Behrman's three-act comedy, *Let Me Hear the Melody.* Melvyn Douglas, a last-minute replacement for an ailing Franchot Tone, co-starred, in a cast which also included Mary Welch (Stella to Quinn's Stanley in *Streetcar* in the national company) and Cloris Leachman. Burgess Meredith staged this production about a movie producer (Quinn), his leading lady and mistress, and a novelist who is induced to write a film for her about Napoleon's sister. This one never got out of Philadelphia.

"Then," notes Quinn, "I played in *Viva Zapata* and felt, for the first time in movies, that I was doing the kind of acting I wanted. I still wasn't making much money, but I said to myself the hell with it—from now on I'm not just going to be anybody." Acting for the first and only time with Marlon Brando, Quinn played Emiliano Zapata's lecherous brother, Eufemio, and in his not overly large role, he established a bullying, blustery character to counterbalance Brando's sullen, inarticulate lead. Here were the stage's *two* Stanley Kowalskis providing a permanent screen record of two divergent yet complementary acting styles, held in check (rather than checkmate) by Elia Kazan, possibly the only director at that time who could accomplish such a task.

The Academy Award he won for his supporting performance notwithstanding, Quinn found only more of the same type of mediocre roles forthcoming that he had left Hollywood to escape in the forties. Having proved himself capable of better things, he still found

is a natural actor and if *The Gentleman from Athens* is a hit, he will take his place among the stars. No one with his force has appeared on our stages since Paul Douglas walked out of radio into the part of the high-shouldered racketeer of *Born Yesterday.* But Mr. Quinn has charm, where Mr. Douglas seemed to lack that quality. He reminds one, too, of Humphrey Bogart, as Bogart was on

the stage in the part of Duke Mantee. But Anthony is also a comedian, and Humphrey was not. . . . You freeze and then melt before Anthony Quinn. Whether he gesticulates as naturally and effectively as he does because director Sam Wanamaker taught him how to do it, or whether he comes by it instinctively, I do not know. But Stanislavski should see him!"

himself cast in insignificant and unimaginative roles, which his artistic integrity forced him to undertake wholeheartedly. There were a pair of Technicolor potboilers for Columbia, *Mask of the Avenger* and *The Brigand,* both directed by his friend Phil Karlson, with whom he had worked on *Black Gold* and who had been assistant director on Quinn's debut film, *Parole.* Quinn was the nastiest of villains in each, which boasted plenty of second-rate excitement and swordplay and a chance to vie with either John Derek or Anthony ("Valentino") Dexter for then-starlet Jody Lawrance in both films.

The five action-crammed, back-lot productions which Anthony Quinn made in 1952 and 1953 were strictly from Universal-International's competently run adventure machine which ground out Technicolor epics for leading men like Gregory Peck, Errol Flynn, Rock Hudson and Jeff Chandler. Quinn turned up as a Portuguese sailor in *The World in His Arms,* Raoul Walsh's sea saga with a curiously strong anti-Russian theme (in keeping, presumably, with the period of the anti-Red, McCarthy-inspired hysteria); a Madagascan pirate in the snappy Errol Flynn swashbuckler, *Against All Flags;* a tribal chief in *Seminole;* a diver with old Paramount stock company confrere, Robert Ryan, in *City Beneath the Sea;* and a native despot in *East of Sumatra.* The last three, however, were directed by Budd Boetticher, later to become a cult director and a good friend of Quinn.

Anthony Quinn made two more films in Hollywood before moving to Europe to begin what has come to be known as his "Italian period." At MGM, he gave an exceptional performance as a cunning, vicious Mexican bandit in John Farrow's *Ride, Vaquero!,* one of Metro's first wide-screen Westerns. Robert Taylor, Ava Gardner and Howard Keel were the stars (Quinn was billed below the title), but it was Quinn who got the notices, giving the picture its occasional moments of distinction. His role of Jose Esqueda is another which he rightly recalls with pride. And finally, he co-starred with Gary Cooper and Barbara Stanwyck (both of whom he had worked with in minor roles in DeMille films) in a small-scale contemporary Western about wildcatting in the oil fields of the Southwest. He played the oil company foreman who gets himself hurled down an oil well by his vicious wife (Stanwyck) who suddenly has eyes for Gary Cooper.

If Quinn's Hollywood career to this time was marked by his countless roles as ethnic heavies and assorted nonwhite characters, the remainder of his professional work on the screen would consist of creative interpretations of, primarily, the ugly, the unfortunate, the battered, the misunderstood. In the spring of 1953 he entered a new phase of his career, professionally and

On the set of *The Magnificent Matador*

personally, in Italy. He made five films there in eleven months and emerged as an international star of the first rank. Not that all of those films were even mediocre, though. He had a small role in a mishmash of Homer's *Ulysses,* which had been intended as Italy's first three-dimensional film and was to have been directed by the veteran German filmmaker, G. W. Pabst. By the time Quinn had signed aboard (in a part in which he is completely wasted if not quite invisible), *Ulysses* was graced with a new script by Ben Hecht, Hugh Grey and Irwin Shaw (and presumably others who demanded anonymity), a new director, Mario Camerini, and a scaled-down budget—it no longer was a 3-D project. Even leading lady Silvana Mangano, wife of co-producer Dino DiLaurentiis, had her roles cut from three to two. Originally she was to play not only Penelope (Ulysses' wife) and Circe, but also Calypso. Homer notwithstanding, Calypso was finally written out.

Next on Quinn's film schedule: a version of *Cavalleria Rusticana*. Like the Rita Hayworth-Glenn Ford *Carmen*, this was to be a dramatic, nonmusical film—and made in 3-D. Quinn maintains that he *did* sing in the film, although he is not to be heard in the version eventually released (in black and white) in the United States under the title *Fatal Desire*. Quinn has also said that "while preparing for the role of Alfio, I was introduced to a young actress named Sophia Loren and, as a matter of fact, I suggested her for the part of Santuzza. The producer, Carlo Ponti, said she wasn't the type and gave the role to May Britt." Subsequently Quinn acted in three films with Sophia Loren.

Following *Cavalleria Rusticana*, Quinn had the male lead in *Donne Proibite*, a dreary little movie about a group of prostitutes who find themselves on the street when their bordello is demolished to make way for a new housing development. One of the girls was played by Giulietta Masina, who introduced Quinn to her husband Federico Fellini. Fellini asked the American actor to look at one of his scripts, dealing with a circus strong man and the feebleminded girl he buys mostly to stooge for him. Quinn was impressed and asked to see something else Fellini had done, and the director showed him *I Vitelloni*, which he had recently completed. (Fellini's only other film was *The White Sheik*, made in 1951, although he had directed sequences in a few of those episodic gems the Italians are adept at turning out, such as *Amore in citta*. His previous credits had been scripts for several Rossellini movies, including *Open City* and *Paisan*, two of the vanguards of Italy's neo-realism movement.)

Quinn agreed to work on the film, which Fellini had entitled *La Strada*, for virtually nothing during the mornings while acting on *Donne Proibite* in the afternoons. "I took an interest of 25 per cent in the picture instead of a salary. If I had kept it in *La Strada*, which made millions, I would have been a rich man. However, my agent at the time saw the film and thought it would be a flop, so I sold my interest in it for $12,000." Quinn on Fellini: "One of the few geniuses I have ever worked with. He's a man who inspires an actor enormously and he fills you with the sense that you're playing something important. You feel when you are doing a picture with him that you are involved in some kind of a film classic."

Few disagree that Quinn's astonishing performance

Admiring his *Lust for Life* Oscar

as Zampano in *La Strada* "made" the actor internationally. Curiously, only once again in his career did Quinn work with one of the acknowledged giants among the European directors of international cinema—Michael Cacoyannis in *Zorba the Greek* a decade later. Aside from his role in the latter, Quinn's award-winning or -nominated performances were for three masters of the American film: Kazan, Minnelli and Cukor.

Quinn returned to the United States briefly in the fall of 1953 to star as Johnny McBride, an amnesiac framed for murder, in Victor Saville's sadistic *The Long Wait*, from the Mickey Spillane novel. It gave Quinn his second starring role (after *Black Gold*) although he was not yet a box-office name—*La Strada* had not yet gone into release. For the greater portion of *The Long Wait*,

Quinn wandered about with an air of incredulity and alternated scenes between relentlessly battering hood Gene Evans and being solaced by four girls, one of whom he figured might be the key to his past. Then the actor once again went to Italy to take the lead in *Attila* opposite Sophia Loren. When finally released in America three years after it had been made, *Attila* received one of those patented exploitation campaigns designed by Joseph E. Levine, the man who previously had unleashed *Hercules* in our neighborhood theaters, and we were treated to an entertainingly distorted view of the Dark Ages. Writing in *The New York Times,* critic Richard Nason felt that "The Hun, played with much grunting, snorting and shouting by Anthony Quinn, takes over Europe with what looks like little more than a large-sized posse," and he called the whole thing "pointless fudge of violence and piety." *Variety*'s "Hawk" found, on the other hand, that "Quinn makes a strong and powerful Attila."

The gulf existing between such diverse portrayals as the cruel Zampano and the blood-thirsty Attila, in virtually successive films, just about summarizes Quinn's erratic career in which lusty, fully realized characterizations, even in movie disasters, and slender roles which shamefully waste the man's acknowledged talents can exist side by side in consecutive movies. Regardless, for Quinn at least, it represented a generous amount of lire from Signores Ponti and DeLaurentiis.

Following completion of *Attila,* Quinn went to Mexico City to again work with director Budd Boetticher (fourth time) and Maureen O'Hara (third time) in a bullfighting picture (third time). In *The Magnificent Matador,* though, Anthony Quinn, now a star, had the title role.

During this period Quinn formed a production company with Kirk Douglas (no productions have been forthcoming) and another with Robert Ryan, under which they (Quinn and Ryan) would tour with readings from *Don Quixote, Macbeth,* etc., under the auspices of producer Paul Gregory. This endeavor also appears to have fallen into limbo, especially with the death of Ryan in 1973. Quinn also was reported to have turned down a $3,000,000 offer to star in a British TV series, *The Man from Lloyd's,* in favor of his own weekly show which would dramatize the story behind the world's great paintings. Once again, the project never got off the drawing board. One successful venture, announced in an article in *The New York Times* in May 1955, was Quinn's sale to MGM of an original screen story, *The Farm,* dealing with a priest's plan to convert a reformatory into a farm for wayward boys. It has yet to be filmed, with an unlikely future in view of MGM's virtually ending filmmaking as of the fall of 1973.

The gangster role, with which Quinn had virtually cornered the market at Paramount fifteen years earlier, provided the focus for the actor's return to Hollywood-style filmmaking in the violent and rather implausible *The Naked Street.* He starred as a bull-headed racketeer who, learning his younger sister (Anne Bancroft) is pregnant with killer Farley Granger's child, fixes the younger hood's release and forces him to marry his (Quinn's) sister. Several critics referred to the variation, via Quinn's role, on the sister-fixation theme which had become somewhat of a staple in the gangster films

At the Oscar ceremonies with Anna Magnani and Yul Brynner

of the thirties before being somewhat phased out during the forties and was now beginning to reappear. Indeed, the characterization created by Quinn—a combination of toughness and brotherly love as well as hatred and vengeance—elicited a degree of sympathy among viewers when he falls to his death from a rooftop while trying to elude the police.

In his succeeding film, though, Quinn played the hero, a gruff, forceful Spanish captain who leads the expedition to settle southern California in the early seventeenth century. The film, *Seven Cities of Gold,* provided a CinemaScope showcase against an adventure background for several of 20th Century-Fox's contract players, among whom Quinn was not one and was therefore not given top billing.

Vincente Minnelli then signed Quinn to play the rather poorly defined and quite brief role of Paul Gauguin in the lavish production of *Lust for Life,* the screen version of Irving Stone's best-selling novel about Vincent Van Gogh. Quinn once again worked with Kirk Douglas, who was given the lead for several reasons including his uncanny likeness to the artist's self-portrait. Of his bit as Gauguin, Quinn has often explained the conception he chose and the efforts he has made to achieve the greatest degree of realism. "It isn't true that I bend a character to fit my own ideas. I have to think myself into a part. As Gauguin, I had to do more than just carrying paintings. I had to go through the same soul-searching he did before he left his wife and children. I myself was almost forty. I had four children. Was *I* happy? Did *I* give a damn what people thought? When I found myself uncaringly walking into a French village with flowers I'd picked, I knew I had established contact with the painter." He was on screen as Gauguin for a mere six minutes, and his Oscar-winning performance ranks among the shortest on film. In accepting his Academy Award, Quinn said, in part, "At the risk of being misunderstood, I'd like to say that, for me, acting has never been a matter of competition with others. I was only competing with myself—and I thank you for letting me win the fight with myself." He also admitted that he'd play any role that is offbeat even though other actors had fatter parts.

One of those offbeat roles was in the gritty little Western, *Man from Del Rio,* and his leading role as Dave Robles remains among his all-time favorites. Quinn was an illiterate Mexican gunman who found himself thrust into the job of sheriff of a small Texas border town. When discussing the film, Quinn pointed out: "I do the inferior pictures because of what the parts demand. I did *Man from Del Rio,* for example, only because my role was a friendless outlaw with no sense of responsibility, a man full of race prejudice. I felt it was something I want to make a comment on."

Quinn's protean career continued into the weird film, *The Wild Party,* in which he was cast as Big Tom Kupfen, "ex-football player, ex-hero, ex-person," human scum who depends on animal strength to exist and satisfy his desires. And then came yet another of those offbeat, psychological Westerns which movies were following television's lead in making. The film, entitled *The Ride Back,* was strikingly similar to a TV drama, *The Long Trail,* in which Quinn had just starred. *The Ride Back* marked co-star William Conrad's debut as a

With Henry Wilcoxon, Mary Pickford and Bob Hope, helping Cecil B. De-Mille celebrate another milestone in 1957

A "Person to Person" TV visit with the Quinns: Christina, Kathleen, Valentine and Duncan with their parents in 1958

producer and was made by The Associates and Aldrich Company, although Robert Aldrich himself had no hand in the film other than as executive producer.

Quinn now entered into the period of first-rank stardom without forsaking his long-time credo of searching out unusual roles to compensate for the lack of romantic leads which twenty years in films never gave him. In Paris he undertook the challenging part of Quasimodo in Jean Delannoy's full-color, wide-screen treatment of *The Hunchback of Notre Dame*. Because RKO Pictures still retained rights to the title, the Victor Hugo tale was filmed under the title *Notre Dame de Paris*. Quinn played his Quasimodo as a more pitiful and less monstrous figure than did Lon Chaney in 1923 and Charles Laughton in 1940, while maintaining the actor's privilege of donning bizarre makeup—a twenty-five-pound hump on his back, orthopedic braces to twist his body, false nose and teeth, five-pound lead weights in his shoes, and other "monster" accouterments. It was Quinn's vigorous performance, together with Gina Lollobrigida's alluring Esmeralda, which provided the production with whatever merits it had.

For veteran director Allan Dwan, Quinn next co-starred in *The River's Edge,* playing the hero against Ray Milland's villain for a change of character, the guide forced by the murderous bank robber to lead the latter over the border into Mexico. Late in 1957, still another direction opened up in Quinn's career. Back on the Paramount lot, he was approached by his father-in-law, whose relationship with Quinn had mellowed during the 1950s. DeMille told Quinn that he was preparing to remake *The Buccaneer* as a musical with Yul

Brynner as Lafitte and that he (DeMille) was not up to directing the project. Brynner himself had been asked to direct as well as star in the film but declined. Quinn suggested that DeMille engage Budd Boetticher for the task, but the veteran producer countered with an offer that Quinn take the job. The idea of transforming the adventure story into a musical was abandoned, but what emerged was, as one critic noted, "an adventure story with the adventure removed." Quinn's propensity was to underdirect the film, taking the heart out of the action scenes and concentrating on character development and atmosphere at the expense of spectacle. If nothing else, Quinn never could be accused of reshooting the DeMille picture scene-for-scene, although he maintains that the $5,000,000 production was less an indication of what he is capable of as a director than other underlying (read "business") factors. "I wasn't even allowed in the cutting room," he had said. "I just set up the cameras and said, 'Roll 'em.' Our business is the only one in which they demand fifty times their investment, and if they don't get it, it's a flop." Quinn *was* given credit, somewhat begrudgingly by many critics, for his creative staging of his battle scenes. "I did the whole battle of New Orleans in a fog and used only thirty-five extras. That's the only place in the picture I expressed myself, and it really turned out well, I think." *The Buccaneer* was produced by DeMille's long-time associate and former leading man, Henry Wilcoxon, "under the personal supervision of Cecil B. DeMille" (as the credits read). It was to be the last film to bear the DeMille name.

In her column of October 11, 1957, Sheilah Graham headlined: "Anthony Quinn has retired as an actor."

In the interview, Quinn was quoted as saying: "After seventy movies, I've had it as an actor. I find directing more exciting, more interesting. I have two more pictures to direct after this, and it would have to be something fantastically fabulous to make me change my mind and act again." Failure is a rather potent mind-changer, and Quinn returned to acting, embarking on the finest phase of his career. In rapid succession, he co-starred in three "women's" pictures: *Wild Is the Wind,* with Anna Magnani; *Hot Spell,* with Shirley Booth; and *Black Orchid,* with Sophia Loren. George Cukor's *Wild Is the Wind* gave Quinn a leading lady as volatile as he and elevated the film from mere melodrama to first-rate sparks-flying entertainment. Academy Award winner Anna Magnani, in the second of her only three American films, received another nomination, and Quinn got his first in the Best Actor category (his two previous awards were for supporting performances). Daniel Mann's *Hot Spell* found Quinn opposite another powerful actress and playing a man who, bored with his small-town family of twenty years, runs off with a teen-aged chippie. "I feel one of the best pieces of work I have done objectively was in this picture," Quinn was quoted as saying sometime later. Martin Ritt's *Black Orchid* teamed Quinn once again with Sophia Loren during the period in which the actress was unsuccessfully being promoted into an "American" star. An unusually subdued Quinn acted the role of a widower who proposes to the widow of a gangster over the strong objections of his own grown daughter. It was grade-A soap opera, distinguished by Quinn's complex characterization.

After assembling all of the Quinns for Edward R. Murrow's "Person to Person" television visit in May 1958, the actor donned cowboy togs for a pair of Westerns, but with that word the similarity between the two ended. The first, John Sturges's vivid and exciting *Last Train from Gun Hill,* Quinn's third film with Kirk Douglas, gave him a traditional role—the cattle boss of a frontier town who learns that his son is the rapist-killer of the wife of his best friend and sheriff of a nearby town. The lines of conflict are drawn in Quinn's decision whether to allow the sheriff to take his son. The second, Edward Dmytryk's *Warlock,* was a star-laden (Richard Widmark, Henry Fonda, Dorothy Malone, et al.) curiosity for its time—a psychological Western with homosexual overtones and a blond Quinn playing a cripple who limps around after Fonda in a rather nebulous relationship. *Warlock* moved into shadowy areas that the public apparently was not yet willing to accept, especially in the conventional realm of the bread-and-butter Western, and Quinn's simmering performance as Tom Morgan, a man "hurt from the inside," went relatively unappreciated.

Then, working once again with George Cukor and Sophia Loren, Quinn co-starred in *Heller in Pink Tights,*

During a break on the set of *The Savage Innocents*

based loosely on the career of Adah Isaacs Menken, the American actress who toured the Old West. Quinn's role is that of the mumbling theatrical manager of the itinerant troupe. His exuberant performance amid the burlesqued tribulations of nineteenth-century-frontier show business (the last script written by Dudley Nichols) distinguished this curiously ignored film into which a great deal of care and first-rate talent was poured. Next, he turned his attentions to Ross Hunter's elegant soap opera, *Portrait in Black,* with Lana Turner at her most adulterous in alluring Jean Louis creations and Quinn as her rather sullen lover and family doctor. Film buffs spotted, among the suds of the lavishly produced melodrama, a touch of nostalgia in the interacting among Quinn, Lloyd Nolan and Anna May Wong, compatriots of the old Paramount stock company two decades earlier.

In the character of Inuk, the Eskimo hunter, in *The Savage Innocents,* Quinn found his most unusual role. The Nicholas Ray film focused on the primitive existence endured by the natives of Canada's extreme north during the early part of the century, and used as its microcosm one man's attempt to feed his family. The sparse dialogue was punctuated by Quinn's "pidgin English-cum-Eskimo," as *Variety* described it.

Returning to the stage once again, Anthony Quinn opened on Broadway on October 5, 1960, starring opposite Laurence Olivier in *Becket*. Quinn played King Henry II and Olivier was the prelate Thomas à Becket, who was murdered in 1170. In an interview, Quinn admitted, "Sir Laurence was one of my giants. I took him on in *Becket* and I got slapped down. But it was good for me. I grew, and I'll go on tackling giants all my life." During the run of *Becket,* in February 1961, Quinn was asked to portray Lincoln in a reading of the president's speeches before a joint session of the New Jersey legislature. When he finally left the Jean Anouilh play on March 25, Olivier assumed the role of the king and Arthur Kennedy stepped into the title part. Quinn's departure was the result of Sam Spiegel's having bought his contract so that the actor might appear as the hawk-nosed tribal chieftan, Auda Abu Tayi, in the spectacle, *Lawrence of Arabia*. After filming the few scenes of his brief role in *Lawrence,* Quinn went to Greece to work on Carl Foreman's stirring adventure classic, *The Guns of Navarone,* injecting into the role of the guerrilla leader, Andrea Stravos, at least a modicum of whatever depth was allowed at the expense of pace and action. Some of Quinn's salary for this film went toward the purchase of a large chunk of the isle of Rhodes (two harbors and an isthmus), which he added to the real estate holdings he already had accumulated in Italy, France and on both coasts of the United States.

Next, it was off to Rome for the starring role in *Barabbas,* the biblical spectacular which Christopher Fry and others had fashioned from Pär Lagerkvist's Nobel Prize-winning novel, filmed previously by Swedish director Alf Sjöberg. The Dino De Laurentiis Tech-nirama 70 spectacular collapsed on the screen under its $10,000,000 budget and its 30,000 extras. Quinn himself acted properly confused as the man whose life was spared when Christ died. While working on the film, the actor became acquainted with Jolanda Addolori, one of the production's wardrobe assistants. The following March, tabloid newspapers headlined: "Anthony Quinn Admits Love Child." The twenty-seven-year-old Miss Addolori had given birth to a son, and Quinn arranged to give the boy his name and to have him baptized at the Basilica of St. Peter in Rome, naming him Francesco Daniele Quinn. The actor made the following statement: "The boy is my son and I am going to acknowledge him. I am not concerned with what people will think as much as with what is good for the boy. I want him to be loved—not to have to go to a psychiatrist at the age of forty-one because he wasn't wanted. I am not flaunting what I have done, and I'm not doing anything for anyone's approval, but I'm not giving in to hypocrisy. I want him to have my name. He will have the same love and attention as all my other children."

Following *Barabbas,* Quinn returned to the United States to star in the film version of Rod Serling's memorable television play, *Requiem for a Heavyweight,* masterfully creating one of his most outstanding characterizations as the washed-up fighter, Mountain Rivera. Several stories have emerged from the set of that film about the difficulties in working with Quinn, and director Ralph Nelson has expressed his feelings in these words: "Tony has great selfishness as a performer. He thinks how a scene can best serve him. Of course, when he's good, he's brilliant, but he just makes it hard for everyone around him." In discussing his own performance in *Requiem,* Quinn has had this to say: "My

At a rehearsal for *Becket* in 1960 with director Peter Glenville, Hilary Beckett producer David Merrick and Laurence Olivier

With Jordan's King Hussein on the set
of *Lawrence of Arabia*

kind of method actor is much more interested in content
than the nonmethod actor. He is a sort of virtuoso who
does his bit and doesn't give a damn if everything is
crumbling about him. I'm concerned with the total comment of the play. Each scene is a piece of the mosaic.
The atmosphere [of *Requiem*], for instance, should be
like a boxing match. It should have the smell of leather
and sweat. Figuratively, it should never get out of the
ring. Once you step out of that atmosphere, it's jarring."

*Barabbas* and *Requiem for a Heavyweight* were
released within days of each other, and the critics had a
field day comparing the actor's performances. The
review in *The New Yorker* said: "Quinn looks like one
of the greatest actors on earth in *Requiem*." Most
knowledgable critics predicted an Oscar for Quinn's
performance as Mountain Rivera, but he failed to receive a nomination. With two films showing concur-
rently in New York and *Lawrence of Arabia* still in the
can, Anthony Quinn then undertook another Broadway
assignment. Co-starring with Margaret Leighton, he

opened on October 25, 1962, in *Tchin-Tchin,* originally
a French avant-garde drama which Sidney Michaels re-
vamped into a wry "American" comedy. Despite Peter
Glenville's sound direction, Quinn complained at the
time that he was unable to find the character he was
playing (a cuckold who takes up with the wife of his
own wife's lover). "When I understand a character," he
told an interviewer, I *become* the character. But for me
this fellow doesn't exist." It was reported that Quinn's
interpretation of Caesario Grimaldi varied from night to
night, from low comedy to dour drama, and that for
weeks he brooded whether to heighten the role's depth
by shaving off his moustache—which he finally did. The
two leads left *Tchin-Tchin* the following April, and the
play continued another four weeks with Jack Klugman
and Arlene Francis in the starring roles.

Michael Cacoyannis, the Greek director, approached
Quinn during the run of *Tchin-Tchin* about filming the
brilliant Nikos Kazantzakis novel *Zorba the Greek,*
which had been kicking around various movie studios

for several years. "Nobody wanted to do it," Quinn recalls. "Burl Ives turned it down. So did Burt Lancaster. They said, 'Who cares about an old man making love to a broken-down old broad?'" With a commitment from Quinn, Cacoyannis went to Paris and bought the book. "We were all in on percentages. We had a small budget, a shoestring. I didn't get a salary or a living allowance, I got a big percentage instead." Quinn's cut is believed to have been one-third.

Shortly before shooting was to begin on Crete, United Artists, which was backing the project, suddenly cut off the budget at $400,000. Quinn remembers: "Michael was nearly in tears. We told United Artists we couldn't make it for less than $750,000. They pulled out. That night, I called Darryl Zanuck and told him how much I needed. He said, 'You've got it!' He didn't even ask to read the script." In the role of the lusty old Greek who insinuates himself into the confidence and companionship of a young British writer whom he teaches to "live" (Quinn feels "Zorba represents the 'life force' that George Bernard Shaw wrote about"), he gave one of the towering performances of the screen, although he admits regretting that the Zorba role tends to overshadow not only his Oscar-winning performances as Eufemio Zapata and Paul Gauguin to say nothing of the roles he has undertaken in the decade since *Zorba the Greek*.

Before audiences saw Quinn in his masterful interpretation of Alexis Zorba (or "Epidemic," as Zorba calls himself, "because everywhere I go people say I louse things up"), they were treated to his bravado performance as Auda in *Lawrence of Arabia*—he was paid $400,000, reportedly, for his brief role—which finally finished editing and went into release in December 1962. He also costarred in *Behold a Pale Horse,* the Fred Zinnemann film made in the Pyrennes, and *The Visit,* which he (Quinn) co-produced. In the former, he's the Falangist police chief who tricks the guerrilla leader, his archenemy for fifteen years, into coming out of hiding across the French border. In the latter, he's the object of the revenge of the world's richest woman whom he had once disgraced. (The Lunts had played the roles on Broadway.) And just prior to beginning work on *Zorba,* Quinn did a cameo in the international co-production *La Fabuleuse Aventure de Marco Polo,* playing a philosophical Kublai Khan. "I was originally scheduled to play a three-minute vignette in the picture (seen in America as *Marco the Magnificent* several years later). Unfortunately, it stretched out to a sequence that I felt was out of keeping with the picture."

In April 1964 Jolanda Addolori gave birth to a second son by Quinn, Daniele Antonio. Quinn bought an Italian villa and placed it in his children's name. *"All my children,"* he has insisted. He has filled the house

A warm greeting for fellow Paramount contract player Robert Preston (bald for his role in *Ben Franklin in Paris*)

with antiques, books (in the thousands) and paintings— Renoir's, Degas's and Quinn's. The villa was an addition to his real estate holdings, which included a house which he designed in Ojai, California. ("Remember, I wanted to be an architect.") On January 21, 1965, after more than twenty-seven years of marriage to Katherine DeMille, they were divorced in Juarez, Mexico, on ground of mutual incompatability. The actor then flew back to the location of his current film project, *A High Wind in Jamaica,* his first swashbuckler since *Against All Flags.* In *High Wind,* Quinn and fellow pirate James Coburn sack a ship and find themselves baby-sitting for a group of children. The picture was summarily dismissed by the critics, who did not think the Quinn film which followed, *Lost Command,* dealing with the French Army's problems in Algeria after its defeat in Vietnam, was any better.

Quinn married Jolanda shortly after Christmas 1965 at his agent's house, with John Cassavetes as best man. At the time, Jolanda was again pregnant. (Their son Lawrence Alexander was born in Italy the following May.) The Quinns wintered in Florida where the Sam Spiegel production, *The Happening,* was being filmed. Quinn's role in this disjointed serio-comedy is that of a retired Mafioso who is accidentally kidnaped by a group of beach bums (and Faye Dunaway) and discovers that nobody will pay the ransom for his release. At the time, Quinn spoke of the character of Roc Delmonico as "a man who's acquired all the status symbols and suddenly loses them all when he's pitched into an impossible situation with these crazy kids. It's an immense and modern theme—the emptiness of loneliness."

While Quinn was working on *The Happening*, he told an interviewer that he was writing a script called *Great Guns* in which he planned to co-star with the Mexican actor Cantinflas. "It's a shame," Quinn has admitted, "that Cantinflas, who's been the greatest guy in movies in most countries, has never been accepted in the United States, and I, an American born in Mexico, have been accepted almost everywhere but in Mexico." The premise of the comedy set below the border just before the 1910 Revolution: Quinn would be seen as a bandit, who would like to settle down to peaceful old age, and Cantinflas would play a mild-mannered milkman with dreams of leading an adventurous life. This mismatched pair shares views and philosophies when thrown together in a gun-running operation. *Great Guns* has yet to be filmed. Similarly, another proposed Quinn project, *Ceferino Namuncura*, also announced during this period, appears to have collapsed. The story had to do with a South American Indian who was made a saint during the latter part of the nineteenth century.

The (second) Quinn clan then began hopscotching the world for various screen projects assembled by production companies of one or more countries. First, there was location shooting in France and Yugoslavia on the ambitious *The 25th Hour*, from the novel by the Rumanian author C. Virgil Gheorghiu, with Quinn starring as a peasant who is successively belabored by Rumanian fascists, German Nazis, Russian Communists and American bureaucrats. Most critics were confused by the proceedings, although Judith Crist called Quinn's performance a "magnificent portrayal." Quinn himself apparently had been confused when originally handed the script, since he told an interviewer, prior to the filming, "It's not a spy story, it's a comedy (!) and I'm excited about it because John Barrymore told me that an actor was lucky to get one comedy in every five parts and here I am with two in a row."

Italy was the next stop for Quinn, where he was given the title role in *The Rover*, the Joseph Conrad tale of an aging pirate bent on breaking the British navy's blockade of Napoleonic France. The film reunited him with Rita Hayworth, his tango partner from *Blood and Sand* more than twenty-five years before. In Mexico, Quinn then undertook the role of folk hero-patriot Leon Alastray in *Guns for San Sebastian*, but even Quinn's colorful performance as the rebel who helps save a Mexican village from being wiped out by Yaqui Indians was not able to give this French-made (in English) adventure film the boost it needed. On Majorca, Quinn became involved in *The Magus*, playing a Greek psychic named Maurice Conchis, a shadowy role in an ambiguous film on which a great deal of production and artistic talent worked in vain.

Anthony Quinn then went to Rome to become pope. An actor gets the opportunity to play the pope about as often as he does to impersonate an Eskimo, let alone Attila the Hun, Paul Gauguin and the hunchback of Notre Dame. No character actor-star can boast of Quinn's range of characterizations. Readying himself for the role of the Russian political prisoner who finds himself elevated to the papacy, the first non-Italian to hold the office in modern times, Quinn began having mixed emotions. "I was in great conflict with myself. I literally went through a psychosomatic experience and

With Ingrid Bergman in Rome to receive the Golden Trapeze Award in 1963

was in the hospital for three weeks. I finally went to director Michael Anderson and asked him, 'How in hell do you play a saint?' He told me, 'A saint is a man who is only competing with God, never his fellow man.' "

For *The Shoes of the Fisherman,* Rome's Cinecitta Studios were converted into the Vatican chambers and religious ceremonies were meticulously recreated. Anthony Quinn himself was properly somber as Pope Kiril, although some of the things the scriptwriters required of him appear to have been questionable. "In considering Pope Kiril, I thought, among other things, of how he'd been working in the Siberian mines and how he would look, dressed in white, in a color film. That white cassock could have made a heavy me look like an elephant, and I had to go way down for that one. When I act, I feel the character's weight is important to me. Don't ask me why, but when I played Kiril, I thought he should weigh 187 pounds, and in playing the pope, I learned the tremendous importance of mind over matter, of trying to be something I wasn't. I became completely subjective. There was even an enormous change in me physically."

Despite Quinn's earnest performance (one critic sarcastically called it just "a series of pious poses and half-smiles") at the head of a large, top-drawer cast of supporting players and "guest stars," including Laurence Olivier as the Russian premier, and despite the technical expertise which went into the lavishly produced film, *The Shoes of the Fisherman* became a box-office disaster, a bitter blow to Metro-Goldwyn-Mayer and an ominous sign of that company's subsequent problems.

The extremes between pious Pope Kiril and bumbling Italo Bombolini are examples of the challenging roles Quinn has accepted with particular relish since the mid-fifties. In Stanley Kramer's *The Secret of Santa Vittoria,* a filthy undershirt, baggy trousers and heavy shoes supplanted the papal cassocks and birettas, and piety gave way to buffoonery with Quinn playing the slovenly mayor of a tiny Italian town who devises a scheme to hide from a Nazi regiment a million bottles of wine—the town's lifeblood. He played Bombolini with a gusto which had been virtually submerged since his Zorba of several years earlier, and undoubtedly the casting of Anna Magnani as his long-suffering wife (actually only a small part in the Robert Crichton novel) was an added incentive. Their bombastic battles as Italo and Rosa provided the core of the film's human relationships among the proud villagers, capturing in the broadest terms the life of a people accidentally caught up in a war. "I've known many Bombolinis in Italy," Quinn said. "The whole key to his character is he has to fool everybody. I've lived in Italy many years, and I know the Italian people well. They seldom give you a straight answer, and I don't mean that as a put-down. It's part

In 1965 with Jolanda Addolori and their sons, Francesco and Daniele

of their charm and the secret of their phenomenal ability to survive. They never commit themselves; they go along with whatever they think you want them to do. That's why they've lost every war—but won every peace."

In 1969 Quinn returned to filmmaking in the United States, where he worked on six of his next seven motion pictures beginning with Daniel Mann's *A Dream of Kings,* shot in Chicago. As the expansive, good-hearted, basically dull-witted Greek-American neighborhood marriage counselor, Matsoukas, Quinn inevitably received critical notices unfavorably comparing this characterization to his Zorba, a comparison, in fact, which found its way into virtually every critique of Quinn's work since that original film creation. The Zorba reference even materialized in reviews of Quinn's next film, *A Walk in the Spring Rain,* in which he again co-starred with Ingrid Bergman. Filmed in the Great Smoky Mountains of Tennessee, it was an idyll of a lusty mountain man and a sophisticated, urban married woman, but notices concerning this romantic drama stressed the point that Quinn plays "a hillbilly Zorba who keeps squirrels in his pockets and spends his nights nursing baby goats."

After making an appearance in *King: A Filmed Record . . . Montgomery to Memphis,* the documentary about Dr. Martin Luther King, Quinn was talked into following fellow actors Richard Burton, Cary Grant and Bette Davis, among others, into recording studios, and what emerged was the Capitol Records album entitled "In My Own Way . . . I Love You," with Quinn reciting romantic lyrics to the accompaniment of a large chorus and orchestra. Surprisingly, the album became a bestseller in Europe, although it remains nothing more than

At another Oscar ceremony, Lila Kedrova pauses to kiss Quinn before accepting her *Zorba the Greek* Academy Award as Best Supporting Actress

a collector's item in the United States.

Quinn's first Chicano role (the contemporary term given to Mexican-Americans) since *Guadalcanal Diary* came in Stanley Kramer's sociologically oriented film, *R.P.M.*, a campus crisis melodrama which came at the tail end of the screen's cycle of "revolutionary" studies. Quinn plays a popular professor who is thrust into the presidency of a West Coast college to replace the man who left under student fire. The film, virtually a nonstop series of nonviolent confrontations (until a little, quite sterile, head-splitting at the climax), provided little for Quinn to do beyond philosophize with student leaders, black activists and college trustees—and occasionally bed down with Ann-Margret, whose role was completely extraneous. Erich Segal's unsubtle screenplay and Kramer's dull direction undermined whatever creativity Quinn injected into his performance as Paco Perez, the forerunner of a series of Quinn-created concerned screen liberals.

Equally as pretentious as *R.P.M.* was *Flap,* a tragicomedy about an American Indian who foments a contemporary uprising to assert the rights of his people. Quinn was stung by the criticism about his performance as the boozing, wenching Flapping Eagle (*Variety* called it "simply an Indian reprise of his Italo Bombolino"). Most of the complaints came in the form of questions about how this "study" could be helpful to anybody's understanding of the American Indian, even in the light of the protests which forced a title change from Clair Huffaker's original novel, *Nobody Loves a Drunken Indian.* Other complaints were about the choice of the distinguished British director, Sir Carol Reed, who, as it turned out, was as right for this picture as was George Sidney to direct *Half a Sixpence.* Quinn admitted while on location that "it's like a goodbye to my youth with this character. Flap is probably the last young man I'll ever play. I'd say he's in his middle thirties, although emotionally he's only twenty."

In September 1970 Quinn returned to television for the first time (except for an occasional talk show appearance to plug a film) in fifteen years, co-starring with Peggy Lee in a "two-man" variety show called "Mr. Anthony Quinn and Miss Peggy Lee." Quinn sang, danced, told jokes, engaged in light banter, and recreated, with Peggy Lee, a scene from *Requiem for a Heavyweight.*

The following January, Quinn began work in Albuquerque on a two-hour telefeature, *The City,* playing another (this time somewhat more valid) Chicano, Thomas Jefferson Alcala. As the mayor of a Southwestern city, described in the publicity blurbs as "the dedicated public official who has been in power sixteen years fighting encroaching computerized living," he overpowered the story with his larger-than-life image. Kay Gardella, television critic for the New York *Daily News,* called him "the kind of strong, masterful person TV needs today."

*The City* became the pilot for Quinn's first TV series during the 1971-72 season, which boasted a stampede of other film stars (James Garner, Shirley MacLaine, James Stewart, Tony Curtis, Glenn Ford) and concentrated more on the personality than on program content. Cleveland Amory, writing in *TV Guide,* felt that "the man who may well be the *best* of the lot is Anthony Quinn. A bull in a china shop even in films, in a TV series he seems even bigger." Noting that Quinn was forced to carry the entire hour-long episodes, critic Amory concluded: "He plays it like Zorba the Quinn. He goes into his part like a river barge and before you know it he has carried you upstream against all obstacles." His Thomas Jefferson Alcala was not a mayor, many critics noted, but a social worker—rumpled, energetic, but *too* involved in the lives of the people. Quinn simply overwhelmed the project with a sort of overkill. "The Man and the City" was cancelled after thirteen weeks.

Shortly after its premiere in September, Quinn did a ninety-minute dialogue with Dick Cavett on Cavett's late-night television program. Using "The Man and the City" as a promotional jumping-off point, Quinn and Cavett began ranging over the actor's long career, and during the course of the discussion, Quinn spoke of plans to produce and star in a film about Henri Christophe, the legendary black Haitian emperor. The film,

With his bride Jolanda at their January, 1966 wedding

Holly. Her article was in the form of a letter to the actor and ran under the headline "Black History Does Not Need Anthony Quinn." She maintained that it is "unthinkable to countenance Anthony Quinn in the role of Christophe" and that "all one asks is that you [Quinn] show a decent regard for the sensibilities and emotional needs of the black community and relinquish the title role to a black actor." Below the Holly letter the *Times* printed Quinn's reply, which began "I detest the vulgarity of the headline in *Variety*. If I pay heed to the people who are trying to keep me from playing Henri Christophe, it's next headline will be 'Blacks Nix Flick With Mex' and that would be really deplorable." He went on to ask Ms. Holly: "Why do you want to relegate me to playing Mexican bandits and redskins who bite the dust? Why can I not play a pope, or an Eskimo, an Indian, a Greek, an Italian—any part where I can make a statement about my life and times? I know the dangerous terrain I'm invading. I have all the qualms any artist has before a blank piece of canvas. It's more fearful than facing a bull in the ring."

On the demise in January 1972 of his abortive TV series, Quinn was more philosophical than bitter. "I thought it was a damned good thing I was trying to do. We've come into a cynical age when nobody buys that anymore. I don't think you can look around the world and say it's not cynical. And whose fault is it? That's the trouble with our kids. You teach them good and they see we don't practice what we preach. Everything's cynicism."

The first four films Quinn made after his excursion into television captured the various movie genres which were in vogue during the late sixties and early seventies: cop-black exploitation orgies, spaghetti Westerns, Mafia pictures and dope-smuggling stories. In the spring of

entitled *Black Majesty,* long had been one of Quinn's projected enterprises, but the casual mention on the Cavett show prompted a probably-not-unexpected backlash which began with a *Variety* article headlined "Filming in Haiti: Quinn Blacks Up" and continued in a lengthy *New York Times* Sunday piece by writer Ellen

A spot of relaxation between scenes for *Guns for San Sebastian*

A preproduction reunion with Laurence Olivier before starting *The Shoes of the Fisherman*

the cast), perhaps because his character was not clearly defined. In addition, he and co-star Yaphet Kotto, despite their billing, had only subsidiary roles, and much was made in critical circles of the fact that an actor of Quinn's stature would become involved with a script so patently racist and a project so extremely violent.

Later in the year, he mimed his way through an Italian Western called *Los Amigos (Deaf Smith and Johnny Ears* in this country), giving what has become the archetypal, expansive Quinn performance—here without words. Then, as many of his acting contemporaries were doing (among them Kirk Douglas, Marlon Brando, Lee J. Cobb, Arthur Kennedy), Quinn gave his godfather interpretation as the aging capo in *The Don Is Dead,* and in early 1974, he undertook the role of the tough bureau chief of the narcotics division working out of the U.S. embassy in Paris in *The Destructors.* Adding to his wide-ranging portrait gallery of roles is that of Julius Caesar in *The Assassination of Julius Caesar,* filmed in late 1972 in Rome for Mexican television.

Anthony Quinn concedes that he works hard for the money. When asked why, a few years ago, he com-

1972, Quinn went to Harlem to produce and star in *Across 110th Street,* based on the Wally Ferris novel. Playing the police precinct commander on the take for years, Quinn turned in a rather subdued performance (compared with the bravura acting of several others in

With sons Daniele and Lorenzo on set of *The Secret of Santa Vittoria* in 1968

Quinn in the 1970s

mented, "Hell, Marlon Brando asked me the same question. I said, 'Marlon, when you buy shoes, you buy one pair. When I buy shoes, I buy eighteen.' " Besides his moviemaking, Quinn's world revolves around his family. "I love children," he is fond of saying. "It was one of the problems with my first wife, whom I adored and still do. When our children were grown, she retired as a mother. But the house was too neat, clean and quiet for me. I said let's adopt some kids, but she wouldn't. Today, I come home and hear 'Daddy, Daddy!' and it's

wonderful. I love making movies, but they don't satisfy me completely. That's why I also write, sculpt and paint. I have my families. It's not working too hard. It's the spirit of man to keep looking for the whys. I'm really rather satisfied."

The skinny kid who shined shoes for pennies on the East Side of Los Angeles and grew up to become an internationally recognized movie star lusts after life as voraciously off the screen as he has done on it. That, on the bottom line, is the essence of Anthony Quinn.

# The FILMS of ANTHONY QUINN

With Alan Baxter (center)

# Parole!

Universal / 1936

CAST: *Russ Whelan,* HENRY HUNTER; *Frances Crawford,* ANN PRESTON; *Richard K. Mallard,* Alan Dinehart; *Bobby Freeman,* Noah Beery Jr.; *Marty Crawford,* Grant Mitchell; *Percy "Okay" Smith,* Alan Baxter; *John Borchard,* Alan Hale; *Joyce Daniels,* Bernadene Hayes; *Rex Gavin,* Berton Churchill; *John J. Driscoll,* Jonathan Hale; *Governor,* John Miltern; *Earl Bigbee,* Selmer Jackson; *Reporter Gregory,* Clifford Jones (Philip Trent); *Dummy Watts,* Frank Mills; *Zingo Browning,* Anthony Quinn; *Warden,* Wallis Clark; *District Attorney,* Edward Keane; *Parole Chairman,* Douglas Wood; *John,* Christian Rub; *Police Chief,* John Kennedy; *Patton,* Frank McGlynn Sr.; *State's Attorney,* Landers Stevens; *Molly Smith,* Zeffie Tilbury; *Parole Board Member Williams,* Stanley Andrews; *Carmody,* Tom Moore; *Special Prosecutor,* Arthur Loft; *Salvatore Arriolo,* William (Billy) Gilbert; *Police Lieutenant,* Guy Usher; *Personnel Manager,* Walter Miller; *Board Chairman,* Thomas Curran; *Psychiatrist,* Ed Reinoch; *Secretary,* Arnold Gray; *Dr. Arthur Carroll,* Harry C. Bradley.

CREDITS: *Director,* Louis Friedlander (Lew Landers); *associate producer,* Robert Presnell; *screenplay,* Kubec Glasmon, Joel Sayre and Horace McCoy; *story,* Kubec Glasmon and Joel Sayre; *assistant director,* Phil Karlstein (Phil Karlson); *camera,* George Robinson; *editor,* Philip Cahn. Running time: 67 minutes.

Making his film debut in a forty-five-second walk-on, Anthony Quinn was seen at the very beginning of the familiar proceedings as Zingo Browning, one of the convicts. His own description of his role, told in a brief two sentences, takes nearly as much time to relate as the part itself: "I was a prisoner in a jail scene right after the opening credits. I was shown laughing, and then I got knifed." *Parole,* sometimes referred to as *Paroles for Sale,* was one of the last directorial efforts of Louis Friedlander before he became Lew Landers, one of the "B" picture workhorse directors at RKO and later at Columbia. His assistant on the film was Philip Karlstein, who later, as Phil Karlson, directed Quinn in a number of properties.

As one of the countless "exposés" of parole system abuses—an expedient plot device and movie staple of the late 1930s, the fast-moving little melodrama was promoted by Universal with the advertising campaign line: "A welcher on society—should he be given a sporting chance?" The welcher was Russ Whelan (Henry Hunter), a young attorney convicted of manslaughter in an auto accident and about to be returned to society. His parole is nearly torpedoed by the murder of stool pigeon Zingo Browning (Quinn) while seated at a prison show near Russ, hard-boiled "Okay" Smith (Alan Baxter), and Russ's cellmate, Marty Crawford (Grant Mitchell), a former lawyer serving time for jury bribing. Russ's parole goes through, but Marty's is delayed on the grounds that he can identify Zingo's killer. Marty, however, arranges for his daughter Frances (Ann Preston) to help Russ get situated on the outside.

Russ reluctantly accepts a job from Okay whose own parole came through dubious channels, and he soon finds himself involved in several shady deals with crooked businessman, Richard Mallard (Alan Dinehart). Realizing his parole will be revoked if his association with Mallard is discovered, Russ tries to quit but is warned by Okay that he'll be implicated in Zingo's murder and returned to prison. With Frances's help, Russ searches for a way to extricate himself from the mess and finds an unexpected ally in Mallard's secretary, Joyce Daniels (Bernadene Hayes), who has fallen for Russ. She turns over to the district attorney (Edward Keane) records implicating her boss in various illegal deals and in parole board manipulations, and through them, Okay's involvement in Zingo's murder. For her efforts, Joyce is murdered by Mallard's henchmen before the police have a chance to round up the gang. Russ is commended and his pardon signed, allowing him to marry Frances and resume his law career with his recently paroled father-in-law.

[ 39 ]

# Sworn Enemy

Metro-Goldwyn-Mayer  /  1936

CAST: *Hank Sherman,* ROBERT YOUNG; *Margaret Gattle,* FLORENCE RICE; *Joe Emerald,* Joseph Calleia; *Dr. Simon Gattle,* Lewis Stone; *Steamer Krupp,* Nat Pendleton; *District Attorney Paul Scott,* Harvey Stephens; *Eli Decker,* Samuel S. Hinds; *Dutch McTurk,* Edward Pawley; *Lang,* John Wray; *Simmons,* Cy Kendall; *Steve Sherman,* Leslie Fenton; *Kreel,* William Orlamond; *Hinkle,* Robert Gleckler; *Greek,* George Regas; *Al,* Duke York; *Landlady,* Lillian Harmer; *Gibbons,* King Mojave; *Gangsters,* Guy Kingsford, Wallace Gregory, Ed Hart and Anthony Quinn; *Lunchstand Man,* George Chandler; *Nick,* Harry Tyler; *Cop,* Jack Daley; *Fight Announcer,* Charley Keppen; *Guard,* George Guhl; *Morris,* Al Hill; *Bergen,* Norman Ainsley; *Policemen,* Tom Mahoney and Robert E. Homans.

CREDITS: *Director,* Edwin L. Marin; *producer,* Lucien Hubbard; *screenplay,* Wells Root; *story,* Richard Wormser; *music,* Edward Ward; *art director,* Frederic

Quinn in center with moustache, and Joseph Calleia (left)

With Joseph Calleia (third left) and Nat Pendleton (center)

Hope; *camera,* Lester White; *editor,* Frank Hull. Running time: 72 minutes.

Quinn's fleeting scene as Zingo Browning in his film debut was a starring role compared to his assignment in this crime melodrama out of MGM's efficient "B" unit. Unlisted in the cast (but spotted by redoubtable film historian and eagle-eyed credit watcher, John Cocchi), Quinn once again had a bit as a gangster, working for crippled crime czar, Joe Emerald (Joseph Calleia).

Robert Young provides the heroics in this smartly paced programmer, as Hank Sherman, chauffeur for local bigwig Eli Decker (Samuel S. Hinds). When Decker is gunned down by gangsters and Hank's brother, Steve (Leslie Fenton), a boxing promoter, is gravely wounded, Hank vows to track down the killers and expose the head man in the local rackets, ably assisted by Decker's secretary, Margaret Gattle (Florence Rice). After being sworn in as a special investigator by the district attorney (Harvey Stephens), Hank is assigned the task of getting enough evidence to incriminate Joe Emerald. (Ed. note: the spare running time in films of this genre allowed for few expository scenes,

such as the hero's qualifications for the job.) Hank takes over his brother's management of boxer Steamer Krupp (Nat Pendleton) and soon makes contact with the rackets boss, who has had an appreciative eye on the fighter. Introducing Margaret to Emerald as a flashy chorus girl, Hank wangles an invitation to Emerald's apartment, where Margaret learns the location of the gangster's safe while Hank has kept him occupied talking the fight game. The material which they hope to find is secreted in a strongbox in Emerald's steam room.

The following night, while Emerald is supposedly at one of Steamer Krupp's fights, Hank and Margaret sneak back to the apartment, planning to break open the safe—with dynamite, if necessary. They find themselves trapped in the steam room, however, when Emerald and his men return unexpectedly. Emerald locks the door and turns up the steam level. Hank, though, manages to brace the dynamite charge next to the steam room door, and Emerald is killed by the explosion as the police burst in the front door to round up the remaining members of the mob. Hank gives the district attorney the evidence vindicating his brother and tying Emerald into the many murders plaguing the city.

With Donald Barry and Charles Murphy

# Night Waitress

RKO Radio / 1936

CAST: *Helen Roberts*, MARGOT GRAHAME; *Martin Rhodes*, GORDON JONES; *Skinner*, Vinton Haworth; *Dorn*, Marc Lawrence; *Torre*, Billy Gilbert; *Mario Rigo*, Donald Barry; *Fong*, Otto Yamaoka; *District Attorney*, Paul Stanton; *Borgum*, Arthur Loft; *Inspector*, Walter Miller; *Hoods*, Anthony Quinn and Charles Murphy; *Cops*, Frank Faylen and Dick Miller; *Blonde*, Barbara Pepper; *Crook*, Ernie S. Adams.

CREDITS: *Director*, Lew Landers; *associate producer*, Joseph Henry Steele; *screenplay*, Marcus Goodrich; *story*, Golda Draper; *art director*, Van Nest Polglase; *camera*, Russell Metty; *editor*, Desmond Marquette. Running time: 57 minutes.

In a second consecutive unbilled role (as with *Sworn Enemy* uncovered by John Cocchi), Quinn received a fast few days' work in the by-now familiar gangster guise. "Romance, dreams, excitement, thrills on the San Francisco waterfront!" RKO promised in its ads, which pigeonholed the film as "the thrill-packed story of a girl alone in a world of man-against-the-law!" In it, Quinn is seen as a vicious hood contracted to rub out squealer Mario Rigo (Donald Barry).

Following her release from prison after innocently becoming involved in a bonds theft, Helen Roberts (Margot Grahame) returns to the job Torre (Billy

Gilbert) had been holding open for her in his waterfront café. She soon finds herself in more trouble when a small-time hood is murdered in the café, where he had been trying to make contact with Martin Rhodes (Gordon Jones), a former rumrunner now operating a charter service with his small ship. Helen once had been in love with Martin and, trying to protect him, refuses to tell the police what she knows of the killing. When they leave, Martin confides that he was being contacted to haul a load of secret cargo on his boat, and with Helen's assistance, he finally learns that the haul was to be stolen gold bullion.

Discovering that a racketeer named Borgum (Arthur Loft) is quite anxious to recover the bullion, and unable to go to the police for help, Helen and Martin are forced to do their own snooping in hopes of locating the loot before Borgum's men close in. Martin soon finds that the gold has been sunk *under* his docked boat and leaves Helen on board while he rushes to get the police. Thinking that the bullion is already on the boat, Borgum sends his henchmen to take over the ship. The gang ties Helen up and heads the ship toward open waters. Martin, aboard a police launch, directs the pursuit and finally overtakes his boat, releasing Helen, capturing Borgum's men, and returning the stolen bullion.

With Gary Cooper and James Ellison

# The Plainsman

Paramount /1936

CAST: *Wild Bill Hickok*, GARY COOPER; *Calamity Jane*, JEAN ARTHUR; *John Lattimer*, Charles Bickford; *Buffalo Bill Cody*, James Ellison; *Louisa Cody*, Helen Burgess; *Jack McCall*, Porter Hall; *Yellow Hand*, Paul Harvey; *Painted Horse*, Victor Varconi; *General Custer*, John Miljan; *Abraham Lincoln*, Frank McGlynn, Sr.; *Van Ellyn*, Granville Bates; *Young Trooper*, Frank Albertson; *Captain Wood*, Purnell Pratt; *Jake*, Fred Kohler, Sr.; *Breezy*, George "Gabby" Hayes; *Dave*, Fuzzy Knight; *Sgt. McGinnis*, Pat Moriarity; *Tony the Barber*, Charles Judels; *Quartermaster Sergeant*, Harry Woods; *A Cheyenne Indian*, Anthony Quinn; *River Gambler*, Francis J. McDonald; *Boy on Dock*, George Ernest; *General Merritt*, George MacQuarrie; *Custer's Courier*, Edgar Dearing; *Secretary of War Stanton*, Edwin Maxwell; *Purser on the Lizzie Gill*, Bruce Warren; *Injun Charley*, Charles Stevens; *Old Veteran*, Francis Ford; *Hysterical Trooper*, Irving Bacon; *Mary Todd Lincoln*, Leila McIntyre; *John F. Usher*, Harry Stubbs; *James Speed*, Davison Clark; *William H. Seward*, Charles W. Herzinger; *Hugh McCulloch*, William Humphries; *Giddeon Wells*, Sidney Jarvis; and Arthur Aylesworth, Douglas Wood, George Cleveland, Lona Andre, Hank Worden, Jonathan Hale, Noble Johnson, Wadsworth Harris, Bud Flanagan (Dennis O'Keefe).

CREDITS: *Producer/director*, Cecil B. DeMille; *executive producer*, William LeBaron; *screenplay*, Waldemar Young, Lynn Riggs and Harold Lamb; based on story by Courtney Riley Cooper, the novel *Wild Bill Hickok* by Frank J. Wilstach, *and material compiled by* Jeanie Macpherson; *music director*, Boris Morros; *original music*, George Antheil; *art directors*, Hans Dreier and Roland Anderson; *special effects*, Farciot Edouart and Gordon Jennings; *camera*, Victor Milner and George Robinson; *editor*, Anne Bauchens. Running time: 113 minutes

Filmed again in 1966 with Don Murray and Abby Dalton.

Anthony Quinn's participation in Cecil B. DeMille's robust spectacular about Wild Bill Hickok, Calamity Jane and Buffalo Bill is one of the career chapters the actor enjoys relating, and a full fifteen pages are devoted to its description in the first installment of his autobiography, *The Original Sin*. By his own account, he obtained the role of "A Cheyenne Indian" (which is the way he is billed) by engaging in an elaborate bluff and convincing DeMille he actually *was* a Cheyenne.

In his role, which lasted less than two minutes, Quinn, dressed in loincloth and head feather and little else, rattled off five pages of Indian-style gibberish, informing Hickok (Gary Cooper) and Buffalo Bill (James Ellison) of the Sioux massacre of General Custer (John Miljan) at the Little Big Horn. DeMille's use of this technique provided an imaginative way of synopsizing the event via one rapid flashback during Quinn's "dissertation." Interestingly, Quinn later would appear in Indian garb—and in much larger roles—in other films about both General Custer and Buffalo Bill.

*The Plainsman* fit snugly into the then well-established mold of filmed American history as seen through the eyes of Cecil B. DeMille, with facts fading away in deference to entertainment value. Wild Bill Hickok, in this case, was occupied with (1) tracking down the villainous John Lattimer (Charles Bickford), who had been selling rifles to the Indians; (2) dodging a rather subdued but overtly marriage-minded Calamity Jane (Jean Arthur); and (3) chiding his old buddy, Buffalo Bill Cody, about settling into domesticity and becoming a bit henpecked. The boisterous proceedings were punctuated with frequent action sequences, Indian attacks, knock-down fights—even the killing of Gary Cooper!

David Lowell Rich's 1966 made-for-television (but released theatrically first) version was a static, routine, Universal back-lot rehash without any of the whooping excitement, cast-of-thousands spectacle and matchless Cooper-Arthur byplay which made DeMille's production the memorable classic it remains.

[ 43 ]

# Swing High, Swing Low

Paramount / 1937

With Fred MacMurray and Carole Lombard

CAST: *Maggie King,* CAROLE LOMBARD; *Skid Johnson,* FRED MacMURRAY; *Harry,* Charles Butterworth; *Ella,* Jean Dixon; *Anita Alvarez,* Dorothy Lamour; *Harvey Howell,* Harvey Stephens; *Murphy,* Cecil Cunningham; *Georgie,* Charles Arnt; *Henri,* Franklin Pangborn; *The Don,* Anthony Quinn; *The Purser,* Bud Flanagan (Dennis O'Keefe); *Tony,* Charles Judels; *Police Chief,* Harry Semels; *Interpreter,* Ricardo Mandia; *Judge,* Enrique DeRosas; *Sleepy Steward,* Chris Pin Martin; *Cock Fight Spectator,* Charles Stevens; *Musselwhite,* Ralph Remley; *Elevator Boy,* Oscar Rudolph; *Manager,* George Sorel; *Justice of the Peace,* George M. Jimenez; *Man in Club,* Lee Bowman; *Man in Club,* Nick Lukats; *Announcer,* Lee Cooley; *Army Surgeon,* Richard Kipling; *Customer,* Esther Howard; *Radio Technician,* Donald Kerr; *Attendant,* William Wright; *Cook,* Spencer Chan; *Santa Claus,* Darby Jones; *Dock Policeman,* Jack Daley.

CREDITS: *Director,* Mitchell Leisen; *producer,* Arthur Hornblow Jr.; *screenplay,* Virginia Van Upp and Oscar Hammerstein II; based on the *play* "Burlesque" by George Manker Watters and Arthur Hopkins, *music director,* Boris Morros; *musical arrangements,* Victor Young and Phil Boutelje; *songs,* Ralph Rainger and Leo Robin, Sam Coslow and Al Siegel, Ralph Freed and Burton Lane; *art directors,* Hans Dreier and Ernst Fegte; *special effects,* Farciot Edouart; *camera,* Ted Tetzlaff; *editor,* Eda Warren. Running time: 97 minutes.

Anthony Quinn obtained the role of the Panamanian Don in this second of three screen versions of the 1927 play, *Burlesque,* through his friendship with Carole Lombard. According to his autobiography, he had impressed the actress with his gutsy attitude on the set of *The Plainsman* and she recommended him to director Mitchell Leisen, who summoned Quinn and explained the part briefly. "It's a nice role. Carole Lombard has been turned down by Fred MacMurray and she meets this attractive Panamanian. She thinks for a moment that maybe she'll fall in love with him. Then Fred comes back and there's a fight. I think it's a very interesting

---

Filmed in 1929 as *The Dance of Life* and in 1948 as *When My Baby Smiles at Me.*

role for you at this stage." It also was spoken only in Spanish.

The story deals with a nightclub singer, Maggie King (Carole Lombard), posing as a hairdresser on a steamer passing through the Panama Canal on its way to San Francisco, and a soldier on canal duty, Skid Johnson (Fred MacMurray), who flirts with her as the ship goes from lock to lock. (Ed. note: Skid Johnson was a dancer in the play and the other film versions, but became a trumpeter here because, in director Leisen's words, "Fred has two left feet when it comes to dancing.") When the ship finally docks, Skid offers to show Maggie the sights and they begin making the rounds of the local cabarets. In one, Skid becomes annoyed when a Latin lothario (Quinn) makes a pass at Maggie, and a barroom brawl ensues, causing Skid to get himself arrested and Maggie to miss her boat. With the help of Skid's roommate Harry (Charles Butterworth), Maggie bails Skid out of jail, and finding herself stranded, decides to move in with the boys. She also arranges a job for Skid and herself at a local spot run by a lady named Murphy (Cecil Cunningham). Skid rapidly becomes a "name" and marries Maggie, not long before he's offered a chance at New York. Skid promises to send for Maggie as soon as he's settled and he heads for the Big Time, accompanied by Anita Alvarez (Dorothy Lamour), a fiery young singer who had worked with him at Murphy's. Skid becomes an overnight smash in New York and quickly becomes a fixture in social circles, usually with Anita on his arm.

When Maggie suddenly turns up, she eyes the situation and tells Skid she's leaving him. Skid, still in love with her, begins to let his career slip and takes to the bottle. News reaches Maggie of Skid's drinking problems, and she rushes to his side when she learns that he is scheduled for an important radio audition but might not be up to it physically. Shaken and ill, Skid manages to find the right notes, with Maggie at his side, to get through the audition. A shadow of his former self, he realizes that there is hope because Maggie will be with him.

# Waikiki Wedding

Paramount / 1937

Quinn (top left) with Bob Burns, George Regas, Shirley Ross, Bing Crosby

CAST:   *Tony Marvin,* BING CROSBY; *Shad Buggle,* BOB BURNS; *Myrtle Finch,* MARTHA RAYE; *Georgia Smith,* SHIRLEY ROSS; *J. P. Todhunter,* George Barbier; *Dr. Victor Quimby,* Leif Erickson; *Everett Todhunter,* Grady Sutton; *Uncle Herman,* Granville Bates; *Kimo,* Anthony Quinn; *Koalani,* Mitchell Lewis; *Muamua,* George Regas; *Assistant Purser,* Nick Lukats; *Priest,* Prince Lei Lani; *Kaiaka,* Maurice Liu; *Mahina,* Raquel Echeverria; *Maile,* Nalani De Clercq; *Lani,* Kuulei De Clercq; *Specialty Dancer,* Miri Rei; *Frame,* Spencer Charters; *Harrison,* Alexander Leftwich; *Tomlin,* Ralph Remley; *Specialty Dancer,* Augie Goupil; *Keith,* Harry Stubbs; *John Durkin,* Pierre Watkin; *Secretary,* Iris Yamaoka; *Radio Operator,* David Newell; *Mrs. Marvin,* Emma Dunn; *1st Policeman,* Robert Emmet O'Connor; *2nd Policeman,* Lalo Encinas; *Bellboy,* Sojin Jr.; *Singer,* Ray Kinney.

CREDITS:   *Director,* Frank Tuttle; *producer,* Arthur Hornblow Jr.; *screenplay,* Frank Butler, Don Hartman, Walter DeLeon and Francis Martin; *story,* Frank Butler and Don Hartman; *music director,* Boris Morros; *orchestrations,* Victor Young; *songs,* Ralph Rainger, Leo Robin and Harry Owens; *choreography,* LeRoy Prinz; *special effects,* Farciot Edouart; *camera,* Karl Struss; *editor,* Paul Weatherwax. Running time: 89 minutes.

Director Mitchell Leisen recommended Anthony Quinn to Frank Tuttle for a Bing Crosby-Martha Raye film he was casting. The role of the bogus native hired by Crosby to stage a fake kidnaping for "atmosphere" provided Quinn with his third consecutive non-English-speaking part and marked the final step in the evolution of the four basic characterizations with which he was to be identified (with few exceptions) during the initial, decade-long phase of his screen career: gangster, Indian, Latin, native.

As a framework primarily for Crosby's crooning and Raye's raucousness, the plot of *Waikiki Wedding* was constructed to give maximum footage to each, as well as to introduce several islands-flavored tunes such as "Blue Hawaii" and the Oscar-winning "Sweet Leilani." Amid all of this, Tony Marvin (Crosby), easygoing publicity man for a pineapple company, is obliged to escort contest winner Georgia Smith (Shirley Ross) on her Hawaiian tour. His buddy, Shad Buggle (Bob Burns), is recruited as companion for her friend, Myrtle Finch (Martha Raye). Tony saunters through his assignment halfheartedly, and Georgia becomes bored and prepares to leave for the States, much to the annoyance of the company sponsoring her trip. Tony is ordered to keep her happy and occupied, and he arranges with a native named Kimo (Anthony Quinn) to have the group of them kidnaped.

The abduction is pulled off by the natives who pretend to be angered by the disappearance of a sacred jewel, and Georgia, entranced by the romantic atmosphere, the ceremonial dances, the moonlight and the music, falls in love with Tony, who ultimately engineers their escape. When Georgia returns to her hotel, though, she discovers that the entire affair was a trick and, furious, she books passage for home. Tony, realizing that he has fallen for Georgia, concocts a series of tricks to keep her from getting on the boat, and, learning that Myrtle has decided to remain and marry Shad, Georgia finally forgives Tony and agrees to his offer of a Waikiki wedding.

With Bing Crosby and players

With Gilbert Roland and Dorothy Lamour

# The Last Train from Madrid

Paramount / 1937

CAST: *Carmelita Castillo*, DOROTHY LAMOUR; *Bill Dexter*, LEW AYRES; *Eduardo de Soto*, GILBERT ROLAND; *Baroness Helene Rafitte*, Karen Morley; *Colonel Vigo*, Lionel Atwill; *Lola*, Helen Mack; *Juan Ramos*, Robert Cummings; *Maria Ferrer*, Olympe Bradna; *Captain Ricardo Alvarez*, Anthony Quinn; *Michael Balk*, Lee Bowman; *Women's Battalion Officer*, Evelyn Brent; *Guard*, Jack Perrin; *Chauffeur*, Frank Leyva; *Officer*, Roland Rego; *Intelligence Officer*, George Lloyd; *Lola's Friend*, Ralf Harolde; *Martin*, Hooper Atchley; *Rosa Delgado*, Louise Carter; *Guard*, Harry Semels; *Mora*, Francis McDonald; *Pedro Elias*, Francis Ford; *Warden*, Charles Middleton; *Second Warden*, Sam Appel; *Clerk*, Stanley Price; *Fernando*, Otto Hoffman; *Announcer*, Henry Brandon; *Waiter*, Maurice Cass; *Gomez*, Harry Worth; *Turnkey*, (Paul) Tiny Newland; *Hernandez*, Rollo Lloyd; *Escaped Prisoner*, Charles Stevens; *Saleswoman*, Bess Flowers; *Government Man*, Harry Woods; *Bit Soldier*, Alan Ladd; *Man Coming from Bungalow*, Cecil B. DeMille.

CREDITS: *Director*, James Hogan; *producer*, George M. Arthur; *associate producer*, Hugh Bennett; *screenplay*, Louis Stevens and Robert Wyler; *story*, Elsie and Paul Harvey Fox; *music director*, Boris Morros; *cam-era*, Harry Fischbeck; *editor*, Everett Douglass. Running time: 85 minutes.

Quinn had his first substantial role in the pivotal part of a Spanish officer assigned to guiding a trainload of first-class passengers to Valencia as the war closes in on Madrid. The film was constructed in the manner of *Grand Hotel*, mixing a modicum of action with a maximum of melodrama and pairing off members of Paramount's serviceable roster of character players and future stars. *Last Train* has been called at various times the first Hollywood look at the Spanish Civil War and the initial World War II movie, but actually it was devoid of any propaganda, point of view or political leanings, and stressed this intentional neutrality in the film's prologue. Quinn himself received his first critical notices for his role as Captain Alvarez, and *The New York Times* ran his photograph alongside its review of the film, in which critic Frank Nugent commented: "The cast is best served by Anthony Quinn as the self-effacing officer." Howard Barnes, on the other hand, felt in his critique in the *New York Herald Tribune* that "Mr. Quinn's sacrificial gestures are noble but unconvincing," and then went on to say that "either the newsreels from Spain have been faked or *Last Train from Madrid* is a

With Karen Morley, Lee Bowman and Gilbert Roland

With Gilbert Roland and Dorothy Lamour

sorry attempt to hitch a threadbare plot onto portentous world happenings."

Among the interesting sidelights regarding the film are these: Gilbert Roland, the nominal lead, insisted that all actors with moustaches shave them so that he would be distinctive; a young Alan Ladd can be seen fleetingly as a soldier; even Cecil B. DeMille himself did a walk-on in this not-quite-an-"A"-film-but-more-than-a-"B."

In *Last Train,* Captain Alvarez (Quinn), assigned by Colonel Vigo (Lionel Atwill) to issue train passes to certain "eligible" people hoping to get to Valencia, finds he is able to help Eduardo de Soto (Gilbert Roland), an old army friend and now a political fugi-

tive, escape from Madrid. Among the train's passengers is Carmelita Castillo (Dorothy Lamour), de Soto's former girlfriend who is now traveling in the company of Alvarez. Her presence is the spark which turns the two friends against one another. Both, though, have a common goal: escape. Colonel Vigo has discovered that Alvarez has aided de Soto and has branded his trusted officer a traitor. Realizing how desperate the situation has become, Alvarez forces his way into Vigo's office and holds his colonel at gunpoint to make sure the train leaves for Valencia safely and is beyond Vigo's control. At dawn, the self-sacrificing Alvarez is discovered and shot, but de Soto and Carmelita are at last free.

With players

# Partners in Crime

Paramount / 1937

With Roscoe Karns

CAST: *Hank Hyer,* LYNNE OVERMAN; *Sim Perkins,* Roscoe Karns; *Odette Le Vin,* Muriel Hutchison; *Nicholas Mazaney,* Anthony Quinn; *Lillian Tate,* Inez Courtney; *Mr. Twitchell,* Lucien Littlefield; *Silas Wagon,* Charles Halton; *Inspector Simpson,* Charles Wilson; *Mabel,* June Brewster; *Mrs. Wagon,* Esther Howard; *Housekeeper,* Nora Cecil; *Mayor Callahan,* Russell Hicks; *Reporter,* Don Brodie; *Photographer,* Archie Twitchell (Michael Branden), *Callahan's Secretary,* Arthur Hoyt; *Cab Driver,* Oscar "Dutch" Hendrian; *Miss Brown,* Ruth Warren.

CREDITS: *Director,* Ralph Murphy; *producer,* Harold Hurley; *screenplay,* Garnett Weston; based on the *novel* "Murder Goes to College" by Kurt Steel; *music,* Boris Morros; *art directors,* Hans Dreier and Robert Odell; *camera,* Henry Sharp; *editor,* Eda Warren. Running time: 66 minutes.

Quinn was relegated to the remarkable Paramount "B" unit for seasoning, and, in thirteen films, worked with one of the best repertory screen troupes of the 1930s— Anna May Wong, Lloyd Nolan, J. Carrol Naish, Akim Tamiroff, Lynne Overman, Roscoe Karns, Philip Ahn, Richard Denning, Robert Paige, and others. Other than Anna May Wong, who nearly always played the virtuous China doll and was, for all practical purposes, the only Oriental leading lady in American films, each member of the company was proficient at playing leads or bits, heroes or heavies. Ironically, Quinn alone was stuck almost exclusively with villain roles because of his menacing looks. In fact, of the thirteen crime programmers he made between 1937 and 1941, he was the hero (and lead) only once—and then he was cast as an Oriental!

And of the thirteen, *Partners in Crime* ranks near the very bottom plotwise. "Bush league" is how *Variety* described it (although the paper singled out the "crackling performance by Lynne Overman"), and Dorothy Manners, then film critic for the New York *Daily News,* felt that "The Bureau of Standards may have a case in the canned nonsense in *Partners in Crime.* The humor specified by recipe is sadly deficient." In this curious combination of comedy and melodrama, Quinn turns up as a political blackmailer with the unlikely name of Nicholas Mazaney. When he and Odette Le Vin (Muriel Hutchison) attempt to extort money from the reform mayoral candidate, private detective Hank Hyer (Lynne Overman), a sardonic gumshoe with an eye for the girls and curiosity for other people's business, stumbles onto their skulduggery. Dating Odette, he discovers that she and Mazaney have been hired by the crooked incumbent mayor (Russell Hicks) to smear his rival with trumped-up bigamy charges. When Odette turns up at the candidate's headquarters and announces that the reformer is actually her father, he is forced off the ticket. Hank, determined that good government must prevail, talks his reporter pal Sim Perkins (Roscoe Karns) into running for the office, and to the astonishment of all, he wins the election. During the victory celebration, however, Sim is suddenly disqualified when it is learned that he is not an American citizen, and he and Hank are kicked out of town for perpetrating a political hoax themselves.

The plot was bungled ("ridiculous to the point of annoyance," as one reviewer saw it) that leading man Lynne Overman was not even in the payoff after trying to rout the blackmailers, get his buddy into the mayor's chair, solve a nonexistent murder and promote a romance. And what the story had to do with its source material, Kurt Steel's novel, *Murder Goes to College,* is another unsolved mystery.

With Lynne Overman, Charles Wilson, Dick Rush, Howard Mitchell, Russell Hicks, Arthur Hoyt

With Anna May Wong

# Daughter of Shanghai

Paramount / 1937

CAST: *Lan Ying Lin*, ANNA MAY WONG; *Otto Hartman*, Charles Bickford; *Andrew Sleete*, Larry (Buster) Crabbe; *Mrs. Mary Hunt*, Cecil Cunningham; *Frank Barden*, J. Carrol Naish; *Harry Morgan*, Anthony Quinn; *James Lang*, John Patterson; *Olga Derey*, Evelyn Brent; *Kim Lee*, Philip Ahn; *Captain Gulner*, Fred Kohler; *Lloyd Burkett*, Guy Bates Post; *Rita (dancer)*, Virginia Dabney; *L. T. Yorkland*, Pierre Watkin; *Secretary*, Archie Twitchell (Michael Branden); *Quan Lin*, Ching Wah Lee; *Jake Kelly*, Frank Sully; *Sam Blike*, Ernest Whitman; *Ah Feng*, Maurice Liu; *Amah*, Mrs. Wong Wing; *Miles*, Paul Fix; *Captain Schwartz*, Charles Wilson; *Sailor*, John Hart; *Lil*, Mae Busch; *Interpreter*, Gino Corrado; *Ship's Officer*, Lee Shumway.

CREDITS: *Director*, Robert Florey; *producer*, Harold Hurley; *screenplay*, Gladys Unger and Garnett Weston; *story*, Garnett Weston; *music director*, Boris Morros; *art directors*, Hans Dreier and Robert Odell; *camera*, Charles Schoenbaum; *editor*, Ellsworth Hoagland. Running time: 61 minutes.

In the first film Quinn made with Anna May Wong, he once again played a goon. This time he was in the employ of J. Carrol Naish, who, because of his dialect proficiencies, was one of the most versatile character actors in films and usually chief menace of the B's. Quinn acted in more films (eight) with Naish than with any other "name" (he did six each with Anna May Wong and Lloyd Nolan). In one of the most curious aspects of *Daughter of Shanghai*, in which Miss Wong went through her familiar "Perils of Pauline" exploits where her escapes are frequent, narrow and strictly incredible, the nominal leading man was Philip Ahn who was relegated to *tenth* billing—following all the villains, heavies and assorted hoods. Marguerite Tazelaar, critic for the *New York Herald Tribune*, said that "the only thing which keeps this picture from being more ridiculous is the dignity Miss Wong's performance lends to the lurid episodes, and also her beautiful delivery of lines," and concluded that "the entire cast puts to shame the plot." Robert Florey's competent direction of the nearly nonstop action and of the exceptional "all-star" cast gave what consequence there was to this melodrama of slave trade in San Francisco's Chinatown.

As the *Daughter of Shanghai* (?), Lan Ying Lin (Wong) swears revenge when the mob kills her father who had refused to help them funnel smuggled aliens through his legitimate business. Her remarkable detective work, with occasional assistance from federal agent Kim Lee (Philip Ahn), leads her to a Central American dive, run by Otto Hartman (Charles Bickford). There she passes herself off as a dancer and learns that the spot is used to transship the aliens to the States. She is soon captured and, together with Kim Lee, who has turned up disguised as a sailor, is tossed aboard a plane piloted by Frank Barden (J. Carrol Naish), who oversees the smuggling operation, and his henchman, Andrew Sleete (Larry Crabbe). She and Kim are to be dumped into the sea, but they save themselves by clinging to pipes in the ceiling of the plane's cargo section as the loading doors are swung open, and return to unmask the racket's mastermind, Mary Hunt (Cecil Cunningham), the wealthy matron who had been one of Lan Ying's father's best customers. While Kim Lee engages in a knockdown fight with Harry Morgan (Quinn), one of Mrs. Hunt's toughs, Lan Ying holds the head of the operation at bay until federal agents can arrive.

With Akim Tamiroff and Fredric March

# The Buccaneer

Paramount / 1938

CAST: *Jean Lafitte*, FREDRIC MARCH; *Gretchen*, FRANCISKA GAAL; *Annette de Remy*, Margot Grahame; *Dominique You*, Akim Tamiroff; *Ezra Peavey*, Walter Brennan; *Beluche*, Anthony Quinn; *Senator Crawford*, Ian Keith; *Governor Claiborne*, Douglass Dumbrille; *Aunt Charlotte*, Beulah Bondi; *Gramby*, Fred Kohler, Sr.; *Captain Brown*, Robert Barrat; *Andrew Jackson*, Hugh Sothern; *Mouse*, John Rogers; *Tarsus*, Hans Steinke; *Collector of Port*, Stanley Andrews; *Dolly Madison*, Spring Byington; *Admiral Cockburn*, Montagu Love; *Marie de Remy*, Louise Campbell; *General Ross*, Eric Stanley; *Captain Lockyer*, Gilbert Emery; *Captain McWilliams*, Holmes Herbert; *Madeleine*, Evelyn Keyes; *Camden Blount*, Francis J. McDonald; *Lieutenant Shreve*, Frank Melton; *Charles*, Jack (John) Hubbard; *Captain Reid*, Richard Denning; *Roxane*, Lina Basquette; *Young Blade*, John Patterson; and Reginald Sheffield, Barry Norton, John Sutton, Mae Busch, Crauford Kent, Ed Brady, James Craig, Stanhope Wheatcroft, Maude Fealy, Paul Fix, Charles Trowbridge, Philo McCullough, Ralph Lewis, Terry Ray (Ellen Drew), Charlotte Wynters, Charles Morton.

Filmed by DeMille in 1958 with Anthony Quinn directing and Yul Brynner starring as Lafitte.

CREDITS: *Producer/director*, Cecil B. DeMille; *executive producer*, William LeBaron; *associate producer*, William H. Pine; *screenplay*, Edwin Justus Mayer, Harold Lamb and C. Gardner Sullivan; based on Jeanie Macpherson's *adaptation* of "Lafitte the Pirate" by Lyle Saxon, *music director*, Boris Morros; *original music*, George Anthiel; *special effects*, Farciot Edouart and Dewey Wrigley; *camera*, Victor Milner; *editor*, Anne Bauchens. Running time: 124 minutes.

In the second of his three pictures for Cecil B. DeMille, Anthony Quinn was cast in the role of Beluche, one of Jean Lafitte's lieutenants, swashbuckling through this colorful if somewhat implausible tale of the nineteenth-century pirate who offered his services to General Andrew Jackson at the Battle of New Orleans. In his autobiography, Quinn confesses that he had been considered for the Lafitte role and that Carole Lombard and agent Charles K. Feldman had interceded in his behalf, but the idea of casting a twenty-one-year-old actor as the seasoned pirate was torpedoed by DeMille's daughter, Katherine. DeMille, according to Quinn, then had hoped to land Clark Gable for the role, but was turned down by Louis B. Mayer. So the veteran producer-director settled on Fredric March, with whom he previously had worked on *The Sign of the Cross*. Although Quinn failed to get the lead in the film, he did marry the boss's daughter and, two decades later, made his debut as a director filming the Technicolor version of the adventure epic.

Told in the grand DeMille manner, despite Frank Nugent's comment in his review in *The New York Times* about it being "a run of DeMille picture," *The Buccaneer* is grand entertainment, spectacularly staged and enthusiastically acted by a typically DeMillian cast of familiar names (except for leading lady Franciska Gaal, introduced herein before drifting into obscurity). According to DeMille, the brazen pirate of the Louisiana bayous, Jean Lafitte, preys on virtually any ship which comes his way but molests no packets flying the American flag. In love with a New Orleans belle, Annette de Remy (Margot Grahame), he tries vainly to break into the city's social circle, even to the point of offering himself and his men to Andrew Jackson for service during the War of 1812.

At the victory ball following the valiant and strikingly successful battle which saved New Orleans for America, Lafitte is honored by Jackson and is about to claim Annette as his bride, when it is learned that Lafitte and his men had burned a boat carrying Annette's younger sister, Marie (Louise Campbell), who was eloping. The buccaneer is thus forced to desert New Orleans once again and return to his pirating in the bayous with his brigands (including Akim Tamiroff, Walter Brennan, Anthony Quinn, among others) and to console himself with the Dutch girl, Gretchen (Franciska Gaal), whom he had rescued sometime before from a vessel he had ransacked, and who had fallen in love with him.

As Beluche

With Fred Kohler, Sr., Akim Tamiroff and Fredric March

With Anna May Wong

# Dangerous to Know

Paramount / 1938

CAST: *Margaret Van Kase,* GAIL PATRICK; *Stephen Recka,* AKIM TAMIROFF; *Mme. Lan Ying,* ANNA MAY WONG; *Inspector Brandon,* Lloyd Nolan; *Philip Easton,* Harvey Stephens; *Nicholas Kusnoff,* Anthony Quinn; *Duncan,* Roscoe Karns; *Mayor Bradley,* Porter Hall; *Butler,* Barlowe Borland; *Mrs. Carson,* Hedda Hopper; *Harvey Greggson,* Hugh Sothern; *John Rance,* Edward Pawley; *Crouch,* Eddie Marr; *Hanley,* Harry Worth; *Councilman Murkil,* Robert Brister; *Senator Carson,* Pierre Watkin; *Mike Tookey,* Garry Owen; *Man,* John Hart; *Judge Parker,* Donald Brian; *Motorcycle Cop,* Stanley Blystone; *Secretary,* Terry Ray (Ellen Drew); *Mrs. Barnett,* Rita La Roy; *Mr. Barnett,* Harvey Clark; *Messenger,* Jack Knoche; *Headwaiter,* Gino Corrado.

CREDITS: *Director,* Robert Florey; *associate producer,* Edward T. Lowe; *screenplay,* William R. Lipman and Horace McCoy; based on the *play* "On the Spot" by Edgar Wallace; *music,* Boris Morros; *art directors,* Hans Dreier and John Goodman; *camera,* Theodor Sparkuhl; *editor,* Arthur Schmidt. Running time: 70 minutes.

As the exotically named Nicholas Kusnoff, Quinn turned up as another hood in the screen version of the Edgar Wallace play, *On the Spot.* For a change of pace, though, he was assigned to the payroll of Akim Tamiroff, the film's star who plays a racketeer and power behind city politics as well as patron of the arts. And for a change, Anna May Wong was given the role of the "other woman," playing Tamiroff's Oriental mistress.

The actress re-created the role she had essayed in the 1930 Broadway version of this lurid melodrama about a gangster who tries to crash society. As the Paramount ad campaign screamed: "This man holds a whole city in his evil grip because he's *Dangerous To Know!*"

Stephen Recka (Tamiroff), suave and cultured rackets king who relaxes by rhapsodizing at his huge theater organ, has amassed a fortune through a lifetime of shady deals and lives in one of the city's showplaces which he leaves in the care of his Chinese "hostess," Mme. Lan Ying (Wong). (Ed. note: Coincidentally or not, Miss Wong's character name in *Daughter of Shanghai* was Lan Ying Lin.) At one of Recka's lavish parties, he meets a high society girl named Margaret Van Kase (Gail Patrick), on whom he forces himself. She rebuffs his advances and introduces him to her fiancé Philip Easton (Harvey Stephens), a bond salesman. Recka proceeds to have the young man kidnaped and threatens to have him framed in a securities theft unless Margaret agrees to marry the rackets boss. On the eve of his wedding, Recka ignores Mme. Ying's pleas not to leave her, and, while he is relaxing with Bach and Handel, she stabs herself after carefully arranging her suicide to look like murder with the evidence pointing to Recka. This is the break sought by Inspector Brandon (Lloyd Nolan), who had been trying doggedly to implicate the crime czar for some time. Brandon has his men round up Nicholas Kusnoff (Quinn), Recka's right-hand man, along with the rest of the gang, and arrests Recka himself for Mme. Ying's death, thus freeing Margaret to marry Philip.

With Evelyn Brent and Roscoe Karns

# Tip-Off Girls

Paramount / 1938

CAST: *Bob Anders,* LLOYD NOLAN; *Marjorie Rogers,* MARY CARLISLE; *Tom Benson,* Roscoe Karns; *Red Deegan,* Larry (Buster) Crabbe; *Joseph Valkus,* J. Carrol Naish; *Rena Terry,* Evelyn Brent; *Marty,* Anthony Quinn; *Scotty,* Benny Baker; *Jason Baardue,* Harvey Stephens; *Sam,* Irving Bacon; *"Boots" Milburn,* Gertrude Short; *Hensler,* Archie Twitchell (Michael Branden); *Blacky,* Barlowe Borland; *George Murkil,* Pierre Watkin; *Drivers,* John Hart, Harry Templeton, Vic Demourelle Jr., Jack Pennick, Ethan Laidlaw and Stanley King; *Louis,* Stanley Price; *Steve,* Phillip Warren; *Pete,* Wade Boteler; *Jim,* John Patterson; *Gus,* Frank Austin; *Police Lieutenant,* Richard E. Allen; *Police Sergeant,* Stanley Andrews; *Hijacker,* Oscar "Dutch" Hendrian; *Nurse,* Barbara Jackson; *Tessie,* Joyce Mathews; *Waitresses,* Ruth Rogers, Laurie Lane, Margaret Randell and Cheryl Walker.

CREDITS: *Director,* Louis King; *associate producer,* Edward T. Lowe; *screenplay,* Maxwell Shane, Robert Yost and Stuart Anthony; *music,* Boris Morros; *art directors,* Hans Dreier and Robert Odell; *camera,* Theodor Sparkuhl; *editor,* Ellsworth Hoagland. Running time: 62 minutes.

Quinn returned to J. Carrol Naish's well-oiled mob for this hour-long melodrama about truck hijackers and their stalwart G-Men nemeses. Trumpeted in ads as "Paramount's thrilling exposé of America's $10-million highway hijacking racket!," the film was originally—and more accurately—titled *Highway Racketeers.* The label under which it was released referred to the females who flagged the trucks to be victimized, although the entire picture actually was, as *The New York Times* described it, "one long conflict between the tough guys who do the hijacking and the tough guys who are out to nab them."

In the film, an association of truckers, led by Joseph Valkus (Naish), turns to the district attorney for help in combating a rash of hijackings threatening the industry. The group is unaware, though, that Valkus himself is the brains behind the crimes. Federal agents Bob Anders (Lloyd Nolan) and Tom Benson (Roscoe Karns) are assigned to the case as undercover men and

Working title: *Highway Racketeers.*

With Lloyd Nolan, Oscar "Dutch" Hendrian, John Hart, Roscoe Karns

With Oscar "Dutch" Hendrian, John Hart, Evelyn Brent, Stanley Price, Larry (Buster) Crabbe

have little trouble infiltrating the gang after they do a professional job of hijacking one of Valkus's own trucks. Anders quickly works his way through the ranks and into Valkus's confidence, and, with the help of the boss's secretary, Marjorie Rogers (Mary Carlisle), he obtains evidence to tie Valkus into the hijackings. Marty (Quinn), one of Valkus's men, catches Anders telephoning information to fellow agents and turns him over to Valkus. Learning of Anders' identity, Valkus has him beaten up, hoping to learn how much information he knows. The boss then orders Anders and Marjorie taken for rides in separate trucks while he

himself plans to surprise the police at the roadblock he knows to have been set up. He and his men pile into one of the trucks, determined to shoot their way past the authorities. Anders, however, manages to free himself in time to thwart their plans in a climactic gun battle and save Marjorie by tracking down the truck she is in and crashing into it.

In his *New York Times* review, critic Bosley Crowther felt that "Told swiftly, in a clean, straight line, and convincingly performed . . . (it) is a good B-plus action picture." It was the first of three consecutive pictures Quinn made with director Louis King.

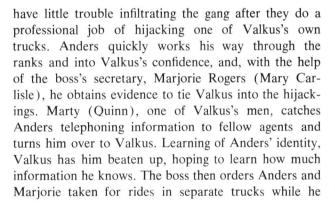

With Oscar "Dutch" Hendrian, Lloyd Nolan, Evelyn Brent, Roscoe Karns

With Lynne Overman

# Hunted Men

Paramount / 1938

CAST:   *Joe Albany,* LLOYD NOLAN; *Jane Harris,* MARY CARLISLE; *Peter Harris,* Lynne Overman; *Henry Rice,* J. Carrol Naish; *Robert Harris,* Delmar Watson; *James Flowers,* Larry (Buster) Crabbe; *Legs,* Anthony Quinn; *Frank Martin,* Johnny Downs; *Mrs. Mary Harris,* Dorothy Peterson; *Virgie,* Louise Miller; *Donovan,* Regis Toomey; *Miss Quinn,* Fern Emmett; *Waiter,* George Davis; *Headwaiter,* Hooper Atchley; *Tiny,* Dick Rich; *Cops,* Dick Rush and J. P. McGowan; *Detective Chief,* John Elliott; *Commissioner,* John Hamilton; *Homicide Squad Chief,* Mitchell Ingraham; *Police Chief,* Wallis Clark; *Police Captain,* Ivan Miller; *Door-*man, Howard Mitchell; *Flower Woman,* Zeffie Tilbury; *Gangster,* Phillip Warren; *Cabbie,* Stanley Price; *Party Guests,* Scott Groves, Edwin Brian and John Hart; *Girls,* Ruth Rogers, Janet Waldo, Laurie Lane and Mary Parker.

CREDITS:   *Director,* Louis King; *producer,* Harold Hurley; *associate producer,* Stuart Walker; *screenplay,* William R. Lipman and Horace McCoy; *based on a play* by Albert Duffy and Marian Grant; *music,* Boris Morros; *art directors,* Hans Dreier and Franz Bachelin; *camera,* Victor Milner; *editor,* Anne Bauchens. Running time: 65 minutes.

Working title: *Crime Gives Orders.*

Quinn's villainy in this well-made little melodrama was

for Lloyd Nolan, a cold-blooded killer who comes under the influence of a normal, decent, American family. The basic plot, here competently handled by director Louis King, has been used countless times in films, probably most successfully in the Bogart picture, *The Desperate Hours*.

In *Hunted Men,* rackets boss Joe Albany (Lloyd Nolan) kills nightclub owner James Flowers (Larry Crabbe) whom he has found to be skimming, but in attempting his getaway, he is knocked down by the car driven by a slightly tipsy Peter Harris (Lynne Overman). Harris believes Albany to be an acquaintance and takes the shaken gunman home with him. There Albany finds himself in the midst of happy, middle-class, God-fearing family. His henchmen, who have followed him to this respectable house on a quiet street, telephone him and urge him to stay there, convincing him that it's a perfect hideout. Albany settles into uneasy domesticity and endears himself to the household, particularly to Harris's daughter Jane (Mary Carlisle), who thinks she's falling in love with him, and to young Robert (Delmar Watson). The hero-worshipping youngster even invites Albany to join his junior G-Man organization. The gang's lawyer Henry Rice (J. Carrol Naish) turns up at the house periodically to keep Albany informed of the police search and suggests that the boss keep his low profile, not realizing that Albany is becoming a sentimentalist. Albany finally identifies himself to the Harris family and promises them safety as long as they keep quiet.

Through snapshots innocently taken by Harris's son, the police trace Albany and surround the house. Desperate, Albany pulls a gun on the Harrises, threatening to fight it out with the police from inside the house. When he sees, however, the heartbreak in young Robert's eyes, he softens and, not wishing to see the family harmed, hands his gun to Harris. He walks out the front door toward the cordon of police unarmed, ignoring their orders for him to raise his hands. Defiantly he taunts the police to fire, and falls before a volley of bullets.

With Lloyd Nolan, Larry (Buster) Crabbe, George Davis, J. Carrol Naish

With Fortunio Bonanova and John Howard

# Bulldog Drummond in Africa

Paramount / 1938

CAST: *Capt. Hugh Drummond,* JOHN HOWARD; *Phyllis Clavering,* HEATHER ANGEL; *Colonel Nielson,* H. B. Warner; *Richard Lane,* J. Carrol Naish; *Algy Longworth,* Reginald Denny; *Tenny,* E. E. Clive; *Deane Fordine,* Anthony Quinn; *Major Grey,* Mathew Boulton; *Baron Nevsky,* Michael Brooke; *Dr. Stern,* William von Brincken; *Acris,* Rollo Dix; *Constable Jenkins,* Forrester Harvey; *McTurk,* Neil Fitzgerald; *First Officer,* Fortunio Bonanova; *Waiter,* Jean De Briac; *Hotel Manager,* Paul Porcasi; *First Man,* Konstantin Shayne; *Second Man,* Rudolf Myzet; *Sergeant,* Evan Thomas; *Phillips,* Leonard Carey.

CREDITS: *Director,* Louis King; *producer,* Harold Hurley; *associate producer,* Edward T. Lowe; *screenplay,* Garnett Weston; based on the *story* "Challenge" by H. C. (Sapper) McNeile; *music,* Boris Morros; *art directors,* Hans Dreier and Earl Hedrick; *camera,* William C. Mellor; *editor,* Anne Bauchens. Running time: 60 minutes.

In the latest in the string of Bulldog Drummond adventures, Quinn is again a loyal henchman for J. Carrol Naish, this time given the task of kidnaping Hugh Drummond's good friend, Colonel Nielson of Scotland Yard. John Howard once more plays the resourceful detective and Reginald Denny and E. E. Clive are back as Algy Longworth and Tenny, respectively. But H. B.

Warner has replaced John Barrymore in the role of Nielson, and Heather Angel, rather than Louise Campbell, plays Drummond's girlfriend, Phyllis Clavering. Undoubtedly Quinn, learning of his assignment on a Bulldog Drummond film, had looked forward to working with his friend and idol, John Barrymore.

The screen version of Sapper McNeile's "Challenge" begins on the eve of Drummond's oft-postponed marriage to Phyllis. Learning that Colonel Nielson has mysteriously disappeared, Drummond quickly discovers that the Scotland Yard inspector has been kidnaped by international spies and taken by plane to Africa. Drummond follows this lead, taking Phyllis, his friend Algy and his valet Tenny with him. In Morocco he is told by the police that he is out of his jurisdiction and is warned to leave. The intrepid Bulldog, instead, launches his own investigation and unmasks the kidnapers as foreign agents Richard Lane (Naish) and his chief henchman Deane Fordine (Quinn). Their plan is to torture their hostage into divulging the secrets of a radio-wave disintegrator which the British government supposedly possesses.

Fordine tries to kill Drummond and his party in the detective's private plane, but is outwitted when Drummond doubles back and lands near Lane's jungle hideout. There he overpowers Fordine and fights off Lane's chained pet lions to reach Nielson, who is tied to a stake in the midst of the beasts. Lane himself becomes a victim of the lions when he falls from a balcony while attempting to flee, and the Drummond party fly off to England to resume wedding plans.

Bosley Crowther cautioned Drummond devotees, in his review, to take the whole thing with a grain of salt and even "take along a whole box and keep shaking it throughout the entire picture. In that way the full and wholesome flavor of a fabulous but exciting film may be enjoyed."

With Michael Brooke, J. Carrol Naish, H. B. Warner, William von Brincken, Michael Vallon

# King of Alcatraz

Paramount / 1938

CAST:  *Dale Borden,* GAIL PATRICK; *Raymond Grayson,* LLOYD NOLAN; *Captain Glennan,* Harry Carey; *Steve Murkil,* J. Carrol Naish; *Robert MacArthur,* Robert Preston (film debut); *Lou Gedney,* Anthony Quinn; *First Mate Rogers,* Richard Stanley (Dennis Morgan); *Bonnie Larkin,* Virginia Dabney; *Nora Kane,* Nora Cecil; *Olaf,* Emory Parnell; *Dixie,* Dorothy Howe; *Radio Operators,* John Hart and Phillip Warren; *Harry Vay,* Richard Denning; *Matthew Talbot,* Porter Hall; *Gus Banshek,* Tom Tyler; *Murok,* Konstantin Shayne; *Pietr Mozda,* Harry Worth; *Dave Carter,* Eddie Marr; *Fred Cateny,* Clay Clement; *Officer,* Monte Blue; *Bill Lustig,* Gustav von Seyffertitz; *"Nails" Miller,* Paul Fix; *Silver,* John Harmon; *Ed Vierick,* Jack Knoche; *First Officer,* Jack Norton; *Second Officer,* Stanley Blystone; *Third Officer,* George Anderson; *Steward,* Eddie Acuff; *Ship Doctor,* Pierre Watkin.

With Galan Galt

CREDITS:  *Director,* Robert Florey; *associate producer,* William C. Thomas; *screenplay,* Irving Reis; *music,* Boris Morros; *art directors,* Hans Dreier and Earl Hedrick; *camera,* Harry Fischbeck; *editor,* Eda Warren. Running time: 56 minutes.

As the shifty-eyed, vicious Leo Gedney, Anthony Quinn was as usual in the employ of sinister J. Carrol Naish in this offbeat comedy-turned-serious gangster gem, directed crisply by Robert Florey. *The New York Times* critic Frank Nugent found it to be "a fresh and remarkably diverting film" and called it "a trim little melodrama, tightly written and logically contrived."

Despite its title, *King of Alcatraz* really had nothing at all to do with The Rock, but dealt with a fugitive public enemy who, with his mob, commits piracy on the high seas. It begins with a light touch, focusing on Raymond Grayson (Lloyd Nolan) and Robert MacArthur (Robert Preston, in his first screen role), rival radio operators on ships owned by Matthew Talbot (Porter Hall) who have a continuous game of one-upmanship. To cure their constant and debilitating bickering, Talbot assigns them to the same ship and warns them to shape up. The nurse on board is Dale Borden

(Gail Patrick), who has dated both men and wants nothing to do with either until each changes his devil-may-care attitude. They all soon learn that the small group of passengers aboard are gangsters, members of the Steve Murkil (Naish) mob, and that the little old lady who had come aboard with them is Murkil himself, recently escaped from Alcatraz. Murkil has his men hijack the ship and orders the captain (Harry Carey) to change course for Central America. Grayson is seriously wounded while trying to overpower the mob, and Dale is allowed to receive instructions by radio on how to remove the bullet.

During the operation, the loyal crew regains the ship and Murkil is killed. One of the bullets, however, has hit MacArthur who has been manning the radio and passing on instructions to Dale. His death clears the way for Grayson to find happiness with the lovely nurse who had saved his life, and honor the traditional fade-out of these wonderfully entertaining all-star nuggets.

For this one in particular, wrote critic Nugent: "Paramount's Robert Florey deserves a round of applause for keeping it spinning so furiously. It just goes to show you can't tell by the title."

With (standing) Nora Cecil, Monte Blue, John Harmon, Paul Fix; (seated) Tom Tyler, Gustav von Seyffertitz, Edward Marr, Harry Worth

# King of Chinatown

Paramount / 1939

CAST: *Dr. Mary Ling,* ANNA MAY WONG; *Frank Baturin,* AKIM TAMIROFF; *The Professor,* J. CARROL NAISH; *Dr. Chang Ling,* Sidney Toler; *Robert Li,* Philip Ahn; *Mike Gordon,* Anthony Quinn; *Dolly Warren,* Bernadene Hayes; *Rep. Harrigan,* Roscoe Karns; *Potatoes,* Ray Mayer; *Interne,* Richard Denning; *Detective,* George Anderson; *Dr. Jones,* Charles Trowbridge; *2nd Interne,* Archie Twitchell (Michael Branden); *Bart,* Eddie Marr; *Fight Announcer,* Pat West; *Investigator,* Guy Usher; *Heath,* Alex Pollard; *District Attorney Phillips,* Pierre Watkin; *Barber,* Sam Ash; *Slugger Grady,* Jimmy Vaughn; *1st Gangster,* Charles B. Wood; *2nd Gangster,* George Magrill; *Mr. Foo,* Chester Gan.

CREDITS: *Director,* Nick Grinde; *producer,* Harold Hurley; *screenplay,* Lillie Hayward and Irving Reis; *story,* Herbert Biberman; *music director,* Boris Morros; *art directors,* Hans Dreier and Robert Odell; *camera,* Leo Tover; *editor,* Eda Warren. Running time: 57 minutes.

This tidy little crime melodrama, a fast fifty-seven minutes under director Nick Grinde, is notable for (1) featuring for the first—and only—time together Paramount's three chief menaces, J. Carrol Naish, Akim Tamiroff and Anthony Quinn; (2) the unusual premise of not only making the leading character a vicious gangster (Tamiroff, in this case), but also constructing the plot to arouse sympathy for him, tried with lesser success in the earlier *Hunted Men,* and other films; (3) introducing topicality into the proceedings: ambulances for the war in China; and (4) becoming virtually the definitive Paramount "B," with the entire stock company, save Lloyd Nolan and Lynne Overman.

Anthony Quinn himself was elevated to a higher level of gangsterdom than in previous roles, as he and fellow rocketeer Naish attempt to wrest the Chinatown protection racket from bad guy Tamiroff.

Frank Baturin (Tamiroff), convinced that one of his henchmen, Mike Gordon (Quinn), has double-crossed him when one of Gordon's fighters throws a match, losing Baturin a bundle, orders his trusted book-keeper, The Professor (Naish), to see that Gordon is taken care of. Gordon escapes, however, and talks The Professor into helping him kill their boss and divide the territory. Baturin is ambushed and, seriously wounded, is rushed to the hospital where his life is saved by Dr. Mary Ling (Anna May Wong), daughter of his long-time enemy, Chang Ling (Sidney Toler). In spite of her hatred for Baturin, Mary nurses him back to health and discovers his innocence in her father's murder. While Baturin is recovering, a bloody crime wave overtakes the city as Gordon and The Professor begin dividing his crime empire. Learning that the rackets boss has not died from his wounds, though, they devise a plan to finish the job.

Back in the safety of his home, Baturin, still under Mary's personal care, proposes marriage. She turns him down, telling him of her plans to devote herself to relief work in China. Grateful, nevertheless, for her tender care, he gives her $50,000 for ambulances and equipment. Later that night, The Professor turns up at Baturin's house, informs his former boss that it was he and Gordon who had murdered Mary's father because he knew too much, and now must take care of Baturin once and for all. Baturin becomes excited when The Professor levels a gun at him and dies of a heart attack.

With Lynne Overman, Joel McCrea and Barbara Stanwyck

# Union Pacific

Paramount / 1939

CAST: *Mollie Monahan,* BARBARA STANWYCK; *Jeff Butler,* JOEL McCREA; *Fiesta,* Akim Tamiroff; *Dick Allen,* Robert Preston; *Leach Overmile,* Lynne Overman; *Sid Campeau,* Brian Donlevy; *Jack Cordray,* Anthony Quinn; *Mrs. Calvin,* Evelyn Keyes; *Duke Ring,* Robert Barrat; *General Casement,* Stanley Ridges; *Asa M. Barrows,* Henry Kolker; *General Grenville M. Dodge,* Francis J. McDonald; *Oakes Ames,* Willard Robertson; *Calvin,* Harold Goodwin; *Sam Reed,* Richard Lane; *Dusky Clayton,* William Haade; *Paddy O'Rourke,* Regis Toomey; *Monahan,* J. M. Kerrigan; *Cookie,* Fuzzy Knight; *Al Brett,* Harry Woods; *Dollarhide,* Lon Chaney Jr.; *General U.S. Grant,* Joseph Crehan; *Mame,* Julia Faye; *Rose,* Sheila Darcy; *Shamus,* Joseph Sawyer; *Bluett,* Earl Askam; *Dr. Durant,* John Marston; *Andrew Whipple,* Byron Foulger; *Jerome,* Selmer Jackson; *Senator Smith,* Morgan Wallace; *Sargent,* Russell Hicks; *Mrs. Morgan,* May Beatty; *General Sheridan,* Ernie Adams; *Oliver Ames,* William J. Worthington; *Governor Leland Stanford,* Guy Usher; *Mr. Mills,* James McNamara; *Governor Stafford,* Gus Glassmire; *Dr. Harkness,* Stanley Andrews; *Rev. Dr. Tadd,* Paul Everton; *Harmonica Player,* Jack Pennick; and Max Davidson, Elmo Lincoln, Lane Chandler, William Pawley, Emory Parnell, Monte Blue, Nestor Paiva, Richard Denning, David Newell, Noble Johnson, Maude Fealy, Stanhope Wheatcroft.

CREDITS: *Producer-director,* Cecil B. DeMille; *executive producer,* William LeBaron; *associate producer,* William H. Pine; *screenplay,* Walter DeLeon, C. Gardner Sullivan and Jesse Lasky Jr.; based on Jack Cunningham's adaptation of the *novel* "Trouble Shooter" by Ernest Haycox; *music score,* Sigmund Krumgold and John Leipold; *art directors,* Hans Dreier and Roland Anderson; *camera,* Victor Milner and Dewey Wrigley; *editor,* Anne Bauchens. Running time: 133 minutes.

In the last of the three films with DeMille, Anthony Quinn plays slimy Jack Cordray, the sartorially splendid right-hand man of villainous Brian Donlevy, doing his boss's hatchet work and getting his early and justly deserved comeuppance at the gun of stalwart Joel

With Joel McCrea and Robert Preston

With Brian Donlevy, Joel McCrea, Harry Woods, Robert Preston

McCrea, whom he had tried to shoot in the back. Quinn received seventh billing in DeMille's traditionally name-laden cast, and of his brief role, he noted: "The part was very small and I found it embarrassing." Dozens of Paramount's "B" roster players were featured in this outstanding epic of railroading in the Old West (Tamiroff, Overman, Preston, Quinn, among others), in support of the stars and a constant factor in making DeMille spectacles film-buffs' delights.

This one, as colorful and rip-roaring as any bearing the DeMille name, dealt with the building of the Union Pacific Railroad. All the bread-and-butter components of the classic Western were included: the good guys, headed by troubleshooter Joel McCrea and his sidekicks Akim Tamiroff and Lynne Overman; the bad guys, led by gambler Brian Donlevy and his motley gang, among whom were Quinn, Robert Barrat, Fuzzy Knight and Harry Woods; the tough-minded heroine, Barbara Stanwyck, here playing the postmistress daughter of veteran railroader J. M. Kerrigan; and the hero's competition, Robert Preston, who works both sides of the road (tracks?) playing both a good guy *and* a bad guy, depending on the more advantageous position at the moment.

Sparing nothing—horses or actors—DeMille gets up a full head of steam in his own unparalleled way immediately after his opening credits crawl into infinity for one of his very best brawling sagas, based on his entertainment-oriented idea of how the men who wanted the railroad built clashed with those who didn't.

With Lane Chandler (standing third left), May Beatty (lifting Quinn's watch) and Blackie Whiteford (seated near right), with players

With J. Carrol Naish, Eric Blore and Anna May Wong

# Island of Lost Men

Paramount / 1939

CAST:    *Kim Ling,* ANNA MAY WONG; *Gregory Prin,* J. CARROL NAISH; *Chang Tai,* Anthony Quinn; *Herbert,* Eric Blore; *Tex Ballister,* Broderick Crawford; *Frobenius,* Ernest Truex; *Professor Sen,* Rudolf Forster; *Hambly,* William Haade; *General Ahn Ling,* Richard Loo; *Sam Ring,* Philip Ahn; *Cafe Manager,* Torben Meyer; *Hindu,* Lal Chand Mehra; *Waiter,* George Kirby; *Blonde,* Vivien Oakland; *Blonde's Escort,* Jack Perry; *1st Tourist,* Ruth Rickaby; *2nd Tourist,* Ethyl May Halls; *Ship's Officer,* Bruce Mitchell.

CREDITS:    *Director,* Kurt Neumann; *associate producer,* Eugene Zukor; *screenplay,* William R. Lipman and Horace McCoy; based on the *play* "Hangman's Whip" by Norman Reilly Raine and Frank Butler; *music director,* Boris Morros; *art directors,* Hans Dreier and

Franz Bachelin; *camera,* Karl Struss; *editor,* Ellsworth Hoagland. Running time: 64 minutes.

The big surprise—and the only one—in this jungle melodrama recounting the further perils of Anna May Wong and the continued villainy of J. Carrol Naish: the casting of Anthony Quinn as the good guy! The Chinese hero! "Six men and a girl, helpless . . . while weird jungle tom-toms beat out the signal for the headhunters' attack!" Paramount's creative advertising copywriters prepared the world for something out of *King Kong* or at the very least *Bring 'Em Back Alive,* while the producers and director Kurt Neumann delivered *Island of Lost Men,* with Naish as the evil exploiter of pursued men in a jungle hideout.

Kim Ling (Wong), daughter of an army general (Richard Loo) who has disappeared with a large sum of his government's money, is determined to learn his whereabouts and to clear his name. Doing a bit of in-

---

Filmed in 1933 as *White Woman,* with Charles Laughton, Carole Lombard and Kent Taylor (in the Quinn role).

With Anna May Wong

When the general is located and Chang is making arrangements for the three to escape, Tex Ballister (Broderick Crawford), an American wastrel, turns up at Prin's hideout and exposes Chang's true identity. Then he tries to extort money from Prin in return for the information and threatens to blow the whistle on the gunrunner's kidnaping and blackmailing activities. Prin tries to silence Tex permanently, but the latter incites an uprising among the natives, and Chang grabs the chance to flee with Kim Ling and the general, as Prin himself is killed.

For the benefit of music devotees; Anna May Wong sang for the first time in films. The song, performed as part of her club act, was "Music on the Shore," written by Frederick Hollander and Frank Loesser, and was *not* nominated for an Academy Award in the year which gave us "Over the Rainbow."

credibly efficient sleuthing, she follows the trail to a seaport town in Central America and obtains a job singing in a smoke-filled dive. There she meets Gregory Prin (Naish), mastermind behind a gunrunning operation, and discovers that he might have further information on her father's activities. She induces Prin to take her to his jungle camp where, she soon learns, he provides a haven for fugitives from the law. One of Prin's henchmen, Chang Tai (Quinn), takes Kim Ling aside when the opportunity presents itself and reveals himself as an undercover agent who also is looking for the general, and tells her that he suspects her father to be held at a trading post further up-river. A short time later, while snooping around the camp, Kim Ling finds the $300,000 her father had been carrying in Prin's quarters and informs Chang Tai who contrives with his boss to be sent to the trading post.

With Anna May Wong

With J. Carrol Naish and Anna May Wong

With Judith Barrett, Morgan Conway,
Clem Wilenchick (Crane Whitley),
Minor Watson

# Television Spy

Paramount / 1939

CAST: *Douglas Cameron,* WILLIAM HENRY; *Gwen Lawson,* JUDITH BARRETT; *James Llewellyn,* William Collier Sr.; *Dick Randolph,* Richard Denning; *Boris,* John Eldredge; *Reni Vonich,* Dorothy Tree; *Forbes,* Anthony Quinn; *Burton Lawson,* Minor Watson; *Carl Venner,* Morgan Conway; *William Sheldon,* Byron Foulger; *Harry Payne,* Chester Clute; *Frome,* Wolfgang Zilzer; *Wagner,* Olaf Hytten; *Amelia Sheldon,* Hilda Plowright; *Caroline Sheldon,* Ottola Nesmith; *Police Sergeant,* Wade Boteler; *Jim Winton,* Archie Twitchell (Michael Branden); *Tamley,* Clem Wilenchick (Crane Whitley); *Grinton,* Monte Vandergrift; *Adler,* Charles L. Lane; *Edgar,* Eric Wilton; *Judge,* E. J. Le Saint; *Senator,* Ivan Miller; *Tommy,* Eugene Jackson.

CREDITS: *Director,* Edward Dmytryk; *associate producer,* Edward T. Lowe; *screenplay,* William R. Lipman, Horace McCoy and Lillie Hayward; *story,* Endre Bohem; *music,* Boris Morros; *art directors,* Hans Dreier and Franz Bachelin; *camera,* Harry Fischbeck; *editor,* Anne Bauchens. Running time: 60 minutes.

Edward Dmytryk, working on his second film, was the director of this incredibly plotted and unbelievably complicated hour-long gangster melodrama, the first of four films on which Quinn—here once again a bad guy—worked with Dmytryk. *Television Spy,* which boils down in the last few minutes simply to boy meets girl via the television screen, received at least a few kind words from the New York *Daily News* reviewer, Dorothy Manners, who hiked out to Brooklyn to catch this gem: "The action is fast, the suspense overplayed. The pic-

With Judith Barrett

James Llewellyn (William Collier Sr.), into viewing a demonstration of long-distance television, the old man is duly impressed and encourages the scientist to perfect the invention, which Llewellyn hopes to donate to the government. Cameron's plans, however, are stolen by foreign agents Reni Vonich (Dorothy Tree) and Forbes (Quinn), who then dupe the scientist's former partner, Burton Lawson (Minor Watson), into re-creating the transmitter from the pilfered blueprints.

Conducing a test telecast sometime later, Cameron discovers a "bootleg" station on the same wavelength, operated by Lawson's daughter, Gwen (Judith Barrett). On a table beside her, Cameron notices, is a set of plans which he recognizes as his own. He demands an explanation from Gwen, but Forbes shuts down the station. Lawson then realizes he has been used by a gang of international spies and that he and Gwen are in grave danger. Cameron, who has fallen in love with Gwen long-distance, cannot believe that she had stolen the plans, and is secretly contacted by Lawson who has evaded Forbes and put his station back on the air. Lawson convinces his former partner that he (Lawson) knew nothing of the theft and urges Cameron to notify the police. As Cameron is about the contact the California authorities from his New York laboratory, Reni and Forbes burst in on him. Llewellyn, watching from another room on a closed circuit (explained as "an interoffice televiser"), sends in help and the spies are disarmed. Cameron then completes his call to California to tell the police where the Lawsons are being held captive. Llewellyn, acting as matchmaker, then introduces Gwen to Cameron formally, using the remarkable new invention called television.

ture itself is a fair-to-middling thriller, but the genius is largely behind the scenes—and his name is Edward Dmytryk . . . who seems to possess magic powers wherein the emotions hold sway over season."

As the title implies, the film pioneered in dealing with the still-infant invention and tied to it intrigue over its control by the American government and foreign interests. When brilliant young scientist Douglas Cameron (William Henry) talks his crusty old sponsor,

With Judith Barrett, Minor Watson, Dorothy Tree, Morgan Conway, John Eldredge

With Louise Campbell and John Miljan

# Emergency Squad

Paramount / 1940

CAST: *Pete Barton*, WILLIAM HENRY; *Betty Bryant*, LOUISE CAMPBELL; *Dan Barton*, Richard Denning; *Chester Miller*, Robert Paige; *Nick Buller*, Anthony Quinn; *Slade Wiley*, John Miljan; *Lt. Murdock*, John Marston; *Editor Joyce*, Joseph Crehan; *Emily*, Catherine Proctor; *Slim*, James Seay; *Matt*, Walter Tetley; *Landlady*, Lillian Elliott; *Callahan*, Jack Kennedy; *Lennie*, Weldon Heyburn; *Jack*, Kenneth Duncan; *Jimmy*, Jimmie Dundee; *Mack*, Stanley Blystone; *Wally*, Wilfred Roberts; *Ada*, Barbara Barondess; *Ada's Son*, Henry Blair; *Fire Captain*, Pat O'Malley; *Bob*, Darryl Hickman; *Mrs. Cobb*, Zeffie Tilbury.

CREDITS: *Director*, Edward Dmytryk; *associate producer*, Stuart Walker; *screenplay*, Garnett Weston and Stuart Palmer; *story*, Robert Musel and Michael Raymond; *music*, Boris Morros; *art directors*, Hans Dreier and Franz Bachelin; *camera*, Stuart Thompson; *editor*, Everett Douglas. Running time: 58 minutes.

In Quinn's second consecutive Edward Dmytryk picture, the two leading men (William Henry and Richard Denning) were the same, while leading lady Louise Campbell stepped in for Judith Barrett. Villains in this outing were Anthony Quinn and John Miljan, whose job in this film was to undermine a tunnel project in order to drive down the value of the tunnel authority's bonds. "The direction is amateurish," considered *Harri-son's Reports,* "and the acting worse, while the characters talk themselves to death."

The title refers to a group of troubleshooters (Henry, Denning and Robert Paige) who take on assignments too tough for others—a plot device used excessively in films and, as practiced in TV's "Emergency," still with us. Nevertheless, the title is rather misleading since the film revolves around the efforts of would-be gal reporter Betty Bryant (Louise Campbell) to land a newspaper job from editor Joyce (Joseph Crehan). She is promised a permanent spot on the paper if she can first come up with a sensational front-page story. Enter the boys from Emergency Squad, who invite her to tag along while they make an important rescue. When she gets the story and subsequently the job she's after, Betty begins digging into the background behind a series of mysterious accidents in a trouble-prone tunnel project, and learns that contractor Slade Wiley (Miljan) and racketeer Nick Buller (Quinn) are tied in with the mishaps.

Wiley and Buller invite Betty to inspect the tunnel with them, timing their guided tour to end just before a new explosion takes place. This way they hope to divert all suspicion from themselves. Their plan backfires, however, when a sudden cave-in traps them and the reporter inside the tunnel with only ten minutes until the scheduled explosion. The Emergency Squad roars into action and stages a hairbreadth rescue of the trio. Betty returns to the paper to file her story, exposing Wiley and Buller and saving the tunnel project.

# Road to Singapore

Paramount / 1940

CAST:    *Josh Mallon,* BING CROSBY; *Mima,* DOR-
OTHY LAMOUR; *Ace Lannigan,* BOB HOPE; *Joshua
Mallon IV,* Charles Coburn; *Gloria Wycott,* Judith Bar-
rett; *Caesar,* Anthony Quinn; *Achilles Bombanassa,*
Jerry Colonna; *Timothy Willow,* Johnny Arthur; *Mor-
gan Wycott,* Pierre Watkin; *Gordon Wycott,* Gaylord
(Steve) Pendleton; *Sir Malcolm Drake,* Miles Mander;
*Zato,* Pedro Regas; *Babe,* Greta Grandstedt; *Bill,* Ed-
ward Gargan; *Fred,* Don Brodie; *Sailor,* John Kelly;
*Sailor's Wife,* Kitty Kelly; *Father,* Roger Gray; *Secre-
tary,* Harry C. Bradley; *Cameraman,* Richard Keene;
*Ninky Poo,* Gloria Franklin; *High Priest,* Monte Blue;
*Ship's Officer,* Cyril Ring; *Dancing Girl,* Carmen D'Antonio; *Society Girl,* Helen Lynd; *Columnist,* Jack Pep-
per; *Bartender,* Arthur Q. Bryan.

CREDITS:    *Director,* Victor Schertzinger; *producer,*
Harlan Thompson; *screenplay,* Don Hartman and Frank
Butler; *story,* Harry Hervey; *music director,* Victor
Young; *songs,* Johnny Burke, James Monaco and Vic-
tor Schertzinger; *choreography,* LeRoy Prinz; *art direc-
tors,* Hans Dreier and Robert Odell; *special effects,* Far-
ciot Edouart; *camera,* William C. Mellor; *editor,* Paul
Weatherwax. Running time: 84 minutes.

The following casting item appeared in the *New York
Herald Tribune* on August 27, 1939: "Anthony Quinn,
son-in-law of Cecil B. DeMille, has been cast for the
part of Dorothy Lamour's dancing partner in *Road
to Singapore.*" Had Quinn seen the one-line release, that
identification after his name undoubtedly would have
caused him no little distress. In the first of the joyous
*Road* pictures (and the first of two in which he appeared), Quinn had ample opportunity to snarl and
glower at Crosby and Hope in his role as the heavy
from whom the boys "rescue" Dorothy Lamour.

On this trek, the boys, here called Josh Mallon
(Crosby) and Ace Lannigan (Hope), are on the run
because Josh is trying to put distance between himself
and his wealthy, marriage-minded girlfriend, Gloria Wy-

With Dorothy Lamour

cott (Judith Barrett). Turning up on the remote island
of Keigoon, where natives speak only Esperanto, they
come across the beautiful sarong-clad Mima (Lamour)
and begin flirting with her, until her jealous dancing
partner and fiancé Caesar (Quinn) drags her off, threatening to kill her. Josh and Ace devise a plan to save
her from her fate at Caesar's hands, and Mima moves
into their shack with them, where she cooks, tidies up,
scrubs and sings for them. When his father (Charles
Coburn) suddenly turns up on the island, along with
Gloria, Josh turns down their pleas that he return to the
States with them, preferring instead to go native, enjoy
the world of ukeleles, native dances and fresh pineapple
juice, and marry Mima.

The plot, naturally, is considerably embellished by
the madcap antics of Paramount's "Rover boys" and
their camaraderie as they compete for Dorothy Lamour's affections—the standard framework for the
loosely scripted *Road* pictures.

With Jerry Colonna, Johnny Arthur
(rear), Benny Innocencio, Fred Mala-
tesia (hidden), Judith Barrett, Bob
St. Angelo, Charles Coburn, Gloria
Franklin, Bing Crosby

# Parole Fixer

Paramount / 1940

CAST: *Scott Britton*, WILLIAM HENRY; *Enid Casserly*, VIRGINIA DALE; *Steve Eddson*, ROBERT PAIGE; *Colette Menthe*, Gertrude Michael; *Bruce Eaton*, Richard Denning; *Francis (Big Boy) Bradmore*, Anthony Quinn; *Mrs. Thornton Casserly*, Marjorie Gateson; *Ross Waring*, Lyle Talbot; *Bartley Hanford*, Harvey Stephens; *Tyler Craden*, Paul McGrath; *Gustave Kalkus*, Richard Carle; *Nellie*, Charlotte Wynters; *Aunt Lindy*, Louise Beavers; *Frank Preston*, Wilfred Roberts; *George Mattison*, Jack Carson; *Edward Bradshaw*, John Gallaudet; *Edward "Slim" Racky*, Eddie Marr; *Ben*, Morgan Wallace; *Bobby Mattison*, Sonny Bupp; *Jimmy Mattison*, Billy Lee; *Randall Porter*, Harry Shannon; *Judge*, Russell Hicks; *Edward Murkil*, Edwin Maxwell; *Mrs. Tilden*, Mary Hart; *Carter*, Olaf Hytten; *Mr. Tilden*, Ed Mortimer; *Florist*, Byron Foulger; *Edward (Florist's Helper)*, Doodles Weaver.

CREDITS: *Director*, Robert Florey; *associate producer*, Edward T. Lowe; *screenplay*, William R. Lipman and Horace McCoy; *based on the novel* "Persons in Hiding" by J. Edgar Hoover; *music*, Boris Morros; *art directors*, Hans Dreier and John Goodman; *camera*, Harry Fischbeck; *editor*, Harvey Johnston. Running time: 57 minutes.

In the third of four films economy-minded Paramount was cleverly able to squeeze from J. Edgar Hoover's book *Persons in Hiding*, Anthony Quinn was cast with a screenful of familiar faces playing, under the competent, fast-paced direction of Robert Florey, another in his growing gallery of baddies—this one named Francis "Big Boy" Bradmore. The Hoover book was carved into a quartet of films (the others: *Persons in Hiding*, *Undercover Doctor* and *Queen of the Mob*) by prolific writers William R. Lipman and Horace McCoy, and they provided work for just about everybody on the "B" roster in one or another of the crime melodramas. *Parole Fixer*, as the title suggests, was billed as an exposé of the inequities of the parole system as practiced by corrupt politicians—in this case, sinister lawyer Paul

With Robert Paige and Virginia Dale

McGrath, who, although given tenth billing, was the film's nominal star.

Lawyer Tyler Craden (McGrath), plotting to get a generous portion of the fortune of flighty social matron, Mrs. Thornton Casserly (Marjorie Gateson), decides he needs "professional" help and pulls strings to have "Big Boy" Bradmore (Quinn) sprung from prison. Not long after his release, Bradmore murders FBI agent George Mattison (Jack Carson), and G-men Scott Britton (William Henry) and Ross Waring (Lyle Talbot) are assigned to the case. Meanwhile, Craden induces Mrs. Casserly to use her influence to obtain petitions demanding the release of another convict, Steve Eddson (Robert Paige). The head of the parole board (Richard Carle), whom Craden has been blackmailing, votes for

Eddson's release, and then arranges for the parolee to become Mrs. Casserly's chauffeur. Eddson, working with Bradmore, kidnaps Mrs. Casserly's daughter, Enid (Virginia Dale), along with Enid's fiancé, Bruce Eaton (Richard Denning). When Mrs. Casserly begins to suspect Eddson of the crime, agents Britton and Waring, who have been zeroing in on Bradmore, get their biggest break by tying in the man they're after with Eddson and finally with Craden himself. The G-men close in on the gang, rescue the young couple, and expose the entire racket, prompting legislation revising parole procedures.

B. R. Crisler, who reviewed the film for *The New York Times* and gave it one quick paragraph, felt that "the subject, like the story, is by now not worth the effort which its cast so heroically expends upon it."

With Bob Hope and Paulette Goddard

# The Ghost Breakers

Paramount / 1940

CAST:    *Larry Lawrence,* BOB HOPE; *Mary Carter,* PAULETTE GODDARD; *Geoff Montgomery,* Richard Carlson; *Parada,* Paul Lukas; *Ramon/Francisco Maderos,* Anthony Quinn; *Alex,* Willie Best; *Havez,* Pedro de Cordoba; *Raspy Kelly,* Tom Dugan; *Martin,* Lloyd Corrigan; *Frenchy Duval,* Paul Fix; *Mother Zombie,* Virginia Brissac; *The Zombie,* Noble Johnson; *Lt. Murray,* Robert Elliott; *Hotel Porter,* James Flavin; *Announcer,* Emmett Vogan; *Telephone Girl,* Kay Stewart; *Interne,* Douglas Kennedy; *Interne,* Robert Ryan; *Elevator Boy,* Jack Hatfield; *Screaming Woman,* Grace Hayle; *Police Sergeant,* James Blaine; *Bellhop,* David Durand; *Ship Porter,* Max Wagner; *Newsboy,* Leonard Sues; *Ship Bellboy,* Jack Edwards; *Drunk,* Jack Norton; *Baggage Man,* Paul Newland; *Headwaiter,* Francisco Maran; *Dolores,* Blanca Vischer.

CREDITS:    *Director,* George Marshall; *producer,* Arthur Hornblow Jr.; *screenplay,* Walter DeLeon; *based on the play by* Paul Dickey and Charles W. Goddard; *music,* Ernst Toch; *art directors,* Hans Dreier and Robert Usher; *special effects,* Farciot Edouart; *camera,* Charles Lang; *editor,* Ellsworth Hoagland. Running time: 82 minutes.

Anthony Quinn played a dual role in this third screen version of the old Broadway chestnut by Paul Dickey and Charles W. Goddard, dealing with the efforts to keep the new owner of a spooky Cuban castle away on the pretext that the place is haunted, while a search proceeds for buried treasure in the dungeon. Quinn, as Latin twin brothers, is among those warning Paulette

Filmed in 1915 with H. B. Warner, as *The Ghost Breaker* (sic) in 1922 with Wallace Reid, and as *Scared Stiff* in 1953 with Dean Martin and Jerry Lewis.

Goddard, the castle's new owner, and Bob Hope, her unwilling companion. Despite Quinn's menacing looks and mysterious comings-and-goings, however, he turns out to be one of the many red herrings in this madcap chase to the hidden silver mine, one of the best Bob Hope movies of the era.

After inheriting Castillo Maldito on Black Island in Cuba, Mary Carter (Paulette Goddard) is warned by Cuban consul Havez (Pedro de Cordoba) not to accept her estate, as every other relative has died a horrible death there. Shortly thereafter, Parada (Paul Lukas), attorney for the estate, offers Mary $50,000 for the property after repeating Havez's predictions. She is determined, though, and books passage that night. Meanwhile, Larry Lawrence (Bob Hope), a radio commentator whose specialty is exposing shady underworld dealings, turns up at Mary's hotel coincidentally, called by gangster Frenchy Duval (Paul Fix), whom Larry was prepared to unmask on his show. As he heads for Frenchy's room, Larry passes Parada's door and pauses; then, spotting one of Frenchy's men, he ducks behind a door just as Ramon Maderos (Quinn), who had just arranged by phone to discuss her castle with Mary, steps into Parada's room, gun in hand and begins spraying the room with bullets. Terrified, Larry pulls out his own gun and fires wildly. Maderos crumples to the floor dead and Larry, in a state of panic, runs into Mary's room and dives into an open steamer trunk. The trunk, with Larry inside is taken to the boat and placed in Mary's stateroom. Aboard ship, Mary learns that Parada has the next stateroom and receives flowers from him, along with another warning note.

When Larry is released from the trunk, he convinces Parada he has been hired by Mary as a ghost-breaker, ridding houses of their haunts. In Havana Mary is introduced to Geoff Montgomery (Richard Carlson), whom she vaguely remembers from a New York cocktail party. Accompanying Geoff to a club, she meets Maderos's twin brother Francisco, who demands to know the circumstances behind Ramon's death, and then warns her that he will see her later. Going alone to the castle, Mary finds that Larry has preceded her, along with his valet Alex (Willie Best). They have seen ghostly figures and heard an organ moaning. Investigating, the three come upon a casket-filled death chamber where suddenly ghosts of Mary's ancestors begin to rise from their coffins. One, it turns out, is Parada, who has been attacked. He mutters about treasures, marching men and "organ the key," and then he dies.

Mary plays on the organ, the notes formed by the feet of figures on the wall. As she does, a casket slides and reveals a tunnel to a silver mine. Francisco Maderos is there. Suddenly Geoff appears, gun in hand, but before he can fire, Alex inadvertently opens a trapdoor, dropping Geoff to his death. It seems Maderos was only protecting the mine, and all ends well, with Mary and Larry planning marriage.

With Paulette Goddard and Richard Carlson

# City for Conquest

Warner Bros.–First National / 1940

CAST: *Danny Kenny,* JAMES CAGNEY; *Peggy Nash,* ANN SHERIDAN; *Old-Timer,* Frank Craven; *Scotty MacPherson,* Donald Crisp; *Eddie Kenny,* Arthur Kennedy; *Mutt,* Frank McHugh; *Pinky,* George Tobias; *Dutch,* Jerome Cowan; *Googi Zucco,* Elia Kazan; *Murray Burns,* Anthony Quinn; *Gladys,* Lee Patrick; *Mrs. Nash,* Blanche Yurka; *Goldie,* George Lloyd; *Lily,* Joyce Compton; *Max Leonard,* Thurston Hall; *Cobb,* Ben Welden; *Salesman,* John Arledge; *Gaul,* Ed Keane; *Doctor,* Selmer Jackson; *Doctor,* Joseph Crehan; *Callahan,* Bob Steele; *Henchman,* Billy Wayne; *Booking Agent,* Charles Lane; *Floor Guard,* Pat Flaherty; *M. C.,* Sidney Miller; *Blonde in Dressing Room,* Ethelreda Leopold; and Lee Phelps, Charles Wilson, Edward Gargan, Howard Hickman, Murray Alper, Dick Wessel, Edward Pawley, Bernice Pilot, William Newell, Lucia Carroll, Dana Dale (Margaret Hayes).

CREDITS: *Producer–director,* Anatole Litvak; *associate producer,* William Cagney; *screenplay,* John Wexley; based on the *novel* by Aben Kandel; *music director,* Leo F. Forbstein; *musical score, Max Steiner; orchestrators,* Hugo Friedhofer and Ray Heindorf; *dialogue director,* Irving Rapper; *art director,* Robert Haas; *dance director,* Robert Vreeland; *special effects,* Byron Haskin and Rex Wimpy; *camera,* Sol Polito and James Wong Howe; *editor,* William Holmes. Running time: 103 minutes.

Under Quinn's new contract with Warner Bros. (he still owed Paramount one picture), he hoped to move into roles with a bit more depth than the countless stock hoods he had been asked to portray before. His first film at his new studio led him to believe things would be somewhat more challenging, and his role of Murray

Burns, the brash, egotistical, smooth taxi dancer who talks Ann Sheridan into dumping Cagney and becoming his dance partner, gave Quinn the opportunity to create more than simply another cardboard character. Arthur Kennedy made his film debut in this picture, and Elia Kazan did one of his rare acting jobs as a slick gangster.

*City for Conquest* was another of the perennially popular "slice of New York life" pictures, this time focusing on Danny Kenny (James Cagney) and Peggy Nash (Ann Sheridan), who grew up together on the Lower East Side. Tired of the squalor and poverty, Peggy is afraid to marry Danny, a truck driver, until he makes something of himself. Besides, she wants to become a professional dancer. Danny decides to become a fighter, both to impress Peggy and to help send his brother Eddie (Kennedy) through music school. Fight manager Scotty MacPherson (Donald Crisp) advises Danny to take boxing seriously, but Danny refuses until he realizes that he might lose Peggy, who had won a cup dancing with a smooth operator named Murray Burns (Quinn). Murray suggests that Peggy team with him professionally, and their act becomes a top theater and club attraction. Sometime later, Peggy and Danny, now both successful, meet again, but Peggy still is unwilling to quit her act with Murray. Danny throws himself into boxing with abandon and decides to go for the big money. During the big fight, Danny is blinded and is forced to give up his career. Peggy is shattered by the events and tells Murray that she's quitting. Googi Zucco (Kazan), Danny's boyhood friend, now a racketeer, kills the crooked trainer of the fighter who blinded Danny, and is himself shot in the process.

With Scotty's help and Eddie's encouragement, Danny opens a newsstand on Broadway and establishes

With Joyce Compton

himself in the neighborhood. His proudest moment is listening to Eddie's Carnegie Hall debut on the radio, with his brother's concerto being dedicated to him. And while rapt in the music, Danny suddenly realizes he is not alone at his little stand—Peggy has returned to him.

With Ann Sheridan and Charles Lane

[ 75 ]

With Edward Pawley, John Howard, Broderick Crawford

# Texas Rangers Ride Again

Paramount / 1940

CAST: *Ellen "Slats" Dangerfield,* ELLEN DREW; *Jim Kingston,* JOHN HOWARD; *Mio Pio,* Akim Tamiroff; *Cecilia Dangerfield,* May Robson; *Mace Townsley,* Broderick Crawford; *Ben Caldwater,* Charley Grapewin; *Carter Dangerfield,* John Miljan; *Joe Yuma,* Anthony Quinn; *Captain Inglis,* William Duncan; *Ranger Blair,* Harvey Stephens; *Ranger Comstock,* Harold Goodwin; *Maria,* Eva Puig; *Palo Pete,* Edward Pawley; *Mandolin,* Eddie Foy Jr.; *Johnson,* Joseph Crehan; *Highboots,* Jim Pierce; *Slide Along,* Monte Blue; *Nevers,* Stanley Price; *Ranger Gilpin,* Tom Tyler, *Ranger Stafford,* Donald Curtis; *Stenographer,* Eddie Acuff; *Eddie,* Robert Ryan; *Girl,* Ruth Rogers; *Announcer,* Gordon Jones.

CREDITS: *Director,* James Hogan; *associate producer,* Edward T. Lowe; *screenplay,* William R. Lipman and Horace McCoy; *music director,* Boris Morros; *art directors,* Hans Dreier and Earl Hedrick; *camera,* Archie Stout; *editor,* Arthur Schmidt. Running time: 67 minutes.

Anthony Quinn wrapped up his lengthy player contract at Paramount with this standard horse opera, reduced to the basic good guys vs. bad guys, boy-meets-girl formula. In this curious combination of the contemporary West and the conventional film Western, much like the Roy Rogers television show of the 1950s in which Roy chased the bad guys in a jeep, Quinn played the steely-eyed half-breed ranch foreman in league with the owner's disgruntled nephew in a covert rustling operation. Crusty May Robson easily stole the film as the feisty owner of the spread, trying to halt the mysterious disappearance of her cattle. Sharp-eyed movie devotees have spotted a young Robert Ryan in a brief role as a curious citizen who, sitting in a car with his girlfriend, spots a truck carrying the stolen beef and trails it.

To put an end to the strange depletion of her herd,

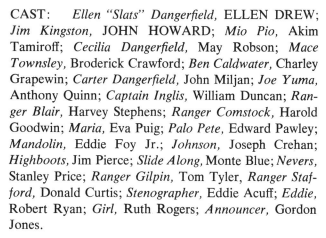

Cecilia Dangerfield (May Robson) enlists the aid of the Texas Rangers, and the assignment to investigate falls to Jim Kingston (John Howard) and Mace Townsley (Broderick Crawford), who turn up incognito at her White Sage Ranch pretending to be saddle tramps looking for jobs. Cecilia's nephew Carter (John Miljan), who runs the spread, turns them over to his foreman, Joe Yuma (Quinn). Yuma hides his suspicions about the strangers and sets them to work mending fences. While they're checking one end of the ranch territory, the rustlers go about their task at the other end, slaughtering the cattle, loading the beef onto trucks, and destroying the carcasses in a secret lime pit. Kingston and Townsley intercept a radio message from Carter Dangerfield to a wholesaler in town. While Townsley is away checking on a lead, Kingston meets Cecilia's highborn niece Slats (Ellen Drew), who falls for the brash stranger as a change from the boredom of isolated ranch life.

When Townsley returns, he and Kingston trail the rustlers to their leader, Joe Yuma, and, while Townsley sneaks aboard the truck hauling the beef, Kingston blockades himself in the ranch house with Cecilia and Slats, together with handyman Mio Pio (Akim Tamiroff) and old-time ranger and long-time friend Ben Caldwater (Charley Grapewin). They prepare for a siege by Yuma and his men. Meanwhile, in town, Townsley slips out of the truck in a huge warehouse and confronts Carter Dangerfield, who is closing a deal with his contact (Joseph Crehan). The rangers arrive to close down the operation, as Townsley and Captain Inglis (William Duncan) ride back to the ranch with a ranger contingent to save Kingston and the Dangerfields. The rangers get their men, Cecilia and Ben decide to rekindle a romance going back fifty years, and Kingston and Slats ride off into the sunset, while trusty Mio Pio takes off in hot pursuit of mean Joe Yuma.

With J. Carrol Naish and Tyrone Power

# Blood and Sand

20th Century–Fox / 1941

CAST: *Juan Gallardo*, TYRONE POWER; *Carmen Espinosa*, LINDA DARNELL; *Doña Sol*, RITA HAYWORTH; *Señora Augustias*, Alla Nazimova; *Manolo de Palma*, Anthony Quinn; *Garabato*, J. Carrol Naish; *Nacional*, John Carradine; *Encarnacion*, Lynn Bari; *Natalio Curro*, Laird Cregar; *Antonio Lopez*, William Montague (Monty Banks); *Capt. Pierre Lauren*, George Reeves; *Guitarist*, Vicente Gomez; *Don Jose Alvarez*, Pedro de Cordoba; *Pedro Espinosa*, Fortunio Bonanova; *Priest*, Victor Kilian; *La Pulga*, Adrian (Michael) Morris; *Pablo Gomez*, Charles Stevens; *Carmen (as a child)*, Ann Todd; *Encarnacion (as a child)*, Cora Sue Collins; *Juan (as a child)*, Rex Downing; *Marquis*, Russell Hicks; *El Milquetoast*, Maurice Cass; *Francisco*, John Wallace; *Gachi*, Jacqueline Dalya; *Manolo (as a child)*, Larry Harris; *Nacional (as a child)*, Schuyler Standish; *Conductor*, Paco Moreno; *Specialty Dancer*, Elena Verdugo; *Friend*, Francis McDonald; *Engineer*, Harry Burns.

Filmed in 1922 with Rudolph Valentino, Lila Lee and Nita Naldi.

CREDITS: *Director*, Rouben Mamoulian; *producer*, Darryl F. Zanuck; *associate producer*, Robert T. Kane; *screenplay*, Jo Swerling; based on the *novel* "Sangre y Arene" by Vincente Blasco Ibañez; *music director*, Alfred Newman; *art directors*, Richard Day and Joseph C. Wright; *camera*, Ernest Palmer and Ray Rennahan; *editor*, Robert Bischoff. Technicolor. Running time: 123 minutes.

Quinn was loaned to 20th Century-Fox for Darryl F. Zanuck's opulent Technicolor remake of the memorable Valentino silent film based on the Ibañez novel. As Manolo de Palma, the boyhood friend, follower and finally successor of Tyrone Power, Quinn solidified in many minds the idea that he was perfect for redoing old Valentino roles. In retrospect, it even appears that Quinn would have made a better Juan Gallardo than did the incredibly handsome, dark-eyed (but non-Latin) Power, who was asked by Mamoulian to play the role as a petulant boor. Quinn's sensual screen tango with Rita Hayworth (conceived by Oscar "Budd" Boetticher and staged by Geneva Sawyer) demonstrated his re-

[ 77 ]

markable agility on the dance floor and remains one of the movie's best remembered moments.

*Blood and Sand* was Rouben Mamoulian's second Technicolor film (Ernest Palmer and Ray Rennahan won Academy Awards for their outstanding color photography), and he filled it resplendently in the gold and pink brocades of Spain, mixing with the elegance of swirling capes in the bullring and the spice of superb supporting performances, most notably by Alla Nazimova as Power's mother and John Carradine as the friend who remains faithful to the end. All the passes and swirls of the bullring were vividly depicted by Mamoulian, but, bowing to the dictates of the Hays Office, no actual thrust of the sword was shown.

Mamoulian begins the film with a thirty-minute prologue, establishing the characters ten years before the main narrative. Juan Gallardo (Power) had been a poor youngster in Seville and son of a bullfighter who had died in the ring. Decidedly illiterate but possessing his father's passion for bullfighting, Juan runs off to Madrid with his boyhood friends, Manolo (Quinn) and Nacional (Carradine). After gaining a reputation of sorts as a minor-league matador, Juan returns to Seville to marry his childhood sweetheart, Carmen Espinosa (Linda Darnell), and then goes on to become the most widely acclaimed matador of the time. Surrounded by leeches, though, Juan remains constantly—but happily—in debt, until the stunning Doña Sol (Rita Hayworth) enters his life. Falling under her seductive spell, Juan begins an affair with her at the expense of both his wife and his career.

Carmen leaves him, but follows the downward trend of his once-blazing star. Doña Sol begins to tire of Juan and casts a sexy eye at the up-and-coming Manolo, who long has stood in his friend's shadow and is now emerging on his own as a ring favorite. The shattered Juan

With Rita Hayworth

returns to Carmen and begs her to take him back, but his newly recaptured success in the ring is cut short by a vicious goring. As he is being carried from the arena, the cheers go up for the new hero of the crowds, Manolo de Palma, and in his dressing room beneath the stands, Juan Gallardo dies.

*Blood and Sand,* with its classic story of love in the moonlight and death in the afternoon, was the first of Quinn's three bullfight movies. He also narrated Budd Boetticher's documentary on the subject, tracing the career of Carlos Arruza, thirty years later.

With Rita Hayworth

# Knockout

Warner Bros. / 1941

CAST: *Johnny Rocket,* ARTHUR KENNEDY; *Angela Grinnelli,* OLYMPE BRADNA; *Gloria Van Ness,* Virginia Field; *Trego,* Anthony Quinn; *Pinky,* Cliff Edwards; *Tom Rossi,* Cornel Wilde; *Louis Grinnelli,* William Edmunds; *Allison,* Richard Ainley; *Pat Martin,* John Ridgely; *Denning,* Frank Wilcox; *Polky,* Ben Welden; *Mrs. Turner,* Vera Lewis; *Monigan,* Charles Wilson; *Doctor,* Edwin Stanley; *First Reporter,* DeWolfe (William) Hopper; *Second Reporter,* Creighton Hale; *Announcer,* Lee Phelps; *Referee,* Al Seymour; *Murphy,* John Kellogg; *Kovacs,* Bill Phillips; *Peters,* David Clarke; *Stanley,* Gaylord (Steve) Pendleton; *Hawkins,* Kid Chissell; *Mrs. Smithers,* Grace Hayle; *Boxers,* Frank Faylen, Paul Phillips and Jack Herrick; *Kent,* Joe Grey.

CREDITS: *Director,* William Clemens; *producer,* Edmund Grainger; *screenplay,* M. Coates Webster; *story,* Michael Fessier; *music,* Heinz Roemheld; *camera,* Ted McCord; *editor,* Doug Gould. Running time: 74 minutes.

Providing a brief respite from the stock hood or gangland torpedo role, Quinn was cast in this little fight

With Cliff Edwards and Arthur Kennedy

With Cliff Edwards and Arthur Kennedy

film as the unscrupulous manager who keeps his young boxer from tossing away a promising (and, for Quinn, lucrative) career for domesticity. As written, the part of Trego the manager was cut from the same piece of cardboard dragged out in innumerable other films, from *Patent Leather Kid* onward. An interesting comparison can be made by examining how the screen had advanced between *Knockout* and Quinn's later sensational role as Mountain Rivera in *Requiem for a Heavyweight* when Jackie Gleason played the manager.

Johnny Rocket (Arthur Kennedy), an up-and-coming fighter, decides to quit the ring at the urging of his bride, Angela (Olympe Bradna), and plans to open a health farm. His manager Trego (Quinn) feels that he is championship material and pressures Johnny into changing his mind. To keep his meal ticket, Trego uses his influence to keep Johnny from finding work else-

where. With proper training and publicity, Johnny fights his way to the top and Trego keeps feeding his ego, introducing him into society and arranging for him to meet lovely socialite sports reporter Gloria Van Ness (Virginia Field). Johnny begins running around with Gloria as his own marriage heads for the rocks, and his spiraling success, combined with dizzying society life, begins to take a toll on him. Figuring Johnny has gone as far as he can in the ring, Trego bets against him, insuring a "fall" by drugging the boxer's mouthpiece. Johnny loses not only the fight but his society girlfriend as well, and he wanders aimlessly with a brain concussion. He finds, at last, that Angela has been waiting for him and lovingly takes him back. With the money she had saved, the two finally are able to open their farm and begin a new life.

With Cliff Edwards, Arthur Kennedy and Tom Garland

With Frank Faylen and Jane Darwell

# Thieves Fall Out

Warner Bros. / 1941

CAST: *Eddie Barnes,* EDDIE ALBERT; *Mary Matthews,* JOAN LESLIE; *Grandma Allen,* Jane Darwell; *Robert Barnes,* Alan Hale; *George Gormsby,* William T. Orr; *Tim Gordon,* John Litel; *Ella Barnes,* Minna Gombell; *Chic Collins,* Anthony Quinn; *Rork,* Edward Brophy; *David Tipton,* Hobart Cavanaugh; *Charles Matthews,* Vaughan Glaser; *Martha Matthews,* Nana Bryant; *Pick,* Frank Faylen; *Kane,* Edward Gargan; *Harry Eckles,* William Davidson; *Cab Driver,* Tom Kennedy; *Blossom,* Etta McDaniel; *Secretary,* Ann Edmonds; *Janitor,* Jack Wise; *Policeman,* Cliff Clark; *Justice of the Peace,* Walter Soderling.

CREDITS: *Director,* Ray Enright; *producer,* Edmund Grainger; *screenplay,* Charles Grayson and Ben Markson; based on the *play* "Thirty Days Hath September" by Irving Gaumont and Jack Sobel; *music,* Heinz Roemheld; *camera,* Sid Hickox; *editor,* Clarence Kolster. Running time: 72 minutes.

Quinn assumed his familiar guise and scowled menacingly at grandma Jane Darwell, but it proved to be no contest in this domestic comedy about a little old lady who beats gangsters at their own game. In this screen version of the Broadway play *Thirty Days Hath September,* which had a brief run in 1938, dozens of familiar faces from Warner Bros.' stock company helped make an entertaining, undemanding hour-plus breeze along.

Unable to get his officious father (Alan Hale) to raise his salary, Eddie Barnes (Eddie Albert) turns to his grandmother (Jane Darwell) for advice. She suggests that he take a loan against an expected inherit-

ance, tied up temporarily in his grandfather's will, and set himself up in business after marrying his girlfriend, Mary Matthews (Joan Leslie). Broker David Tipton (Hobart Cavanaugh) offers Eddie $31,000 for the legacy, and then he turns around and sells it to racketeer Chic Collins (Quinn). Collins immediately goes back to Eddie's father and threatens him and his wife unless he buys back the investment at the inflated Collins price. Grandma Allen, anxious to see Eddie and Mary's romance succeed, then goes into action, leading Collins to believe that she is the beneficiary. Collins has her kidnaped, but is unprepared for the consequences. As an ardent fan of radio serials, Grandma outwits Collins's gang with her knowledge of gangster slang and angles and tricks Collins himself into returning her papers. For all of her meddling, Grandma is able to reconcile the family and see to it that Eddie and Mary are married, with the folks' blessings and a big raise.

With Jane Darwell and Frank Faylen

With Roland Drew and Dick Purcell

# Bullets for O'Hara

Warner Bros. / 1941

CAST: *Patricia Van Dyne*, JOAN PERRY; *Mike O'Hara*, ROGER PRYOR; *Tony Van Dyne*, Anthony Quinn; *Elaine Standish*, Maris Wrixon; *McKay Standish*, Richard Ainley; *Richard Palmer*, DeWolfe (William) Hopper; *Marjorie Palmer*, Joan Winfield; *Wicks*, Dick Purcell; *Bradford*, Roland Drew; *Maxwell*, Joseph King; *Steve*, Victor Zimmerman; *Judge*, Hobart Bosworth; *Swartzman*, Hank Mann; *Lamson*, Sidney Bracy; *Jim*, Kenneth Harlan; *Weldon*, Frank Mayo; *G-Man*, Jack Mower; *Police Matron*, Leah Baird; *Mayme*, Jean Maddox; *Jury Foreman*, Creighton Hale; *Prosecutor*, Frank Ferguson; *Kettering*, Alexander Leftwich; *Minister*, George Irving; *Bellboy*, William Roberts; *Messengers*, Murray Alper and Billy Wayne.

CREDITS: *Director*, William K. Howard; *associate producer*, William Jacobs; *screenplay*, Raymond Schrock; *story*, David O. Selznick and P. J. Wolfson; *music*, Heinz Roemheld; *camera*, Ted McCord; *editor*, James Gibbons. Running time: 50 minutes.

Anthony Quinn found himself badly miscast as a pseudosociety gunman in this routine crook melodrama, filmed earlier as *Public Enemy's Wife*, with Cesar Romero in the role. The film itself has become a standard joke among Quinn and his friends, and obviously is considered one of his most forgettable, even though everybody involved took the ludicrous proceedings seriously. *Variety* commented disparagingly that "The husband is Anthony Quinn, whom any regular filmgoer would instantly recognize as a mobster from the first glimpse," although it took his society wife more than a year before learning of his criminal activities. Rose Pelswick, critic for the *New York Journal-American*, dismissed the film summarily, noting that "Anthony Quinn, wearing his hat in the early George Raft manner, is the

---

Filmed in 1936 as *Public Enemy's Wife* with Pat O'Brien, Margaret Lindsay and Cesar Romero.

With Joan Perry

menace." Virtually the only notable element about the film was that the original story was co-authored by David O. Selznick! The "O'Hara" of the title, incidentally, is the detective who is trailing Quinn, not Quinn himself—which further confuses the silly goings-on.

Thinking that her husband is wealthy, socialite Patricia Van Dyne (Joan Perry) is shocked to learn he is actually a crook, and is further humiliated when he robs their friends Elaine (Maris Wrixon) and McKay (Richard Ainley) while they are all vacationing together. Tony (Quinn) forces Patricia to accompany him back to Chicago, trailed by detective Mike O'Hara (Roger Pryor). After warning his wife not to talk, Tony runs out on her and goes into hiding. Patricia is arrested for complicity, but her friends attest to her innocence in the crime. Freed, she divorces Tony, and O'Hara goes to work on her, carrying on a phony romance and finally convincing her to go through a mock marriage with him to bring Tony out of hiding. The gangster, learning of the wedding, kidnaps his ex-wife, but is trailed by O'Hara to a boat where Tony is killed in a shootout. O'Hara then talks Patricia into a wedding ceremony—this one real.

With unidentified players

# They Died With Their Boots On

Warner Bros.-First National / 1941

CAST: *George Armstrong Custer,* ERROL FLYNN; *Elizabeth Bacon Custer,* OLIVIA de HAVILLAND; *Ned Sharp,* Arthur Kennedy; *California Joe,* Charley Grapewin; *Samuel Brown,* Gene Lockhart; *Crazy Horse,* Anthony Quinn; *Major Romulus Taipe,* Stanley Ridges; *General Philip Sheridan,* John Litel; *William Sharp,* Walter Hampden; *General Winfield Scott,* Sydney Greenstreet; *Fitzhugh Lee,* Regis Toomey; *Callie,* Hattie McDaniel; *Lt. Butler,* G. P. Huntley Jr.; *Captain Webb,* Frank Wilcox; *Sergeant Doolittle,* Joseph Sawyer; *Senator Smith,* Minor Watson; *President U.S. Grant,* Joseph Crehan; *Salesman,* Irving Bacon; *Captain McCook,* Selmer Jackson; *Corporal Smith,* Eddie Acuff; *Captain Riley,* George Eldredge; *Station Master,* Spencer Charters; *Clergyman,* Hobart Bosworth; *Colonel of 1st Michigan,* Russell Hicks; *Major Smith,* Hugh Sothern; *Lt. Davis,* John Ridgely; *Lt. Roberts,* Gig Young; *Mrs. Sharp,* Aileen Pringle; *Mrs. Taipe,* Anna Q. Nilsson; *Grant's Secretary,* Frank Ferguson.

CREDITS: *Director,* Raoul Walsh; *producer,* Hal B. Wallis; *associate producer,* Robert Fellows; *screenplay,* Aeneas MacKenzie and Wally Kline; *music director,* Max Steiner; *art director,* John Hughes; *camera,* Bert Glennon; *editor,* William Holmes. Running time: 140 minutes.

One curious note about Quinn's career is the minute number of real-life figures he has portrayed in relationship to the extraordinary number of roles he has undertaken. And of the authentic figures he did get to play, virtually all, save possibly Attila the Hun, were on the periphery of history. His first—after thirty films—was Crazy Horse, the famed Indian chief of the Oglala Sioux who became second in command to Sitting Bull and was involved in the Little Big Horn massacre of General Custer and the Seventh Cavalry. In Raoul Walsh's robust, two-hour-and-twenty-minute, entertainment-oriented retelling of Custer's remarkable career, Quinn played Crazy Horse as a vigorous, proud chief, conceived in the white man's image and given, in all probability, grossly inaccurate lines to recite under highly romanticized conditions. It did make for splendid adventure of almost unequaled scope, and audiences tended to overlook the factual lapses and fanciful historical rearrangements for the diversion of exciting entertainment and colorful performances. And there was the unmatched dash of Errol Flynn as Custer to neatly carry the whole thing along. Quinn was to work with Flynn in one more film, as he was to do with director Raoul Walsh.

*They Died With Their Boots On,* the screen's first full-fledged attempt at spanning the career of General George Armstrong Custer, followed the flamboyant officer's story from his hazing as a West Point plebe to the legendary massacre by Sitting Bull's braves in 1876, weaving interludes of romance into the lulls between cavalry charges and Indian attacks. "Mr. Walsh," wrote Thomas M. Pryor in his review in *The New York Times,* "spared neither men, horses nor Errol Flynn's General Custer in kicking up the dust of battle." It remains one of the screen's grandest epic adventures.

With Lynn Bari and Cornel Wilde

# The Perfect Snob

20th Century-Fox / 1941

CAST: *Dr. Mason,* CHARLIE RUGGLES; *Martha Mason,* CHARLOTTE GREENWOOD; *Chris Mason,* LYNN BARI; *Mike Lord,* CORNEL WILDE; *Alex Moreno,* Anthony Quinn; *Freddie Browning,* Alan Mowbray; *Nibsie Nicholson,* Chester Clute; *Witch Doctor,* LeRoy Mason; *Waiter,* Jack Chefe; *Driver,* Biddle Dorsey; *Baggage Man,* Matt McHugh; *Chauffeur,* Charles Tannen.

CREDITS: *Director,* Ray McCarey; *producer,* Walter Morosco; *screenplay,* Lee Loeb and Harold Buchman; *music director,* Emil Newman; *art directors,* Richard Day and Albert Hogsett; *camera,* Charles Clarke;

*editor,* J. Watson Webb. Running time: 62 minutes.

In this lightweight comedy out of 20th Century-Fox's "B" unit headed by Sol Wurtzel, veterans Charlie Ruggles and Charlotte Greenwood deftly and quite easily stole the picture from workhorse starlet Lynn Bari, up-and-coming Cornel Wilde, and Quinn, who again was cast as a Latin type, and again played the hero's friend—an extension, minus the intensity, of his role in *Blood and Sand.*

This marshmallow revolved around the efforts of a young golddigger who, with her mother's blessings, sets her cap for the wealthiest man she can find. Following

With Charlotte Greenwood and
Lynn Bari

graduation from a fashionable girls' school, Chris Mason (Lynn Bari) runs off to Hawaii with her mother (Charlotte Greenwood) to snag a rich husband. When her down-to-earth father (Charlie Ruggles) learns that she has become engaged to millionaire Freddie Browning (Alan Mowbray), he decides to take matters into his own hands and to put some sense into the heads of both Chris and her mother. He goes to Hawaii and hires handsome young fisherman Mike Lord (Cornel Wilde) to break up the courtship. Mike actually is the wealthy owner of a sugar plantation, but keeps the news a secret as he goes about his assignment, falling in love with Chris himself. She also melts, even though Mike tells her finally that he'd been paid for breaking up her wedding plans. Chris, though, is still intent on marrying for money, and Mike, still not letting on about his own millions, decides to test her love. He arranges to have his business partner, Alex Moreno (Quinn), invite the family to the plantation, pass himself off as the sugar tycoon, and make a play for Chris. Believing Alex to be the owner of the sumptuous estate, Chris falls for his smooth Latin charm, and Alex informs Mike that he's in love with Chris himself and that it's now every man for himself. Mike now is obliged to once again break up the mismatched couple, with the help of Chris's father and a well-placed right to the jaw.

With Cornel Wilde

With Edward G. Robinson, Broderick Crawford, Edward Brophy, Joseph Downing

# Larceny, Inc.

Warner Bros.–First National / 1942

CAST: *Pressure Maxwell,* EDWARD G. ROBINSON; *Denny Costello,* Jane Wyman; *Jug Martin,* Broderick Crawford; *Jeff Randolph,* Jack Carson; *Leo Dexter,* Anthony Quinn; *Weepy Davis,* Edward Brophy; *Homer Bigelow,* Harry Davenport; *Sam Bachrach,* John Qualen; *Mademoiselle Gloria,* Barbara Jo Allen (Vera Vague); *Aspinwell,* Grant Mitchell; *Hobart,* Jack C. (Jackie) Gleason; *Oscar Engelhart,* Andrew Tombes; *Smitty,* Joseph Downing; *Mr. Jackson,* George Meeker; *Anton Copoulos,* Fortunio Bonanova; *Warden,* Joseph Crehan; *Florence,* Jean Ames; *McCarthy,* William Davidson; *Buchanan,* Chester Clute; *Carmichael,* Creighton Hale; *Officer O'Casey,* Emory Parnell; *Umpire,* Joe Devlin; *Batter,* John Kelly; *Convicts,* Jimmy O'Gatty and Jack Kenney; *1st Guard,* Eddy Chandler; *Chuck,* Oscar "Dutch" Hendrian; *Mugsy,* Bill Phillips; *Ballplayers,* Hank Mann, Eddie Foster, Cliff Saum and Charles Sullivan; *2nd Guard,* James Flavin; *Driver,* Charles Drake; *Woman,* Vera Lewis; *Young Man,* Ray Montgomery; *1st Customer,* Lucien Littlefield; *Secretary,* Grace Stafford, *2nd Customer,* DeWolfe (William) Hopper; *Policeman,* Pat O'Malley.

CREDITS: *Director,* Lloyd Bacon; *producer,* Hal B.

Wallis; *associate producers,* Jack Saper and Jerry Wald; *screenplay,* Everett Freeman and Edwin Gilbert; based on the *play* "The Night Before Christmas" by Laura and S. J. Perelman; *music director,* Adolph Deutsch; *art director,* John Hughes; *camera,* Tony Gaudio, *editor,* Ralph Dawson. Running time: 95 minutes.

This little comedy-melodrama gem, produced by Hal B. Wallis, for whom Anthony Quinn would work often over the years, has the interesting premise of Quinn's menacing Edward G. Robinson, of all people, and matching him scowl for scowl, snarl for snarl. Quinn is in at the beginning (in prison garb) and at the end to help resolve the situation and, inadvertently, to assure that Robinson and friends go straight.

On the eve of their parole from Sing Sing, Pressure Maxwell (Robinson) and Jug Martin (Broderick Crawford), playing in the final baseball game of the prison season, are approached by Leo Dexter (Quinn). Dexter wants them to join him in a planned bank job he's to pull as soon as he gets out. Pressure and Jug decline because of prior commitments: they plan to open a dog track. On the outside, they discover that their partner Weepy Davis (Edward Brophy) has lost the slot machines on which their investment had been riding. Reluctantly Pressure decides to knock over the bank Dexter had told them about, and he buys a small leather-goods store next to the bank, planning to have Jug and Weepy tunnel in while he operates a legitimate business upstairs. Surprisingly, Pressure enjoys unexpected success as a shopkeeper, establishing himself among his business neighbors. His niece, Denny Costello (Jane Wyman), is proud of him, as is the hotshot salesman, Jeff Randolph (Jack Carson), whose best customer turns out to be Pressure.

Still the robbery plans proceed, and word reaches Leo Dexter in prison. Enraged when he learns that Pressure and his boys are cutting him out, Dexter stages a prison break and bursts in on his former prison cohorts on Christmas Eve. Brandishing a gun, he assumes direction of the robbery preparations and forces Jug and Weepy to keep digging. Pressure does his utmost to stall Dexter until he can think of a way to attract the police, but Dexter refuses to be stopped. He has a number of dynamite charges prepared, but too many sticks are used and the shop itself is destroyed. The police arrive to escort Dexter back to Sing Sing, and, with nobody else aware that the robbery plans were actually theirs, Pressure and his cronies are left to start business anew—as upstanding citizens.

With Harry Strang (with gun) and Emory Parnell (right, holding Quinn)

With Bing Crosby and Bob Hope

# Road to Morocco

Paramount / 1942

CAST: *Jeff Peters,* BING CROSBY; *Princess Shalmar,* DOROTHY LAMOUR; *Turkey Jackson,* BOB HOPE; *Mullay Kasim,* Anthony Quinn; *Mihirmah,* Dona Drake; *Ahmed Fey,* Mikhail Rasumny; *Hyder Khan,* Vladimir Sokoloff; *Neb Jolla,* George Givot; *Oso Bucco,* Andrew Tombes; *Yusef,* Leon Belasco; *Kasim's Aides,* Jamiel Hasson and Monte Blue; *Handmaidens,* Louise LaPlanche, Theo de Voe, Brooke Evans, Suzanne Ridgeway, Patsy Mace, Poppy Wilde and Yvonne DeCarlo; *Arabian Waiter,* Ralph Penney; *Arabian Buyer,* Dan Seymour; *English Announcer,* Brandon Hurst; *Chinese Announcer,* Richard Loo; *Russian Announcer,* Leo Mostovoy; *Bystander,* Edward Emerson; *Dancer,* Sylvia Opert; *Nubian Slave,* Blue Washington; *Specialty Dancer,* Rita Christiani; *Pottery Vendor,* Michael Mark; *Sausage Vendor,* Nestor Paiva; *Idiot,* Stanley Price; *Arab Giant,* Robert Barron; *Warriors,* Harry Cording and Dick Botiller; *Guards,* George Lloyd and Sammy Stein; *Knife Dancers,* Vic Groves and Joe Jewett; *Fruit Stand Proprietor,* Cy Kendall; *Voice for Lady Camel,* Sara Berner; *Voice for Man Camel,* Kent Rogers.

CREDITS: *Director,* David Butler; *associate producer,* Paul Jones; *screenplay,* Frank Butler and Don Hartman; *music director,* Victor Young; *songs,* Johnny Burke and James Van Heusen; *art directors,* Hans Dreier and Robert Usher; *camera,* William C. Mellor;

With Jamiel Hasson, Dona Drake,
Dorothy Lamour, Monte Blue

*editor,* Irene Morra. Running time: 83 minutes.

Quinn was invited back to the Paramount lot for another go at Bing Crosby and Bob Hope, and, with his sinister countenance exotically framed in a white burnoose, he once again traded insults with the boys and vied with them for the ultimate prize, Dorothy Lamour. Other than stooging for the stars, Quinn was on hand merely to growl at Crosby, ogle Miss Lamour, and toss such epithets at Hope as "you long-nosed son of a one-eyed donkey!" When not otherwise occupied, he was seen riding to and fro on his trusty steed while wielding a menacing scimitar. The screen trek to Morocco was loaded with the obligatory sight gags which made the *Road* pictures models of nonstop hilarity. One such interlude placed Quinn, the evil chieftain, in the "nodding room" of his lavish palace. There countless heads, resting upon ornate columns, nod their unending consent as Quinn makes his solitary decisions. This time, two extra heads have joined the enthusiastic agreers, as Crosby and Hope, whom Quinn has been stalking, choose this unfortunate location in which to hide out.

The potpourri of delicious nonsense begins when Jeff Peters (Crosby) and Turkey Jackson (Hope) are shipwrecked off the coast of Africa and swim ashore, making their way to a native bazaar. Wandering in search of food, they find themselves in the center of an attack by sheik Mullay Kasim (Quinn), who has come to claim his intended bride Princess Shalmar (Lamour). The boys take refuge in a restaurant, where Jeff sells Turkey into slavery for $200 to pay for the sumptuous meal they have just devoured. Regretting his actions, Jeff goes looking for his buddy and finds him in the throne room of the palace, with his head resting on Princess Shalmar's lap. Turkey tries to discredit Jeff, but the princess reproaches him, for she has taken an immediate liking to Jeff. She explains, though, that she plans to marry Turkey, and then tells Jeff in confidence that the prophets have forecast that her first husband will live only a week. Meanwhile Kasim learns of the marriage and arrives to claim the princess for himself. She appeases the sheik by telling him of the prophecy and that she really wants him for her lifelong mate. When the princess's prophet discovered he has made a mistake, Shalmar immediately agrees to marry Jeff.

Kasim is told of her plans and kidnaps her, while his men take Jeff and Turkey into the desert and abandon them. The two wander about until finally coming upon Kasim's hidden camp, where a huge wedding feast is under way. Jeff and Turkey cause a squabble between Kasim and a visiting chieftain, and in the ensuing tribal warfare, the boys escape with the princess. Later, aboard a New York-bound ship, Turkey enters the power room, thinking it's the restroom, and lights a match. Jeff, Turkey and the princess find themselves shipwrecked once again, adrift in a small raft.

All the elements of exotically situated comedy—papier-mâché palm trees, turbaned villains, dancing girls in scanty attire, even talking camels—combined to make this, in the words of one camel, "the screwiest picture I was ever in."

With Tyrone Power, George Sanders and players

# The Black Swan

20th Century–Fox / 1942

CAST: *James Waring,* TYRONE POWER; *Margaret Denby,* MAUREEN O'HARA; *Capt. Henry Morgan,* Laird Cregar; *Tommy Blue,* Thomas Mitchell; *Capt. Billy Leech,* George Sanders; *Wogan,* Anthony Quinn; *Lord Denby,* George Zucco; *Roger Ingram,* Edward Ashley; *Don Miguel,* Fortunio Bonanova; *Captain Graham,* Stuart Robertson; *Fenner,* Charles McNaughton; *Speaker,* Frederick Worlock; *Chinese Cook;* Willie Fung; *Higgs,* Charles Francis; *Bishop,* Arthur Shields; *Majordomo,* Keith Hitchcock; *Captain Blaine,* John Burton; *Captain Jones,* Cyril McLaglen; *Daniel,* Clarence Muse; *Clerk,* Olaf Hytten; *Sea Captains,* Charles Irwin, David Thursby and Frank Leigh.

CREDITS: *Director,* Henry King; *producer,* Robert Bassler; *screenplay,* Ben Hecht and Seton I. Miller; based on the *novel* by Rafael Sabatini; *music,* Alfred Newman; *art directors,* Richard Day and James Basevi; *camera,* Leon Shamroy; *editor,* Barbara McLean. Technicolor. Running time: 82 minutes.

Having concluded his contract with Warner Bros., Anthony Quinn moved on to 20th Century-Fox and was assigned for the second time to a Tyrone Power adventure spectacle. In the rip-roaring, swashbuckling, Technicolor adaptation of Rafael Sabatini's classic novel, Quinn turned up as the blackguard Wogan, curly haired, scarfaced, black-patched chief mate of dastardly George Sanders. Sanders himself was nearly unrecognizable in a flaming red wig and thick beard. Under Henry King's guidance, high adventure was mixed with dazzling swordplay, lusty romance, brawling camaraderie and rococo rhetoric, as the dashing seventeenth-century pirate Jamie Waring (Power) crossed swords with merciless Billy Leech (Sanders), while making the Caribbean free for English shipping and Jamaica's new governor, former pirate Henry Morgan (Laird Cregar).

Jamie, along with his friend Tommy Blue (Thomas Mitchell), are made Morgan's personal aides, as the new governor asks that all pirate activities in the area be ended. When Leech ignores Morgan's pleas, Jamie is

With Tyrone Power (second left) and George Sanders (center)

assigned the task of bringing him in. Learning that Margaret Denby (Maureen O'Hara), daughter of the former governor, is helping Leech, Jamie kidnaps her as he takes pursuit of Leech's ship, *The Black Swan*. Without his main fleet and heavy firepower, Jamie realizes he cannot beat Leech, so he resorts to a ruse, telling Leech that he has broken with Morgan and wants to join the pirates and plunder on *The Black Swan*. He passes off Margaret as his wife, but Leech sees through the plan and confiscates Jamie's ship, and, with his own crew, under Wogan, Leech sails against Morgan under the Union Jack. Jamie dives overboard and, at a crucial moment, severs the ship's rudder, causing it to run aground. Jamie frees Tommy Blue and his men and they engage Leech's crew in battle. In a climactic duel, Jamie gives the villainous Leech his comeuppance and the reign of pirate terror in the Caribbean is ended in Maracaibo harbor. Jamie then returns to claim the lovely Margaret as his bride.

A decade later, in another swashbuckler, Anthony Quinn and Maureen O'Hara both would have roles as pirates, with Quinn once again a black-hearted villain.

Quinn seated (left center) with Tyrone Power (left), George Sanders (center), Laird Cregar (with pistol), Thomas Mitchell (right)

With Hank Bell

# The Ox-Bow Incident

20th Century–Fox / 1943

CAST: *Gil Carter,* HENRY FONDA; *Donald Martin,* Dana Andrews; *Rose Mapen,* Mary Beth Hughes; *Mexican,* Anthony Quinn; *Gerald Tetley,* William Eythe; *Art Croft,* Henry (Harry) Morgan; *Ma Grier,* Jane Darwell; *Old Man,* Francis Ford; *Judge Tyler,* Matt Briggs; *Arthur Davies,* Harry Davenport; *Major Tetley,* Frank Conroy; *Jeff Farnley,* Marc Lawrence; *Darby,* Victor Kilian; *Monty Smith,* Paul Hurst; *Pancho,* Chris Pin Martin; *Joyce,* Ted (Michael) North; *Mr. Swanson,* George Meeker; *Miss Swanson,* Almira Sessions; *Mrs. Larch,* Margaret Hamilton; *Butch Mapes,* Dick Rich; *Bartlett,* Stanley Andrews; *Greene,* Billy Benedict; *Gabe Hart,* Rondo Hatton; *Winder,* Paul Burns; *Sparks,* Leigh Whipper; *Moore,* George Lloyd; *Jimmy Cairnes,* George Chandler; *Red,* Hank Bell; *Mark,* Forrest Dillon; *Alec Small,* George Plues; *Sheriff,* Willard Robertson; *Deputy,* Tom London.

CREDITS: *Director,* William A. Wellman; *producer,* Lamar Trotti; *screenplay,* Lamar Trotti; *based on the novel* by Walter Van Tilburg Clark; *music director,* Cyril J. Mockridge; *art directors,* Richard Day and James Basevi; *camera,* Arthur Miller; *editor,* Allen McNeil. Running time: 75 minutes.

In William Wellman's grim, uncompromising study of mob rule, set in the Old West, Anthony Quinn is the doomed Mexican who is lynched with his companions, Dana Andrews and Francis Ford, as suspected rustlers. In his role, Quinn attempts to pass himself off as an ignorant cowboy with a series of "No sabe" answers to the campfire interrogation. When he finally drops this ruse, he reveals himself as a knowledgeable tough-talking herder who fearlessly digs a bullet from his own leg after being wounded attempting to escape. Aside from this lengthy scene, however, he has little to do except demonstrate courage as the noose is placed around his neck. Quinn's greatest benefit was exposure in what has subsequently been elevated to classic status in cinema history. In order to make this picture, director Wellman had to promise Darryl F. Zanuck he'd do two films sight unseen *(Thunder Birds* before it, *Buffalo Bill* following), and from an outstanding cast headed by nominal star Henry Fonda, he extracted an extraordinary ensemble performance.

With Francis Ford and Dana Andrews
on horses

Almost as soon as they ride into a small Western town, Gil Carter (Fonda) and his sidekick Art Croft (Henry Morgan) become unwilling observers of an event triggered by the reported killing of a local rancher by cattle rustlers. A mob gathers to seek revenge and is whipped to a frenzy by Major Tetley (Frank Conroy) in a firebrand speech. Under his leadership, a sheriff's posse heads into the hills and comes upon the campfire of three tired cowboys (Andrews, Quinn and Ford), and on the basis of circumstantial evidence, Tetley exhorts the mob into an on-the-spot trial. Despite the pleas of a few dissenters, a guilty verdict is quickly reached and a triple lynching is performed.

Later, back in town, the news of the rancher's killing is found to have been a mistake, and the townsfolk are forced to live with their deed, as Carter reads to them the contents of a pitiful last letter one of the doomed men had written to his family shortly before the lynching.

With Dana Andrews, Francis Ford, Rondo Hatton, Jane Darwell, Chris-Pin Martin (rear), Marc Lawrence, Paul Hurst, Stanley Andrews, Frank Conroy

[ 93 ]

# Guadalcanal Diary

20th Century–Fox / 1943

CAST: *Father Donnelly*, PRESTON FOSTER; *Sgt. Hunk Malone*, LLOYD NOLAN; *Taxi Potts*, WILLIAM BENDIX; *Captain Davis*, RICHARD CONTE; *Soose*, ANTHONY QUINN; *Pvt. Johnny Anderson*, Richard Jaeckel (film debut); *Captain Cross*, Roy Roberts; *Colonel Grayson*, Minor Watson; *Ned Rowman*, Ralph Byrd; *Butch*, Lionel Stander; *Correspondent*, Reed Hadley; *Lt. Thurmond*, John Archer; *Tex*, Eddie Acuff; *Sammy*, Robert Rose; *Weatherby*, Miles Mander; *Dispatch Officer*, Harry Carter; *Major*, Jack Luden; *Lieutenant*, Louis Hart; *Captain*, Tom Dawson; *Colonel Thompson*, Selmer Jackson; *Japanese Officer*, Allen Jung; *Prisoner*, Paul Fung.

CREDITS: *Director*, Lewis Seiler; *producer*, Bryan Foy; *associate producer*, Islin Auster; *screenplay*, Lamar Trotti; based on Jerry Cady's adaptation of the *novel* by Richard Tregaskis; *music director*, Emil Newman; *original music*, David Buttolph; *art directors*, James Basevi and Leland Fuller; *camera*, Charles Clarke; *editor*, Fred Allen. Running time: 93 minutes.

This was Anthony Quinn's first war movie (*i.e.,* his first in uniform) and the only one he made fighting for "our side." In his role as Soose, he portrayed a Mexican-American marine private who is the lone survivor of a

As Soose

dangerous patrol on Guadalcanal. The film version of Richard Tregaskis's best-selling book about the U.S. Marines in the South Pacific still ranks among the more memorable patriotic screen tributes, but it will undoubtedly be best remembered, by film devotees at least, as the movie in which Richard Jaeckel made his debut as a green teen-ager named Chicken (and appears to have not aged in the succeeding three decades as an actor).

Producer Bryan Foy's pre-deRochemont documentary-oriented unit at Fox turned out a stirring action drama under director Lewis Seiler. What unpatriotic criticism there was was aimed at the scriptwriters, who, Bosley Crowther, for one, felt, "have all too freely rigged up a patent fiction to fit the pattern of the film." And in commenting on the performers themselves, he found that "Anthony Quinn acts with that grim determination so familiar in actors who 'seek revenge.' "

*Guadalcanal Diary* was filmed at Camp Pendleton in California and peopled, at least in the leading roles, by stock service types: the tough talking ex-cabbie from Brooklyn (William Bendix), the heroic priest (Preston Foster), the no-nonsense top sergeant (Lloyd Nolan), the courageous captain (Richard Conte), the company clown (Lionel Stander), and others. Despite these familiar figures and faces, the production maintains its credibility as a factual account of the well-publicized marine invasion of August 1942, which began four months of bitter fighting to take the island.

With Robert Rose and Preston Foster

# Buffalo Bill

20th Century–Fox / 1944

CAST: *Buffalo Bill,* JOEL McCREA; *Louisa Cody,* MAUREEN O'HARA; *Dawn Starlight,* LINDA DARNELL; *Ned Buntline,* Thomas Mitchell; *Sergeant Chips,* Edgar Buchanan; *Yellow Hand,* Anthony Quinn; *Senator Frederici,* Moroni Olsen; *Murdo Carvell,* Frank Fenton; *General Blazier,* Matt Briggs; *Mr. Vandevere,* George Lessey; *Sherman,* Frank Orth; *Trooper Clancy,* George Chandler; *Tall Bull,* Chief Many Treaties; *Medicine Man,* Nick Thompson; *Crazy Horse,* Chief Thundercloud; *President Theodore Roosevelt,* Sidney Blackmer; *Barber,* William Haade; *Queen Victoria,* Evelyn Beresford; *Doctor,* Edwin Stanley; *President Hayes,* John Dilson; *Maid,* Cecil Weston; *Bellboy,* Merrill Rodin; *Crippled Boy,* Vincent Graeff; *Editor,* Fred Graham.

CREDITS: *Director,* William A. Wellman; *producer,* Harry A. Sherman; *screenplay,* Aeneas MacKenzie, Clements Ripley and Cecile Kramer; *story,* Frank Winch; *music director,* Emil Newman; *original score,* David Buttolph; *art directors,* James Basevi and Lewis

With Joel McCrea and William Haade

Creber; *special effects,* Fred Sersen; *camera,* Leon Shamroy; *editor,* James B. Clark. Technicolor. Running time: 90 minutes.

In this sprawling, romanticized biography of Colonel William Frederick "Buffalo Bill" Cody, combining melodramatic slush with vivid, screen-sweeping excitement, William Wellman gave Quinn his best opportunity to essay his "noble savage" characterization. The role as Indian Chief Yellow Hand remains the most memorable Quinn performance during this phase of his career, and his hand-to-hand, fight-to-the-death sequence with Buffalo Bill remains one of the films highlights. Wellman admits that the study of the famed frontiersman deals with legend rather than truth because Zanuck wanted a spectacular, slam-bang Western about a great American hero. Spectacular it was, although many have felt that it dwelt somewhat too long on the incidents concerned with Cody's romance and marriage.

Joel McCrea's Cody is a scout who saves the life of a U.S. senator (Moroni Olsen) and his daughter Louisa (Maureen O'Hara) from attacking Indians. Escorting them to a nearby army post, he is introduced to railroad magnate Schuyler Vandervere (George Lessey) and New York journalist Ned Buntline (Thomas Mitchell), who have come to the frontier seeking the aid of the army in forcing the Cheyennes from the land needed by Vandervere to build his railroad. Cody warns them that the Indians will fight rather than move, but the post commander promises to provide troops. Under the leadership of their chief, Yellow Hand (Quinn), a longtime friend of Cody, the Indians ambush the troops and take the senator hostage.

Risking his life to free the senator, Cody promises Yellow Hand that he'll guarantee an equitable peace treaty. The senator returns to Washington, while Louisa remains behind to marry Cody, who soon is approached to head a new company formed to sell buffalo robes. With the beginning of the great buffalo massacre, the Indians, protesting the destruction of the animals but receiving no satisfaction, attack and wipe out General Custer and his Seventh Cavalry. Cody is asked by the army to act as a scout, but Louisa threatens to walk out if he takes the job. Cody leaves and Louisa returns to Washington with their baby. In the wilderness, Cody and his patrol intercept the Indians at War Bonnet Creek, and, to gain time for the troops to move up, he challenges Yellow Hand to a death fight. Cody is victorious and the demoralized Indians are about to fall back when Dawn Starlight (Linda Darnell), Cody's squaw before his marriage, reorganizes them and fearlessly leads them against the troops. She is killed in the ensuing battle, and the Cheyennes are routed.

Cody's exploits have been chronicled by Ned Buntline, who has succeeded in making Buffalo Bill a legend back East, and, to his amazement, the frontiersman is called to Washington to receive the Congressional Medal. On his arrival in the capital, Cody learns that his son is dying of diphtheria and blames Louisa for the boy's death. A celebrity in Washington, Cody is brought to New York by Vandervere for a testimonial dinner, but finds himself duped and denounces the financier, who mounts a campaign to discredit Cody. To ensure a fair deal for the Indians, however, Cody remains in the East, but learns that he is both penniless and friendless.

Ned convinces him to put his talents with a gun to use, and Cody becomes a marksman at a shooting gallery, leading to an idea on a grander scale—to bring Indians to the East in a Wild West show, gaining Cody international acclaim as Buffalo Bill.

With Joel McCrea

With Preston Foster

# Roger Touhy, Gangster

20th Century–Fox  /  1944

CAST:  *Roger Touhy*, PRESTON FOSTER; *Basil "The Owl" Banghart*, Victor McLaglen; *Daisy*, Lois Andrews; *Captain Steve Warren*, Kent Taylor; *George Carroll*, Anthony Quinn; *Joe Sutton*, William Post Jr.; *Smoke Reardon*, Henry (Harry) Morgan; *Cameron*, Matt Briggs; *Riley*, Moroni Olsen; *Agent Drake*, Reed Hadley; *Gloria*, Trudy Marshall; *Agent Kerrigan*, John Archer; *Troubles O'Connor*, Frank Jenks; *Ice Box Hamilton*, George E. Stone; *Agent Boyden*, Charles Lang; *Mason*, Kane Richmond; *Comic in Theater*, Frank Orth; *McNair*, George Holmes; *Clanahan*, Ralph Peters; *Frank Williams*, Roy Roberts; *Lefty Rowden*, John Harmon; *Maxie Sharkey*, Horace McMahon; *Barnes*, Edmund MacDonald; *Edward Latham*, Cy Kendall; *Prison Guard Briggs*, William Pawley; *Ralph Burke*, Murray Alper; *Principal Keeper*, Selmer Jackson; *Warden*, Joseph Crehan; *Court Clerk*, Byron Foulger; *Judge*, George Lessey; *Priest*, Addison Richards; *Patrolman*, Ralph Dunn; *Farmer*, Arthur Aylesworth; and Dick Rich, Joey Ray, Ferris Taylor, William Haade, Jim Farley, William Ruhl, Thomas Jackson, Stanley Blystone, Charles Wilson, Ralf Harolde, Herbert Ashley, Ivan Miller, Grant Withers.

CREDITS:  *Director*, Robert Florey; *producer*, Lee Marcus; *screenplay*, Crane Wilbur and Jerry Cady; *story*, Crane Wilbur; *music director*, Emil Newman; *original score*, Hugo W. Friedhofer; *art directors*, James Basevi and Lewis Creber; *special effects*, Fred Sersen; *camera*, Glen MacWilliams; *editor*, Harry Reynolds. Running time: 65 minutes.

Anthony Quinn was cast, almost routinely, as a convict in the fictionalized "biography" of the controversial Prohibition era racketeer whose real-life exploits were infinitely more interesting than those depicted in this standard gangster melodrama. Touhy's story was slapped together by 20th's "B" unit to ride the wave of topicality of his sensational, short-lived escape, together with most of his gang, from Stateville Penitentiary, Joliet, Illinois, in October, 1942. The original version of the thriller, crisply directed by Robert Florey, was given its first—and probably only—showing on July 12, 1943, to a VIP and prisoner audience at Stateville.

Because of FBI protests that, in several instances, its agents' work in Touhy's recapture was credited instead to local authorities, the studio was obligated to withdraw the film for retakes, reediting and additional footage. At the same time, it was forced to fight a restraining order brought by Touhy's lawyers, claiming the screenplay "defamed" him and its advertising portrayed him as "a vicious law violator and gangster." What emerged when *Roger Touhy, Gangster* was finally put into nationwide release in June, 1944, was a formula cops-and-robbers movie aimed at the Saturday afternoon popcorn crowd, with only the real names of Roger Touhy and his lieutenant, Owl Banghart, standing out among the myriad of fictional people and events.

The screen Touhy was to have been portrayed by Lloyd Nolan, who suddenly refused to play the role on the eve of production. Kent Taylor was rushed into the breach as Touhy, and Preston Foster was assigned the part of the chief detective. At the last minute, a decision was made to have the two actors swap roles, and they soon were reciting the banal dialogue, in most cases out of the sides of their mouths. An exchange between Touhy and his cellmate (played by Quinn) typifies the level of the script, as Touhy, pacing his cell, bemoans angrily: "Ninety-nine years! They give me ninety-nine years! I can't do ninety-nine years!" He is placated by Quinn with the advice: "Well, do as much as you can, Roger."

The authentic story of Roger (The Terrible) Touhy dates back to the Chicago gang wars of the early 1930s, when he was arrested for the kidnaping of onetime confidence man, John (Jake the Barber) Factor, and the demand for $50,000 ransom. Although he contended at his trial that the kidnaping had been a hoax perpetrated by Factor, Touhy was sentenced to ninety-nine years in prison, along with his gang. The mass escape Touhy masterminded in 1942 returned his name to the headlines, where it stayed until his recapture two months later. (The film was begun while he and his gang were still at large.) Two members of the mob were killed in a shoot-out with the FBI, and Banghart himself was sent to Alcatraz with the boast that no jail could hold him because six had not in the past. Touhy was returned to Stateville with an additional one hundred years tacked onto the original sentence.

A postscript to the Touhy story: he was paroled on November 24, 1959, after serving nearly twenty-six years. Twenty-three days later, while walking along Chicago's West Side with his bodyguard, he was ambushed by two assassins and killed by five shotgun blasts.

With George E. Stone, Victor McLaglen, Preston Foster (on ladder), John Harmon, Herbert Ashley, Ivan Miller, Frank Jenks

With Sheila Ryan

# Ladies of Washington

20th Century–Fox / 1944

CAST: *Carol*, TRUDY MARSHALL; *Dr. Mayberry*, RONALD GRAHAM; *Michael Romanescue*, ANTHONY QUINN; *Jerry*, SHEILA RYAN; *Stephen*, Robert Bailey; *Helen*, Beverly Whitney; *Adelaide*, Jackie Paley; *Investigator*, Carleton Young; *Mother Henry*, John Philliber; *Vicky O'Reilly*, Robin Raymond; *Amy*, Doris Merrick; *Betty*, Barbara Booth; *Frieda*, Jo-Carroll Dennison; *Marjorie*, Lillian Porter; *Lt. Lake*, Harry Shannon; *Nellie*, Ruby Dandridge; *Inspector Saunders*, Charles D. Brown; *Mr. Crane*, Pierre Watkin; *Mrs. Crane*, Nella Walker; *Dorothy*, Inna Gest; *Nurse*, Rosalind Keith; *Susan*, Edna Mae Jones; *Ensign*, Bert McClay; *Watchman*, J. Farrell MacDonald; *Clerk*, Byron Foulger; *Nurses' Aide*, Mary Field; *Bit Woman*, Bess Flowers; *Mr. Wethering*, Harry Depp; *Sergeant Martin*, Lee Shumway.

CREDITS: *Director*, Louis King; *producer*, William Girard; *screenplay*, Wanda Tuchock; *music director*, Emil Newman; *original score*, Cyril Mockridge; *art directors*, James Basevi and Leland Fuller; *special effects*, Fred Sersen; *camera*, Charles Clarke; *editor*, Nick Di-Maggio. Running time: 61 minutes.

It was in this unobtrusive "B" film combining an amalgam of topical comedy and lurid melodrama that Anthony Quinn played his first romantic lead and, as the publicity noted, received his first screen kiss. The production, curiously promoted with catch lines such as "It's the year's surprise laugh picture!" and "Share the roars . . . with their 'Share-the-Man' plan!" played the housing shortage in wartime Washington for laughs against a background of adultery, blackmail, suicide, murder and smooth-talking foreign agents, personified by Quinn in his role as Michael Romanescue, a Nazi spy.

Encountering difficulty finding a place to stay in Washington, Jerry (Sheila Ryan) is invited by her college classmate Carol (Trudy Marshall) to the "hen coop," a cooperative shared by a group of government girls. There Jerry soon alienates her roommates with her high-toned attitude. Just coming from an affair with Mr. Crane (Pierre Watkin), a steel magnate who decided to return to his wife, Jerry fakes a suicide attempt to smear his name. Her plan backfires when Carol's fiancé, Dr. Mayberry (Ronald Graham), learns Jerry's motives and shields Crane's name from the papers. Mayberry's assistant, Stephen (Robert Bailey), takes Jerry home from the hospital and begins taking a personal interest in her. She two-times him, though, by carrying on an affair with a handsome foreigner, Michael Romanescue (Quinn), who showers her with expensive gifts, although he has no visible means of support. Romanescue tells her that he's been offered a great deal of money for Crane's war production figures and induces her to get him into Crane's office.

While attempting to open the safe, Romanescue is shot, but manages to kill the watchman. Jerry helps him escape and telephones Stephen for help, passing off Romanescue as her brother. Stephen gets them both to Dr. Mayberry's houseboat, where he unsuccessfully performs surgery on Romanescue. When the police find Romanescue's body, they discover that he had been operated on by an experienced surgeon. Mayberry is implicated since his boat was used, and he is held for questioning. Realizing, however, that Stephen is probably involved, Mayberry decides to shield his friend,

As Michael Romanescue

despite Carol's pleas. At the "hen coop," one of the girls discovers Romanescue's ring among Jerry's belongings, and Carol does some fancy sleuthing, uncovering the link between Jerry and Romanescue, who is discovered to have been a foreign agent. Confronted with the evidence, Jerry breaks down. Stephen, absolved of the murder, is held for failure to report the death, and Mayberry is freed and prepares to marry Carol in a "hen coop" ceremony.

With Jackie Paley, Jo-Carroll Dennison, Doris Merrick, Lillian Porter (seated), Robin Raymond, Sheila Ryan (seated)

As Al Jackson

# Irish Eyes Are Smiling

20th Century–Fox / 1944

CAST: *Edgar Brawley*, MONTY WOOLLEY; *Mary "Irish" O'Brien*, JUNE HAVER; *Ernest R. Ball*, DICK HAYMES; *Al Jackson*, Anthony Quinn; *Lucille Lacey*, Beverly Whitney; *Stanley Ketchel*, Maxie Rosenbloom; *Belle La Tour*, Veda Ann Borg; *Betz*, Clarence Kolb; *Opera Singers*, Blanche Thebom and Leonard Warren; *Stage Manager*, Chick Chandler; *Specialty Dancer*, Kenny Williams; *Headwaiter*, Michael Dalmatoff; *Prima Donna*, Marian Martin; *Song Plugger*, Charles Wil-liams; *Sparring Partner*, Art Foster; *Electrician*, George Chandler; *Irish Woman*, Mary Gordon, *Purser*, Emmett Vogan; *Steward*, Pat O'Malley; *Militant Wife*, Minerva Urecal; *Barker*, Arthur Hohl; *Doorman*, J. Farrell Mac-Donald; *Harry*, Eddie Acuff.

CREDITS: *Director*, Gregory Ratoff, *producer*, Damon Runyon; *screenplay*, Earl Baldwin and John Tucker Battle; *story*, E. A. Ellington; *music director*,

With June Haver

Alfred Newman; *songs,* Mack Gordon and James Monaco; *choreography,* Hermes Pan; *art directors,* Lyle Wheeler and Joseph C. Wright; *special effects,* Fred Sersen; *camera,* Harry Jackson; *editor,* Harmon Jones. Technicolor. Running time: 90 minutes.

Quinn adapted his standard tough-guy characterization to fit Damon Runyon's distinctive conception of a Broadway sharpie in this formula Technicolor musical from 20th Century-Fox about a couple whose road to the bright lights is strewn with the usual musical comedy thorns and misunderstandings and a generous helping of songs. Only through courtesy could this opulent production, designed to make June Haver 20th's newest star, be considered the screen biography of Ernest R. Ball, who wrote the title song. Dick Haymes, here posing as the Irish songwriter, sang dreamily in the style which made him number-two stylist of the day after Frank Sinatra, and Monty Woolley, the film's nominal star, was his familiar, well-loved self, here masquerading as a show-business type for plot purposes, dispensing his expected profundities and making side bets with gambler Anthony Quinn.

After being kicked out of the Cleveland Conservatory of Music, Ernest Ball (Haymes) tries to sell one of his ballads at the local burlesque house, where he mistakes chorus girl Mary "Irish" O'Brien (June Haver) for the star—and falls madly in love with her. Irish has just been fired and goes to New York to try her luck. Ball follows, after earning his train fare in the boxing ring, and finds work as a song plugger while searching for Irish. While performing in a small club, Ball is heckled by theatrical manager Edgar Brawley (Woolley) and gambler Al Jackson (Quinn), who are entertaining the toast of Broadway, Lucille Lacey (Beverly Whitney). Annoyed, Ball discards the music he'd been playing and sings one of his own ballads. The tune catches Lucille's fancy and she offers to sing it in her show at the Palace, making Ball an overnight success.

Sometime later, Ball is entering a restaurant where he's to dine with Brawley and Jackson, and finds Irish working as a hatcheck girl. Over drinks, Brawley bets Jackson that he can make a star, within three months, of the first girl to come out of the ladies' lounge. Brawley had arranged for Lucille to emerge, but Irish is pushed out and falls at Ball's feet. Humiliated, she races from the club, but Brawley vows to make good on his bet. Jackson takes a sudden interest in Brawley's protégé and persuades her to accept a starring part in a Havana show. Ball tries vainly to stop her, but Jackson manages to get her aboard ship, where he tells her that there is no revue and that the trip was a ploy to keep Brawley from winning the bet. Irish manages to get ashore, is reunited with Ball, opens in Brawley's show and helps popularize the composer's songs.

# Where Do We Go from Here?

20th Century–Fox / 1945

CAST: *Bill,* FRED MacMURRAY; *Sally,* JOAN LESLIE; *Lucilla,* JUNE HAVER; *Genie (Ali),* Gene Sheldon; *Indian Chief,* Anthony Quinn; *Benito,* Carlos Ramirez; *General George Washington,* Alan Mowbray; *Christopher Columbus,* Fortunio Bonanova; *Hessian Colonel,* Herman Bing; *General Rahl,* Otto Preminger; *Kreiger,* Howard Freeman; *Benedict Arnold,* John Davidson; *Old Lady,* Rosina Galli; *Dutch Councilman,* Fred Essler; *Army Doctor,* Cyril Ring; *Elderly Wife,* Hope Landin; *Burgher,* Joe Bernard; *Dutchman,* Walter Bonn; *Sergeant,* Max Wagner; *German Lieutenant,* Arno Frey; *Soldier,* Larry Thompson; *Minister,* Norman Field.

CREDITS: *Director,* Gregory Ratoff; *producer,* William Perlberg; *screenplay,* Morrie Ryskind; based on the *story* by Morrie Ryskind and Sig Herzig; *music directors,* Emil Newman and Charles Henderson; *original score,* David Raksin; *songs,* Ira Gershwin and Kurt Weill; *art directors,* Lyle Wheeler and Leland Fuller; *special effects,* Fred Sersen; *camera,* Leon Shamroy; *editor,* J. Watson Webb. Technicolor. Running time: 77 minutes.

In perhaps his silliest role—at least his most inconsequential one—Anthony Quinn emerged in Gregory Ratoff's oddball musical fantasy about American history in the guise of the Indian chief who sold the island of Manhattan to Fred MacMurray for twenty-four dollars and change. Satirical comedy and stooge-playing is not Quinn's forte; a little tongue-in-cheek villainy, it is agreed, appears to be his limit in the comedy genre. In *Where Do We Go from Here?,* Quinn was in and out with dispatch.

This bit of Technicolor escapism, for which Kurt Weill and Ira Gershwin wrote several forgettable songs to tie together the fragmented episodes of history, was touted as "the funniest picture ever set to music!" 20th Century-Fox apparently felt that those accepting that

With June Haver and Fred MacMurray

With June Haver and Fred MacMurray

premise would also buy the one about a stalwart 4-F (MacMurray) who would give anything to get into uniform, and with the help of an Arabian Nights-type genie (Gene Sheldon), finds himself marching through history.

First, he's slogging through a snowstorm with George Washington's army and, though miraculous "hindsight," tries to warn the general against Benedict Arnold. Next, he's a sailor aboard the *Santa Maria,* stepping off onto the New World ahead of Christopher Columbus. Finally, he's bargaining agent for the Dutch in the famous New York land transaction of our early history. Through all the adventures, he continues to be involved with two young ladies (Joan Leslie and June Haver) who look suspiciously like the girls he knew at the USO where he had been a dishwasher. All the while, of course, the genie keeps trying to get him to the correct century and into the marines, where MacMurray is last seen, striding along as the two girls wave to him from the curb.

With Ruth Warrick and players

# China Sky

RKO / 1945

CAST: *Dr. Gray Thompson,* RANDOLPH SCOTT; *Dr. Sara Durand,* RUTH WARRICK; *Louise Thompson,* ELLEN DREW; *Chen Ta,* Anthony Quinn; *Siu Mei,* Carol Thurston; *Colonel Yasuda,* Richard Loo; *Little Goat,* Ducky Louie; *Dr. Kim,* Philip Ahn; *Chung,* Benson Fong; *Magistrate,* H. T. Tsiang; *Charlie,* Chin Kuang Chow; and James Leong, Jimmy Lono. Owen Song, Gerald Lee, George Chung, Bob Chinn, Layne Tom, Jr., Harold Fong, Jung Lim, Moy Ming, Audrey Chow, Kermit Maynard, Weaver Levy, Charles Lung, Albert Law.

CREDITS: *Director,* Ray Enright; *producer,* Maurice Geraghty; *executive producer,* Jack L. Gross; *screenplay,* Brenda Weisberg and Joseph Hoffman; based on the *novel* by Pearl S. Buck; *music director,* C. Bakaleinikoff; *original score,* Roy Webb; *art directors,* Albert S. D'Agostino and Ralph Berger; *camera,*

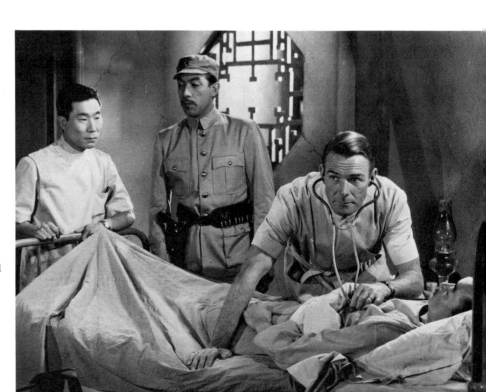

With Philip Ahn, Randolph Scott and Richard Loo

Nicholas Musuraca; *special effects,* Vernon L. Walker; *editors,* Gene Milford and Marvin Coil. Running time: 78 minutes.

Graduating to the next plateau—second male lead— Quinn was cast as a Chinese guerrilla leader in the filming of Pearl Buck's novel, which RKO turned into a standard marital triangle drama set against the struggle of the Chinese to regain their homeland during World War II. "As Chen Ta," *New York Times* critic Thomas Pryor wrote, "Anthony Quinn sounds more Latin than Chinese. And in a climactic flourish of action, filled with the spirit of 'head 'em off at Eagle Pass,' Chen Ta and warriors charge down from their mountain hideaway to rescue the village from a force of Jap paratroopers." Randolph Scott, as the good American doctor, retained his stony-faced dignity throughout, doubtlessly envying Quinn for his frequent action sequences and wishing to devote more energy to winning the war, like John Wayne and Errol Flynn.

The action takes place in a remote hill village serving as supply base for Chen Ta (Quinn), where a pair of heroic American doctors (Scott and Ruth Warrick) patch up the villagers after each Japanese bombing. When Dr. Gray Thompson goes back to America briefly on a fund-raising mission, his associate, Dr. Sara Durand, carries on valiantly, but is shocked when he returns with a lovely bride, Louise (Ellen Drew). Selfish, rich and spoiled, Louise immediately becomes jealous of Sara and, unnerved by the continuous air raids, she tries to talk Gray into taking her back to the States. Gray tells her that it's now impossible, that they are surrounded. Into this romantic situation comes Chen Ta with a wounded prisoner, a Japanese colonel (Richard Loo). Learning that the doctor treating him

As Chen Ta

(Philip Ahn) is half Japanese and that Louise desperately wants to leave the village, the colonel inveigles the doctor into having Louise send a coded telegram in her husband's name asking that a plane be sent in. Louise complies eagerly, and the message secretly calling for a Japanese attack on the village goes out, while Gray and Sara are at Chen Ta's guerrilla camp treating the wounded. Within hours, enemy paratroopers begin dropping into the village and Louise is killed in the ensuing battle. Chen Ta's men swoop in to wipe out the attackers, and Gray, hiding his grief but finally realizing his true love for Sara, joins his assistant in tending the wounded.

Critic Pryor felt that "RKO undoubtedly meant good will in producing this film as an expression of American friendship for China, but it seems to us that this is a case where 10,000 words would have been better than one picture."

With Richard Loo (on floor) and Philip Ahn (center)

[ 105 ]

With Angel Cruz, John Wayne and Lawrence Tierney

# Back to Bataan

RKO / 1945

CAST: *Colonel Joseph Madden,* JOHN WAYNE; *Captain Andres Bonifacio,* Anthony Quinn; *Bertha Barnes,* Beulah Bondi; *Dalisay Delgado,* Fely Franquelli; *Sergeant Biernesa,* J. Alex Havier; *General Homma,* Leonard Strong; *Major Hasko,* Richard Loo; *Colonel Kuroki,* Philip Ahn; *Maximo,* Ducky Louie; *Spindle Jackson,* Paul Fix; *Buenaventura Bello,* Vladimir Sokoloff; *Japanese Captain,* Abner Biberman; *Japanese Announcer,* Benson Fong; *Lt. Commander Waite,* Lawrence Tierney; *General Wainwright,* John Miljan; *Corporal Cruz,* Angel Cruz; *Lt. Colonel Roberts,* Ray Teal; *Major McKinley,* Ken McDonald; *Teacher,* Erville Alderson; *Aides,* Bill Williams and Edmund Glover.

CREDITS: *Director,* Edward Dmytryk; *producer,* Robert Fellows; *associate producer,* Theron Warth; *screenplay,* Ben Barzman and Richard Landau; *story,* Aeneas MacKenzie and William Gordon; *music director,* C. Bakaleinikoff; *original score,* Roy Webb; *art directors,* Albert S. D'Agostino and Ralph Berger; *special effects,* Vernon L. Walker; *camera,* Nicholas Musuraca; *editor,* Marston Fay. Running time: 97 minutes.

In his second consecutive action war movie for RKO, Quinn again was cast as a guerrilla leader, this time in the Philippines, helping John Wayne clear the enemy from the islands in advance of General MacArthur's return. Playing Captain Andres Bonifacio, grandson of the legendary Filipino patriot, Quinn was forced by the scriptwriters to spend much of the film moping around and mooning over his girlfriend, whom he thinks has been collaborating with the enemy. Only when John Wayne proves to him otherwise does he revert to being the courageous fighter he's expected to be.

The film opens with an exciting reenactment of the real-life freeing of American prisoners from the jungle POW camp at Cabanatuan, as the narrator, in stirringly patriotic tones, praises the selfless deeds of the audience and those of the valiant Filipinos fighting the hidden war. Then, in flashback, *Back to Bataan* races into standard heroic, gun-and-glory fiction with the underdogs fighting fiercely against the usual insuperable odds.

Colonel Joseph Madden (Wayne) is ordered to the Luzon hills to organize native guerrillas, and, in need of a patriot around whom to rally the men, he rescues Andres Bonifacio (Quinn) from the Japanese. Thinking

With Fely Franquelli

his sweetheart Dalisay Delgado (Fely Franquelli) is aiding the enemy by her frequent broadcasts, Andres is embittered and refuses to lead his people to further slaughter. Madden, disobeying orders, tells him that the girl is actually aiding the resistance movement secretly. Inspired, Andres agrees to lend his support and, under Madden's leadership, the guerrillas step up their hit and run campaign against the enemy. Alarmed over increasing resistance, General Somma (Leonard Strong) has two of his senior officers (Philip Ahn and Richard Loo) increase pressure on the local villagers, and Bertha Barnes (Beulah Bondi), an American teacher, is forced to give up her school and take refuge in Madden's guerrilla camp. One of her pupils, Maximo (Ducky Louie), accompanies her and volunteers to become a spy. As

the guerrilla movement grows, the Japanese decide to "liberate" the Filipinos, and Madden chooses the occasion to stage an attack. Maximo is captured and tortured until he agrees to lead the Japanese to the guerrilla camp, but he manages to force the truck carrying the officers and a detachment of soldiers over a cliff.

After several months of hardships, the daring natives are resupplied and, hearing news of the imminent American landings on Leyte, Madden organizes a surprise attack on the local Japanese post to prepare the way for the American troops and to help secure their beachhead.

*Back to Bataan* was the third of four pictures on which Quinn worked with director Edward Dmytryk. Only with Robert Florey did the actor make more films.

With Fely Franquelli and H. W. Gim

# California

Paramount / 1946

CAST: *Jonathan Trumbo,* RAY MILLAND; *Lily Bishop,* BARBARA STANWYCK; *Michael Fabian,* BARRY FITZGERALD; *Pharaoh Coffin,* George Coulouris; *Mr. Pike,* Albert Dekker; *Don Luis Rivera y Hernandez,* Anthony Quinn; *Whitey,* Frank Faylen; *Booth Pennock,* Gavin Muir; *Pokey,* James Burke; *Padre,* Eduardo Ciannelli; *Colonel Stuart,* Roman Bohnen; *Elvira,* Argentina Brunetti; *Senator Creel,* Howard Freeman; *Wagon Woman,* Julia Faye; *Town Marshal,* Alan Bridge; *Blacksmith,* Bud Geary; *Piano Player,* Pepito Perez; *Abe Clinton,* Crane Whitley; *Pennock's Partner,* Joey Ray; *Elwyn Smith,* Tommy Tucker; *Elwyn's Mother,* Frances Morris; *Emma (Town-Matron),* Minerva Urecal; *2nd Matron,* Virginia Farmer; *Higgins,* Sam Flint; *Willoughby,* Stanley Andrews; *Starks,* Don Beddoe; *Barrett,* Harry Hayden; *President Polk,* Ian Wolfe; *Eddie the Cashier,* Phil Tead; *Reb,* Ethan Laidlaw; *Old Woman,* Gertrude Hoffman; *Mike the Dealer,* Lester Dorr; *Jessie,* Francis Ford; *Stranger,* Rex Lease.

With George Coulouris and Barbara Stanwyck

With Howard Freeman
and George Coulouris

CREDITS: *Director,* John Farrow; *producer,* Seton I. Miller; *screenplay,* Frank Butler and Theodore Strauss; *story,* Boris Ingster; *music director,* Victor Young; *songs,* E. Y. Harburg and Earl Robinson; *art directors,* Hans Dreier and Roland Anderson; *special effects,* Gordon Jennings; *camera,* Ray Rennahan; *editor,* Eda Warren. Technicolor. Running time: 97 minutes.

In John Farrow's muscular Western recounting some of the state's early history, Anthony Quinn had a peripheral role and was quite subdued as a dignified Spanish marquis being wooed by the nefarious George Coulouris in a grandiose scheme to usurp the territory for himself as the pioneers are voting on statehood. His few scenes late in the film follow the obligatory elements of good screen Westerns—brawls, shootouts, card games, rugged heroes, sinister plotters, and a smoldering romance between Ray Milland, playing a stalwart adventurer, and Barbara Stanwyck, as the spitfire lady gambler.

In the epic migration westward, Jonathan Trumbo (Milland), a cynical soldier of fortune, is hired by Michael Fabian (Barry Fitzgerald) to guide Fabian's wagon train to California. Over Trumbo's objections, Lily Bishop (Stanwyck), a gambling lady, is permitted to join the train, and she and Trumbo are attracted to one another through mutual distrust. When word of a California gold strike reaches the train, wagons begin deserting and Trumbo is seriously injured trying to stop the rush. Trumbo and Fabian finally reach California, and find Lily the reigning gambling queen, backed by former slave trader Pharaoh Coffin (Coulouris), now one of the territory's most powerful men. Coffin heads a political group attempting to turn California into an independent empire.

Trumbo challenges Lily to a card game and wins her saloon, but Coffin recovers it at gunpoint and has Trumbo run out of town. Meanwhile Lily moves into Coffin's lavish hacienda and promises to marry him. Recovering from his beating, Trumbo returns and, with Fabian, rallies the pioneers, who elect Fabian as delegate to the Monterey Convention where statehood is being debated. Fabian's impassioned plea helps swing the vote which promises to bring California into the Union. For his efforts, he is shot down by Coffin's angered followers. Trumbo and the pioneers quell the threatened rebellion and stage a bold assault on Coffin's hacienda. Taking on the greedy tyrant personally, Trumbo is saved at the last minute by Lily, who shoots Coffin as he is about to kill Trumbo.

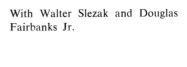

# Sinbad the Sailor

RKO / 1947

CAST: *Sinbad*, DOUGLAS FAIRBANKS, Jr.; *Shireen*, MAUREEN O'HARA; *Melik*, Walter Slezak; *Emir*, Anthony Quinn; *Abbu*, George Tobias; *Pirouze*, Jane Greer; *Yusuf*, Mike Mazurki; *Auctioneer*, Sheldon Leonard; *Aga*, Alan Napier; *Moga*, John Miljan; *Muallin*, Barry Mitchell; *Slave Master*, Glenn Strange; *Commoner*, George Chandler; *Mercenary*, Louis-Jean Heydt; *Kahn of Basra*, Cy Kendall; *Captain of the Guard*, Hugh Prosser; *Crier at Execution*, Harry Harvey; *Lancer Guard*, George Lloyd; *Camel Drover*, Paul Guilfoyle; *Dancing Girls*, Jean Lind, Mary Bradley, Norma Creiger and Vonne Lester; and Phil Warren, Nick Thompson, Billy Bletcher, Lida Durova, Dolores Costelli, Milly Reauclaire, Teri Toy, Joan Webster, Leslie Charles, Norma Brown, Ann Cameron, Jamiel Hasson, Al Murphy, Bill Shannon, Dave Kashner, Max Wagner, Norbert Schiller, Eddie Abdo, Wade Crosby, Charles Stevens, Gordon Clark, Ben Welden.

CREDITS: *Director*, Richard Wallace; *producer*, Stephen Ames; *screenplay*, John Twist and George Worthington Yates; *music director*, C. Bakaleinikoff; *original score*, Roy Webb; *art directors*, Albert S. D'Agostino and Carroll Clark; *special effects*, Vernon L. Walker and Harold Wellman; *camera*, George Barnes; *editors*, Sherman Todd and Frank Doyle. Technicolor. Running time: 117 minutes.

Anthony Quinn was at his most humorously malevolent and scenery-chewing best as the wicked emir menacing dashing Douglas Fairbanks Jr. and lustfully eyeing gorgeous Maureen O'Hara in this sumptuous Arabian

Nights fantasy. Splashy costumes, luxuriant sets, and breathtaking harem girls joined with the elegant Fairbanks tongue-in-cheek bravado to disguise the virtually invisible plot, which revolved around the apocryphal *eighth* voyage of the most famous of all legendary sailors.

Relating another of his exotic tales to a group of spellbound friends gathered around him on a lonely beach, Sinbad recalls how he and his first mate, Abbu (George Tobias), had boarded a storm-tossed ship and found the crew dead. After saving the vessel from the rocks, Sinbad locates a chart while rummaging through the captain's cabin and discovers that it pinpoints the site of a fabulous hidden treasure. Before Sinbad and Abbu can reach land, however, the chart mysteriously disappears. When they drop anchor in Daibul, the ship is confiscated and put up for auction, but Sinbad, passing himself off as a royal prince, outbids a lovely woman, Shireen (Maureen O'Hara), for the craft and pays for it by picking the auctioneer's pocket—and tossing in a handsome tip as well.

Sinbad makes a date with Shireen for that night, but he barely escapes death at the hands of a mysterious swordsman on the way to their meeting. Sinbad finds Shireen in the palace of the evil Emir of Daibul (Quinn), who is about to kill the handsome adventurer. Shireen saves Sinbad's life by introducing him as roy-

alty to the skeptical emir. Sinbad, in turn, kidnaps Shireen and heads out to sea. The emir furiously takes pursuit, sinks Sinbad's ship and captures the pair. Sinbad is ordered to death, but is once again saved, this time by Melik (Walter Slezak), a crafty Mongolian who confesses that he had been the barber on the ship Sinbad had saved and that it was he who had killed the crew and later stolen the map. Melik then strikes a deal with both Sinbad and the emir to share the treasure, which lies under the ruined palace of Alexander the Great in the land of Deryabar. When the three arrive there with Shireen, Sinbad, still pretending to be a prince, reveals his real identity and warns the emir that Melik is planning to double-cross them. Refusing to believe this, the emir has Sinbad and Shireen dragged off while he and the Mongolian gather up the gems. Melik suddenly dies from the "phony" poison he had drunk as part of a ritual to discredit Sinbad.

Sinbad meanwhile escapes with Shireen and captures the emir's ship. The emir himself is killed while trying to retake his vessel, and Sinbad sets sail with Shireen and the treasure. As Sinbad finishes his tale, he hurls a fistful of gems onto the beach, scattering them among his rapt audience. The jewels immediately turn to sand as a laughing Sinbad calls his friends fools for believing such a tall story—and once again sails off with Shireen.

With Douglas Fairbanks Jr. and Maureen O'Hara

With Teresa Wright

# The Imperfect Lady

Paramount / 1947

CAST: *Clive Loring*, RAY MILLAND; *Millicent Hopkins*, TERESA WRIGHT; *Lord Belmont*, Sir Cedric Hardwicke; *Rose Bridges*, Virginia Field; *Jose Martinez*, Anthony Quinn; *Mr. Hopkins*, Reginald Owen; *Lord Montglyn*, Melville Cooper; *Inspector Carston*, Rhys Williams; *Mr. Mallam*, George Zucco; *Sam Travers*, Charles Coleman; *Mr. Rogan*, Miles Mander; *Gladstone*, Gordon Richards; *Lord Chief Justice*, Edmond Breon; *Henderson*, Frederick Worlock; *Malcolm Gadby*, Michael Dyne; *Lucy*, Joan Winfield; *Mrs. Gunner*, Lilian Fontaine; *Bobby*, Leyland Hodgson; *Butler*, Olaf Hytten; *Barrister*, Jack H. Lee; *Barrister*, Major Sam Harris; *Kelvin*, Gavin Muir; *Chimney Sweep*, Ted Billings.

CREDITS: *Director*, Lewis Allen; *producer*, Karl Tunberg; *screenplay*, Karl Tunberg; *story*, Ladislas Fodor; *music*, Victor Young; *song* "Piccadilly Lily" by Jay Livingston and Ray Evans; *choreography*, Billy Daniels and Josephine Earl; *art directors*, Hans Dreier and Franz Bachelin; *special effects*, Farciot Edouart; *camera*, John F. Seitz; *editor*, Duncan Mansfield. Running time: 97 minutes.

The Quinn role in this romantic period drama, set in Victorian England, was somewhat more pivotal to the plot than several which had recently preceded it. He gives a sincere, straightforward performance as a sensitive Spanish concert pianist whose involvement in a murder becomes the crux of what *The New York Times'* Bosley Crowler described as "a silly, bumptious and balmy tale which is a particularly gauche excursion into the never-never land of English swells." Crowther further noted that "as the much put-upon Spanish gentleman, Anthony Quinn is plain funny, that's all." Which is not what either Lewis Allen conceived in his rather leisurely direction or Karl Tunberg considered in his unconvincing screenplay.

When Clive Loring (Ray Milland), a liberal noble-

With Ray Milland, Teresa Wright and
Virginia Field

man seeking election to Parliament, falls in love with music hall dancer Millicent Hopkins (Teresa Wright), his brother, Lord Belmont (Sir Cedric Hardwicke), warns him against getting too involved and then tells Millicent that marriage to her will jeopardize Loring's career. She reluctantly drops out of Loring's life and resumes her own career. One night, after leaving the theater, she is mistaken for a prostitute and, trying to avoid arrest, seeks refuge in the apartment of gallant Jose Martinez (Quinn), a concert pianist. The following morning, after her departure, Martinez is arrested on suspicion of killing a pawnbroker. He tries to clear himself but cannot find the girl whose name and address he does not know.

While the police search for the witness to corroborate his story, Millicent is again located by Loring, now a member of Parliament, who insists that they marry at once. Her photo is published in the papers and Martinez, recognizing Millicent, identifies her as the missing witness. The police question her, but she denies knowing Martinez, fearing that the facts about her overnight stay in his apartment will be misunderstood. When the accused pianist is brought to trial for murder, Millicent is torn by her conscience. She leaves Loring and makes a dramatic appearance at court to exonerate Martinez. Her confession creates a scandal. Loring is compelled to resign his position, his career ruined, but believing in his wife's innocence, he is determined to stand by her.

With Teresa Wright

With Katherine DeMille

# Black Gold

Allied Artists / 1947

CAST: *Charley Eagle*, ANTHONY QUINN; *Sarah Eagle*, KATHERINE DeMILLE; *Ruth Frazer*, Elyse Knox; *Stanley Lowell*, Kane Richmond; *Davey*, Ducky Louie; *Bucky*, Raymond Hatton; *Col. Caldwell*, Thurston Hall; *Jonas*, Alan Bridge; *Dan Toland*, Moroni Olsen; *Davey's Father*, H. T. Tsiang; *Judge Wilson*, Charles Trowbridge; *Monty*, Jack Norman (Norman Willis); *Schoolboy*, Darryl Hickman; *Themselves*, Clem McCarthy and Joe Hernandez.

CREDITS: *Director*, Phil Karlson; *producer*, Jeffrey Bernard; *screenplay*, Agnes Christine Johnson; *story*, Caryl Coleman; *music director*, Edward J. Kay; *art director*, E. R. Hickson; *camera*, Harry Neumann; *editor*, Roy Livingston. Cinecolor. Running time: 90 minutes.

*Black Gold* marks the dividing point separating Quinn from the forty-six screen roles which had preceded his portrayal of Charley Eagle. Totally an "Anthony Quinn movie," it provided him with a lovingly enacted, sympa-

thetic role in a quietly effective film. Unfortunately, its well-meant intentions, human pathos and excitement were vitiated by shoddy production one step up from Hollywood's so-called Poverty Row, in this case, Monogram Pictures. While the picture itself failed to excite critics or audiences, Quinn's performance drew considerable mention from many reviewers, confirming impressions gleaned from his previous roles. *Variety*, for one, spoke of "standout work by Anthony Quinn as the

With Katherine DeMille and Ducky Louie

With Ducky Louie, Jonathan Hale,
Kane Richmond, Elyse Knox

Indian. The actor demonstrates that all he needs to pack
a wallop is the proper role. Here he has it and makes it
socko." The *New York Herald Tribune* found Quinn's
characterization "a strong, persuasive portrait." Quinn's
wife, Katherine DeMille, acted opposite him in their
only film together, beautifully balancing his illiterate
Indian oil tycoon with her performance as his understanding well-educated wife.

Charley Eagle (Quinn), riding one day near the
Texas-Mexico border, finds an unconscious Chinese
boy (Ducky Louie), who had been thrown from his
horse. The boy's father, who had been trying to smuggle
them into the United States, was shot in the attempt.
Charley takes the boy home where he and his wife set
about adopting the lad, and breed the stallion he had
been riding with Charley's own mare.

Induced by Dan Toland (Moroni Olsen), an unscrupulous manager, Charley enters his mare in a claiming race, which the horse wins. Charley, though, is
unfamiliar with racetrack technicalities, and is dazed
when Toland claims the mare for $500. With an old
friend and horse trainer, Bucky (Raymond Hatton),
Charley sneaks the horse away from Toland's paddocks,
leaving $500 in its place. Oil is struck on Charley's land
the night his mare gives birth to a colt, and Charley
names him Black Gold. Bucky and Davey, Charley's
adopted son, team up in training the colt, which Charley
eventually enters in the Kentucky Derby. Charley's sudden death is a stunning blow to the youngster, who
courageously insists on riding Black Gold himself, winning the Derby despite Toland's tricks to get the horse
and his jockey to lose.

With Ducky Louie and Katherine DeMille

With Ducky Louie and Kane
Richmond

# Tycoon

RKO / 1947

CAST: *Johnny Munroe*, JOHN WAYNE; *Maura Alexander*, LARAINE DAY; *Frederick Alexander*. Sir Cedric Hardwicke; *Miss Braithwaite*, Judith Anderson; *Pop Mathews*, James Gleason; *Enrique "Ricky" Vargas*, Anthony Quinn; *Fog Harris*, Grant Withers; *Joe*, Paul Fix; *Chico*, Fernando Alvarado; *Curly Messenger*, Michael Harvey; *Holden*, Harry Woods; *Señor Tobar*, Charles Trowbridge; *Chavez*, Martin Garralaga; and Sam Lufkin, Wayne McCoy, Frank Leyva, Joe Dominguez, Tom Coffey, John Eberts, Sheila Raven, Diane Stewart, Clarise Murphy, Fred Aldrich, Brick Sullivan, Jane Adrian, Rudolph Medina, Al Murphy, Trevor Bardette, Argentina Brunetti, Max Wagner, Lucio Villegas, Blanca Vischer.

CREDITS: *Director*, Richard Wallace; *producer*, Stephen Ames; *screenplay*, Borden Chase and John Twist; based on the *novel* by C. E. Scoggins; *music director*, C. Bakaleinikoff; *original score*, Leigh Harline; *art directors*, Albert S. D'Agostino and Carroll Clark; *special effects*, Vernon L. Walker; *camera*, Harry J. Wild and W. Howard Greene; *editor*, Frank Doyle. Technicolor. Running time: 128 minutes.

Despite the merits of this action-and-romance feature set high in the Andes and designed specifically for John Wayne-styled heroics, Anthony Quinn drew an ill-de-

With Laraine Day and John Wayne

With Sir Cedric Hardwicke

fined, virtually extraneous role as *another* Latin—an engineer and troubleshooter working for his rich uncle, Sir Cedric Hardwicke, while keeping an approving eye on cousin Laraine Day's romance with Wayne. (How Englishman Hardwicke and American Laraine Day came to be related to Chilean Anthony Quinn, while Australian Judith Anderson hovered as an all-knowing duenna, only writers Borden Chase and John Twist can answer.) And thanks to the script, Quinn's character remained so hazy throughout the film, the actor was able to slip away easily from moviemaking at production's end almost without notice in search of new dimensions for his career on the Broadway stage. Four years would elapse before Quinn again was seen on the screen.

Johnny Munroe (Wayne) contracted with his partner, Pop Mathews (James Gleason), to build a tunnel for tycoon Frederick Alexander (Hardwicke), linking his tin mines in the mountains to the coast, wants to bridge a river instead. Alexander would rather go the more economical route *through* the mountain, and his refusals to provide additional funds to insure the safety of Munroe's men causes increasing friction. The tension is heightened when Munroe falls for the boss's daughter Maura (Laraine Day), whom the stalwart American builder had spotted during a weekend of carousing in town. After encouraging Munroe, Maura begins meeting him regularly without her father's knowledge, but with the help of her duenna (Judith Anderson), who doubles as the tycoon's secretary, and Ricky Vargas (Quinn), Maura's cousin and her father's chief engineer.

Angered when he discovers Maura's liaisons, Alexander tries to break Munroe by withholding supplies, but Munroe doggedly continues his assignment. When Alexander learns that Maura is still seeing Munroe in secret, and in fact spent the night with him when both became lost in the jungle, he arranges a shotgun marriage, and Maura goes to live in the construction camp. Munroe's preoccupation with his work distresses her, and when one of the workers is accidentally killed in a tunnel cave-in, she becomes totally disillusioned and returns to her father. Munroe, enraged by Alexander's continuing obstructions, deliberately dynamites the tunnel and announces he'll instead complete his contract by building a railroad *over* the turbulent river. He rushes the bridge steelwork in such dangerous fashion that Pop Mathews and Fog Harris (Grant Withers), their construction boss, quit in disgust.

Reluctantly admiring Munroe for his tenacity while keeping informed by Ricky of the work's progress, Alexander offers to extend the American's contract, but Munroe refuses to accept any favors. With only one remaining span to be set in place, Munroe finds his bridge endangered by floodwaters, but almost single-handedly he manages to save the structure, with last-minute assistance from Pop Mathews and his old crew. Recognizing Munroe's bravery and ability, Alexander arranges a reconciliation between his daughter and her husband, assures Munroe of a new contract, and gives them his blessings before running off to Vermont with his faithful secretary.

With Mel Ferrer

# The Brave Bulls

Columbia / 1951

CAST: *Luis Bello,* MEL FERRER; *Raul Fuentes,* ANTHONY QUINN; *Linda de Calderon,* MIROSLAVA; *Pepe Bello,* Eugene Iglesias; *Eladio Gomez,* Jose Torvay; *Raquelita,* Charlita; *Yank Delgado,* Jose Luis Vasquez; *Loco Ruiz,* Alfredo Aguilar; *Monkey Garcia,* Francisco Balderas; *Jackdaw,* Felipe Mota; *Enrique,* Pepe Lopez; *Little White,* Jose Meza; *Goyo Salinas,* Vicente Gardenas; *Abundio de Lao,* Manuel Orozco; *Tacho,* Esteve Dominguez; *Policarpe Cana,* Silviano Sanchez; *Lara,* Francisco Reigura; *Don Alberto Iriate,* E. Arozamena; *Rufino Vega,* Luis Corona; *Señora Bello,* Esther Laquin; *Chona,* M. del P. Castillo; *Alfredo Bello,* Juan Assaei; *Indio,* Delfino Morales; *Lala,* Rita Conde; *Don Tiburcio Balbuenna,* Roman Diaz Meza; *Mamacita,* Fanny Schiller; *Don Felix Aldemas,* Fernando del Valle.

CREDITS: *Producer-director,* Robert Rossen; *associate producer,* Shirley Miller; *screenplay,* John Bright; based on the *novel* by Tom Lea; *art directors,* Cary Odell and Frank Tuttle; *costumes,* Jean Louis; *camera,* Floyd Crosby and James Wong Howe; *editor,* Henry Batista. Running time: 108 minutes.

Quinn began what is generally considered Phase Two of his screen career by sandwiching a role in Robert Rossen's bullfighting film classic between two stage productions of *A Streetcar Named Desire* (the lengthy road tour and the subsequent Broadway "return engagement"). In the part of Raul Fuentes, the shrewd, practical manager of the fear-ridden matador (Mel Ferrer), Quinn contributed a realistic performance, polished to a sheen from the rough-edged distant cousin of *Knockout* a decade removed. Of his portrayal in this subsidiary role, the critic for the *New York Herald Tribune,* Howard Barnes, said: "Anthony Quinn stands out as the fighter's manager, a practical yet flippant fellow who sees through all of Bello's pretenses but appreciates his talents." Bosley Crowther, commenting in *The New York Times,* called Quinn's performance "racy and rugged."

Although Mel Ferrer is the nominal star, Quinn does get a few love scenes with leading lady Miroslava (the noted Mexican actress from Czechoslovakia who not long afterwards committed suicide), the girlfriend the manager gets to make a play for his most expensive property and number-one meal-ticket. With the excep-

With Mel Ferrer

With Miroslava

tion of Ferrer himself, whose wooden acting provides the film with its greatest liability, the flavor of the bullfight game and its devotees and hangers-on was superbly captured by director Rossen, his technicians, and his virtually all-Mexican cast, Quinn included. (It was Quinn's first movie made in his native country).

*The Brave Bulls,* made in the spring of 1950, was not released until nearly a year later, and Columbia Pictures then had difficulty marketing it, primarily be-

cause Robert Rossen had become caught up in the infamous Hollywood witch-hunt resulting from the Red scare of the era. The film remains a critical success but a financial failure, and occupies a niche as one of the lesser-appreciated screen classics.

Luis Bello (Ferrer) is the leading matador in Mexico, idolized by the public and worshiped by his younger brother, Pepe (Eugene Iglesias), who aspires to follow in Luis's footsteps. After a horrible goring in the ring, Luis begins to doubt his ability and finds himself overcome with a gnawing fear. His slick manager, Raul Fuentes (Quinn), instills him with a degree of confidence and induces him to resume his career. As an incentive, Raul introduces Luis to Linda de Calderon (Miroslava), a sultry blonde with whom the matador soon falls in love, unaware that she's really Raul's girlfriend. At Luis's next ring appearance, he is jeered by the crowd when he displays fear while winning a clumsy victory over the bull.

Luis's mental confusion becomes even more severe when Raul and Linda are killed in an automobile accident following a tryst, and the famed matador becomes a complete coward. Totally demoralized, Luis nevertheless agrees to fulfill an engagement in a small town arena where his brother Pepe is making his debut as a matador. Overtaken by fear, he performs like an amateur and is roundly booed. When Pepe is gored by a ferocious bull in the next contest, though, Luis rushes back into the ring and overcomes his fear of death with a brilliant performance. He leaves the arena to thunderous applause, filled with renewed confidence and courage.

With Miroslava and Mel Ferrer

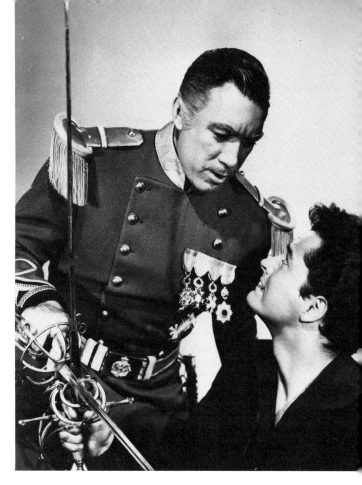

With John Derek

# Mask of the Avenger

Columbia / 1951

CAST: *Capt. Renato Dimorna*, JOHN DEREK; *Viovanni Larocca*, ANTHONY QUINN; *Maria D'Orsini*, JODY LAWRANCE; *Colardi*, Arnold Moss; *Rollo D'Anterras*, Eugene Iglesias; *Jacopo*, Dickie LeRoy; *Zio*, Harry Cording; *Signor Donner*, Ian Wolfe; *Baron Marchese*, Carlo Tricoli; *Marco*, David Bond; *Count Dimorna*, Wilton Graff; *Non-Commissioned Officer*, Tristram Coffin; *First Guard*, Ric Roman; *Artillery Major*, Philip Van Zandt; *Officer*, Chuck Hamilton; *Rudolpho*, Mickey Simpson; *Woman Busybody*, Belle Mitchell; *Market Woman*, Minerva Urecal; *Farmer*, Trevor Bardette; *Majordomo*, Lester Sharpe; *Col. Von Falker*, Gregory Gay.

CREDITS: *Director*, Phil Karlson; *producer*, Hunt Stromberg; *screenplay*, Jesse Lasky Jr.; *story*, George Bruce; *adaptation*, Ralph Bettinson and Philip MacDonald from "The Count of Monte Cristo" by Alexandre Dumas; *music director*, Morris Stoloff; *original score*, Mario Castelnuovo-Tedesco; *art director*, Harold MacArthur; *costumes*, Jean Louis; *camera*, Charles Lawton Jr.; *editor*, Jerome Thoms. Technicolor. Running time: 83 minutes.

This energetic, flashy little costumed horse opera crammed with all manner of derring-do performed by a dauntless adventurer righting wrongs, all in the name of Monte Cristo, was the first of twin mini-epics in which Quinn dispensed the treachery in his deliciously evil style. Both are virtually interchangeable, save for the leading man, the costumes and the locale. In *Mask of the Avenger,* wrote *Variety,* "Quinn makes a realistic heavy as the traitorous military governor." As such, in time-honored tradition, he's unmasked by fearless John Derek (who *is* masked) after one hour and twenty-three minutes of night-riding, wall-scaling, midnight assignations, political skulduggery, heroic quests and frequent swordplay. As one of those snappy, well-paced action fillers Columbia was turning out in the decade after the war, this one boasted excellent color, tight direction by Quinn's friend Phil Karlson, elegant production values— and, as the *New York Herald Tribune* bemoaned, "an asinine script." The *Trib*'s critic complained that "such fine actors as Anthony Quinn and Arnold Moss are hurled into the fray as top-heavy villains, but they only make the nonsense look more ridiculous."

Returning to his home town on the Austrian-Italian border after a tour of duty in the war against Austria in 1848, Captain Renato Dimorna (John Derek) learns that his father has been branded a traitor and executed. Dimorna is attacked by the townsfolk because of his suspected crime, but is rescued by Viovanni Larocca (Quinn), the military governor of the province. Although grateful, Dimorna becomes suspicious of Larocca, who, with his aide, Colardi (Arnold Moss), has been conducting a reign of terror. Larocca subsequently accuses Dimorna's friend, Rollo D'Anterras (Eugene Iglesias), of treachery and takes him prisoner after killing his family. Dimorna secretly leaves Larocca's palace and, black-masked and cloaked, begins a series of daring forays to harass Larocca. He rescues his sweetheart, Maria D'Orsini (Jody Lawrance), from Larocca's guards and then returns to free Rollo. With a small group of loyalists, Dimorna vows to expose Larocca as

As Viovanni Larocca

the real traitor, but before they can act, Larocca surrenders the town to the Austrians. His hand prematurely forced, Dimorna and his men retake the town, but Rollo is killed in the assault on the garrison as Larocca tries to flee, taking Maria as hostage. Dimorna follows but is injured during a sword fight with Larocca and falls from his horse. Larocca prepares to finish him off as Maria seizes a sword and keeps him at bay. Dimorna recovers from the stunning blow and kills the traitor.

With Wilton Graff

With Jean Peters

# Viva Zapata!

20th Century–Fox / 1952

CAST: *Emiliano Zapata,* MARLON BRANDO; *Josefa Espejo,* JEAN PETERS; *Eufemio Zapata,* ANTHONY QUINN; *Fernando Aguirre,* Joseph Wiseman; *Don Nacio,* Arnold Moss; *Pancho Villa,* Alan Reed; *La Soldadera,* Margo; *Don Francisco Madero,* Harold Gordon; *Pablo,* Lou Gilbert; *Señora Espejo,* Mildred Dunnock; *Huerta,* Frank Silvera; *Aunt,* Nina Varela; *Señor Espejo,* Florenz Ames; *Zapatista,* Bernie Gozier; *Colonel Guajarado,* Frank De Kova; *General Fuentes,* Joseph Granby; *Innocente,* Pedro Regas; *Diaz,* Fay Roope; *Lazaro,* Will Kuluva; *Old General,* Richard Garrick; *Don Garcia,* Harry Kingston; *Officer,* Ross Bagdasarian; *Husband,* Leonard George; *Fuentes's Wife,* Fernanda Eliscu; *Captain,* Abner Biberman; *Commanding Officer,* Phil Van Zandt; *Garcia's Wife,* Lisa Fusaro; *Nacio's Wife,* Belle Mitchell; *Overseer,* Ric Roman; *Hernandez,* Henry Silva; *Eduardo,* Guy Thomajan; *Rurale,* George J. Lewis; *Senior Officer,* Henry Corden; *New General,* Nester Paiva; *Captain,* Robert Filmer.

CREDITS: *Director,* Elia Kazan; *producer,* Darryl F. Zanuck; *screenplay,* John Steinbeck; based on the *novel* "Zapata the Unconquered" by Edgcumb Pichon; *music director,* Alfred Newman; *original music,* Alex North; *art directors,* Lyle Wheeler and Leland Fuller; *camera,* Joe MacDonald; *editor,* Barbara McLean. Running time: 113 minutes.

Under the guidance of his old friend, Elia Kazan, Quinn gave his greatest performance to date, winning his first Academy Award as Best Supporting Actor for his outstanding portrayal of Eufemio Zapata, the swaggering, lecherous, bullying brother of the legendary twentieth-century Mexican hero. This was Marlon Brando's third picture after his stage creation of Stanley Kowalski, and Quinn's second, and through his consummate acting skills, Quinn prevented himself from being upstaged by the dynamic film newcomer, creating in Eufemio a gutsy characterization which, despite its brevity, was not overshadowed by Brando's Emiliano Zapata. Most of the critical acclaim, naturally, went to Brando, and then to Kazan, while Quinn contented himself with incisive one-line raves, like Bosley Crowther's: "As the wild, weak-willed brother of Zapata, Anthony Quinn does a dandy, rawboned job," and again in Crowther's Sunday piece: "Quinn is superb as Zapata's brother." Similarly, *Newsweek* decided that "Quinn gives one of the most effective performances in his long screen career." As in William Wellman's *The Ox-Bow Incident* and, to a lesser extent, in Robert Rossen's *The Brave Bulls,* but most especially in Elia Kazan's *Viva, Zapata!,* Quinn's vivid portrayals of doomed men remain as acting lessons to students of the art who more often than not screen the great film classics before moving onto other works.

The Oscar which Quinn won for his performance was presented at the same ceremony at which his father-in-law also accepted an Academy Award (as producer of *The Greatest Show on Earth).* Unfortunately, Quinn himself was out of the country seeking wider film horizons on the Continent, and was unable to relish the moment firsthand.

*Viva, Zapata!* is the study, according to screenwriter John Steinbeck, of the illiterate Mexican peasant revolutionary who for ten years led guerrilla uprisings against dictators and presidents. It begins near the close of the thirty-four-year reign of President Porfirio Diaz (Fay Roope), when Emiliano Zapata (Brando) becomes spokesman for the dispossessed peons, protesting the unending land-grabbing by local real estate barons. Burning with a sense of injustice, the simple Emiliano, together with his brother Eufemio (Quinn), begins leading forays from the hills after they and the villagers are attacked by a squad of the irked Diaz militia and watch as men, women and children are indiscriminately shot down.

Zapata switches his allegiance to Francisco Madero (Harold Gordon), the exiled politician who has sworn

With Margo

to lead a revolution against Diaz, but following the uprising which deposes the dictator-president, Zapata becomes disillusioned when land reforms are not forthcoming. Zapata turns against the gentlemanly, well-intending Madero when it becomes apparent that the new president is actually a pawn for a powerful military clique headed by General Huerta (Frank Silvera). Returning once again to his people, Zapata soon joins forces with Pancho Villa (Alan Reed), who stages his own counter-revolution and presses the presidency on Zapata. Now Zapata himself must listen to the demands of the peasant delegations, and he soon learns that his own brother has been branded a land-grabber. Eufemio, heady with power by association, has become a drunken mini-dictator who dies in a fight over a woman after being reprimanded by Emiliano. Sinking to despondency, Zapata is soon set up for assassination by the intellectual, fanatic revolutionary, Fernando Aguirre (Joseph Wiseman), who sells him out to Huerta and the military.

With Margo, Lou Gilbert and Marlon Brando

With Ian MacDonald and Anthony Dexter

# The Brigand

Columbia / 1952

CAST: *Carlos Delargo/King Lorenzo*, ANTHONY DEXTER; *Prince Ramon*, Anthony Quinn; *Princess Teresa*, Jody Lawrance; *Countess Flora*, Gale Robbins; *Triano*, Carl Benton Reid; *Captain Ruiz*, Ron Randell; *Monsieur De LaForce*, Fay Roope; *Carnot*, Carleton Young; *Major Schreck*, Ian MacDonald; *Doctor Lopez*, Lester Matthews; *Baroness Isabella*, Barbara Brown; *Sultan*, Walter Kingford; *Don Felipe Castro*, Donald Randolph; *Doña Dolores Castro*, Mari Blanchard; *Archbishop*, Holmes Herbert; *King's Secretary*, David Bond; *Majordomo*, George Melford; *Mustapha*, Dale Van Sickel; *Page*, Eduardo Cansino Jr.

CREDITS: *Director*, Phil Karlson; *producer*, Edward Small; *screenplay*, Jesse Lasky Jr.; *story*, George Bruce; *music director*, Morris Stoloff; *original score*,

With Anthony Dexter and Ian MacDonald

With Fay Roope and Carl Benton Reid

With Fay Roope and Gale Robbins

Mario Castelnuovo-Tedesco; *art director,* Robert Peterson; *costumes,* Jean Louis; *choreography,* Eugene Loring; *assistant director,* Carter DeHaven Jr.; *camera,* W. Howard Greene; *editor,* Jerome Thoms. Technicolor. Running time: 94 minutes.

Like *Mask of the Avenger,* both in form and in plot, *The Brigand* provided Quinn more footage for his deliciously evil culprit characterization, crossing swords this time with *two* Anthony Dexters. Noteworthy is the fact that the adversaries in this medium-budgeted Technicolor swashbuckler were the actor who once had been approached to become the new Valentino and the actor whose biggest claim to screen fame was *being* Valentino. This film, like *Mask of the Avenger,* had its vague roots in the Dumas novel, *The Count of Monte Cristo,* with enough fudging and script inanities to sidestep comparisons.

When Moroccan-born desert adventurer Carlos Delargo (Dexter) is brought home to stand trial for killing a government official in a duel over the man's wife, his remarkable resemblance to the king (also Dexter) causes Prime Minister Triano (Carl Benton Reid) to bring Delargo to the monarch's attention. When the king is seriously wounded in an assassination attempt by his ambitious cousin Prince Ramon (Quinn), Delargo is urged to masquerade as the king until the latter recovers. Princess Teresa (Jody Lawrance), scheduled to marry the king, falls in love with Delargo, upsetting Ramon's scheme to take the throne, but he soon becomes suspicious and has his mistress, Countess Flora (Gale Robbins), learn the truth. Ramon discovers where the real king is being hidden and kills both him and Flora. Delargo bursts in and, in a clanging duel, kills Ramon and his henchmen, and then returns to the palace where Teresa and the prime minister vow to keep the secret that Delargo is not in fact the King.

With Ian MacDonald, Fay Roope and Carleton Young

[ 125 ]

# The World in His Arms

Universal–International / 1952

CAST: *Jonathan Clark,* GREGORY PECK; *Countess Marina Selanova,* ANN BLYTH; *Portugee,* ANTHONY QUINN; *Deacon Greathouse,* John McIntire; *Mamie,* Andrea King; *Prince Semyon,* Carl Esmond; *Mme. Anna Selanova,* Eugenie Leontovich; *General Ivan Vorashilov,* Sig Ruman; *Eustace,* Hans Conreid; *William Cleggett,* Bryan Forbes; *Eben Cleggett,* Rhys Williams; *Ogeechuk,* Bill Radovich; *Paul Shushaldin,* Gregory Gay; *Peter,* Henry Kulky; *Seamen,* Gregg Barton, Gregg Martell, Carl Andre, George Scanlon, Carl Harbaugh and Frank Chase; *Lilly,* Eve Whitney; *Lena,* Millicent Patrick; *Jose,* Syl Lamont; *Nicholas,* Leo Mostovoy; *Shanghai Kelley,* Wee Willie Davis.

CREDITS: *Director,* Raoul Walsh; *producer,* Aaron Rosenberg; *screenplay,* Borden Chase; *based on the novel* by Rex Beach; *additional dialogue,* Horace McCoy; *music,* Frank Skinner; *art directors,* Bernard Herzbrun and Alexander Golitzen; *camera,* Russell Metty; *editor,* Frank Gross. Technicolor. Running time: 104 minutes.

As the crafty, thieving schooner captain, Portugee, Anthony Quinn gave one of those high-spirited, full-bodied performances which were to rapidly become identified with him during the 1950s. Storming about, needling fellow captain Gregory Peck, challenging all comers to a drinking match or a wrestling bout, ready for a brawl in any port, laughing lustily in defeat or bragging in victory, Quinn cut a vivid figure in Raoul Walsh's lively adventure epic about life on the nineteenth-century Barbary Coast in San Francisco. The film's highlight was an exceptionally well-staged, windswept race between two sealers from San Francisco to the Pribilofs off the coast of Alaska, making the brawling and romancing which preceded it seem somewhat pale. Although most critics viewed this robust film simply as Grade-A adventure out of Universal-International's then-current he-man mold of muscular derring-do, a few questioned the anti-Red theme woven into the plot which talked at some length about the need for Russian expansionism (through Alaska) to check American imperialism. In any event, critics like Bosley Crowther enjoyed the colorfully escapist *The World in His Arms* for its entertainment value, with *The New York Times* reviewer feeling that Quinn "plays a Portuguese captain as though he were animated by hot-feet and rum."

In San Francisco after a successful seal hunt, Jonathan Clark (Gregory Peck) and his crew end up in the same hotel as Countess Marina Selanova (Ann Blyth) and her entourage. Marina is Russian royalty on the run from imminent marriage to an ambitious Czarist prince (Carl Esmond) and hoping to reach Sitka where her uncle (Sig Rumann) is governor general. Learning that Jonathan has a boat and crew ready, she begs him to take her to Alaska after first being rebuffed by his seal-poaching rival, Portugee (Quinn), who had been unable to raise a crew. Unaware that she is royalty, Jonathan falls for her while giving her a midnight tour of San Francisco (ed. note: the situation is strikingly similar to the Peck-Audrey Hepburn relationship not long afterwards in *Roman Holiday*), and even talks her into marrying him. On the eve of their wedding, her impatient Russian fiancé steams into the harbor on a gunboat, kidnaps Marina and her retinue, and sails for Alaska, vowing to behead her uncle unless their originally planned marriage takes place.

Learning too late that Marina is gone, Jonathan gets drunk and loses his money following a knock-down fight with Portugee. Then he brashly offers to race Portugee to Alaska, with the winner getting the other's ship and entire seal catch. Jonathan's schooner edges past Portugee's rig into the sealing grounds, where the Russians seize the ships, men and cargos. Jonathan and Portugee

With Gregory Gaye

are charged with poaching, but are set free at Marina's request after her prince extracts her promise to marry him. The two sea captains are escorted by troops back to their ships, but they sneak back to the governor's residence in time to disrupt the wedding ceremony. Jonathan kills the prince while Portugee directs the destruction of the Russian gunboat, permitting Jonathan to sail back to America with Marina (*i.e.,* the world) in his arms.

With Gregory Peck

With Maureen O'Hara

# Against All Flags

Universal–International / 1952

CAST: *Brian Hawke,* ERROL FLYNN; *Spitfire Stevens,* MAUREEN O'HARA; *Roc Brasiliano,* Anthony Quinn; *Princess Patma,* Alice Kelley; *Molvina MacGregor,* Mildred Natwick; *Captain Kidd,* Robert Warwick; *Gow,* Harry Cording; *Harris,* John Alderson; *Jones,* Phil Tully; *Sir Cloudsley,* Lester Matthews; *Williams,* Tudor Owen; *Captain Moisson,* Maurice Marsac; *Captain Hornsby,* James Craven; *Barber,* James Fairfax; *Swaine,* Michael Ross; *Hassan,* Bill Radovich; *Crop-Ear Collins,* Paul Newland.

CREDITS: *Director,* George Sherman; *producer,* Howard Christie; *screenplay,* Aeneas MacKenzie and Joseph Hoffman; *based on an* original story *by* Aeneas MacKenzie; *music director,* Hans J. Salter; *art directors,* Bernard Herzbrun and Alexander Golitzen; *cam-*

*era,* Russell Metty; *editor,* Frank Gross. Technicolor. Running time: 83 minutes.

Joining, or more precisely opposing, Errol Flynn in another eye-popping swashbuckler, Quinn made as villainous a pirate captain as ever shivered a timber and made the going as nasty as possible for freebooter Flynn, who's out to eliminate the scourge to His Majesty's Navy of the Madagascan pirates in 1700. Quinn not only crosses swords with the athletic corsair but also puts himself in league with fiery female pirate captain Maureen O'Hara (this was their third of four films together), while director George Sherman kept proceedings moving at breakneck speed and, when the action threatened to flag, introduced a variety of brisk hand-to-hand combat sequences.

In order to break the pirate hold on Madagascar, Brian Hawke (Flynn), a British naval officer acting as a secret agent, is officially whipped aboard a merchant-

Filmed in 1967 as *The King's Pirate* with Doug McClure, Jill St. John and Guy Stockwell.

[ 128 ]

With Errol Flynn

man to make it appear that he has cause for desertion. With two companions, he jumps ship and heads for the island, planning to sabotage the pirates' shore guns and signal a British man-of-war to enter the harbor. Ashore, the men are immediately captured and brought before the pirates' governing board. Captain Roc Brasiliano (Quinn) demands death, but Spitfire Stevens (Maureen O'Hara) votes him down. Hawke join Roc's crew as navigator for the buccaneer's raid on the ship of the emperor of India, aboard which is the emperor's daughter, Princess Patma (Alice Kelley). Over Hawke's objections, Roc puts Patma and her harem girls on the auction block, and when Hawke tries to buy the princess, a jealous Spitfire outbids him and takes the girl home.

Hawke, meanwhile, succeeds in his original mission, but is captured by Roc and his men before he can escape. The irate Spitfire decrees that Hawke and his companions be tied to stakes on the incoming tide to be devoured by huge man-eating crabs.

Spitfire then does a turnabout and frees Hawke while pretending to stab him, and the two slip aboard Roc's brigantine which has been given safe passage past the man-of-war because the Indian princess is being held hostage. Hawke surprises Roc on the bridge and engages him in a duel with rapier and pikestaff, killing the blackguard, saving the princess, subduing the pirate stronghold, guaranteeing the trade route for the British merchant fleet, winning amnesty and sailing into the Technicolor sunset with Spitfire.

*Against All Flags* was the first of the five action-filled Technicolor films Quinn made for Universal-International during 1952-53. It was made prior to *The World in His Arms* but delayed when Errol Flynn broke his ankle shortly before shooting was completed, causing a five-month delay in production, during which time Quinn moved on to other assignments. When the film was remade in 1967, Guy Stockwell enacted the role Quinn had originated, but the new version, entitled *The King's Pirate,* was played strictly for laughs.

With Errol Flynn

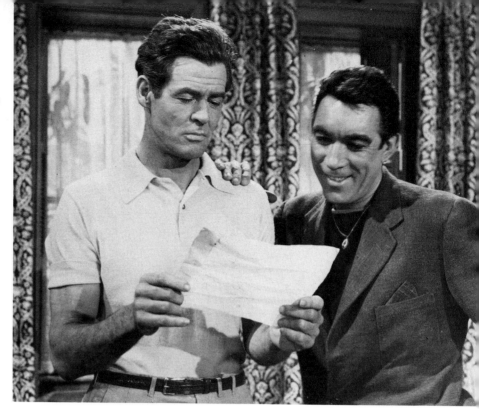

With Robert Ryan

# City Beneath the Sea

Universal–International / 1953

CAST: *Brad Carlton*, ROBERT RYAN; *Terry McBride*, MALA POWERS; *Tony Bartlett*, ANTHONY QUINN; *Venita*, SUZAN BALL; *Captain Meade*, George Mathews; *Dwight Trevor*, Karel Stepanek; *Mama Mary*, Hilo Hattie; *Calypso*, Lalo Rios; *Djion*, Woody Strode; *Martin*, Tommy Garland; *Kirk*, Michael Dale; *Kip*, Leon Lontoc; *Maru*, Bernie Gozier; *Captain Clive*, John Warburton; *Mme. Cecile*, Barbara Morrison; *Mendoza*, Peter Mamakos; *Calypso Singer*, LeRoi Antoine; *High Priest*, George Hamilton; *Half-Caste*, Marya Marco; *Waiter*, Gerado De Corovia; *Ship Steward*, Michael Ferris; *Marie*, Sherry Moreland; *Helen*, Elizabeth Root.

CREDITS: *Director*, Budd Boetticher; *producer*, Albert J. Cohen; *screenplay*, Jack Harvey and Ramon Romero; based on the *story* "Port Royal, the Ghost City Beneath the Sea" by Harry E. Rieseberg; *music director*, Joseph Gershenson; *art directors*, Alexander Golitzen and Emrich Nicholson; *camera*, Charles P. Boyle; *editor*, Edward Curtiss. Technicolor. Running time: 86 minutes.

With Karel Stepanek and Robert Ryan

Acting with Robert Ryan, whose own career had started during the Paramount days when Anthony Quinn was specializing in gangster portrayals, Quinn here was given equal billing as a fellow deep-sea diver bent on salvaging a gold bullion shipment in the West Indies. As noted by *The New York Times*, "Messrs. Ryan and Quinn spent most of the time swapping coy badinage with the appreciative ladies, now and then puttering around, and just as unimpressively, below the surface." The story itself was framed against a colorfully historic

In action as Tony Bartlett

With Suzan Ball

event: the destruction in 1692 by earthquake and tidal wave of the onetime pirate stronghold in Port Royal, Jamaica, with the burial of millions of dollars in sunken gold. Harry E. Rieseberg had written a fascinating chronicle of it, but the inspired story apparently was set aside by the scriptwriters in favor of (again quoting *The New York Times* critic) "a dull, transparent excuse for some familiar juvenile muscularity and streamlined amour." In *City Beneath the Sea,* Quinn worked for the first of many times with director Budd Boetticher.

Divers Brad Carlton (Ryan) and Tony Bartlett (Quinn) are hired by Dwight Trevor (Karel Stepanek) to locate the hulk of a ship which had sunk off the coast of Jamaica with millions in gold bullion. Carlton and Bartlett charter a banana boat belonging to Terry Mc-Bride (Mala Powers) for the diving operations and spend days in a fruitless search until Trevor finally calls a halt to it. After paying off the boys, Trevor then contacts Captain Meade (George Mathews), the supposedly drowned skipper of the sunken ship who knows the exact location of the wreck. Their plan is to grab the treasure for themselves after the company which owns the ship is satisfied that the cargo is in fact lost. Neither Trevor nor Meade, though, trusts the other, and Bartlett is approached by Meade with a $50,000 offer to recover the gold. Bartlett makes his dive at the spot Meade has designated and locates the wreck in the middle of the legendary sunken city of Port Royal. Surfacing, Bartlett holds up Meade for one-third of the loot.

Carlton, meanwhile, has fallen for Terry and is relaxing on her boat when voodoo drums begin beating. Mama Mary (Hilo Hattie), a Jamaican who works for Terry, tells them that the natives are restless because the forbidden city beneath the sea has been entered by a foreigner and the voodoo gods are angry. Back at their room, Carlton learns the truth when his partner asks him to join Meade's scheme to take the gold. After angering Bartlett by turning him down, Carlton goes to Trevor with the information, unaware that Trevor is as crooked as Meade, and is hired to dive for the treasure himself. Sailing to the wreckage sight in Terry's boat, Carlton goes over the side and quickly locates the hulk. While he's on the bottom, Bartlett and Meade pull alongside Terry's boat. At gunpoint, Meade orders Trevor to continue with the operation. When Trevor balks, Meade shoots him and then points the gun at Bartlett, threatening to cut off Carlton's air supply unless the diver sends up the gold. Suddenly an underwater earthquake occurs, almost as predestined by voodoo superstition, trapping Carlton as the sunken city collapses around him. The force of the earthquake tosses Meade overboard, and Bartlett quickly dons diving gear and rushes to his partner's assistance. Later, as they are about to sail for the States with their girlfriends—Carlton with Terry, Bartlett with Venita, a singer in a local club—they receive a legitimate offer to finish the salvage operation they had begun for Trevor.

With Sherry Moreland, Robert Ryan and Elizabeth Root

With Barbara Hale

# Seminole

Universal–International / 1953

CAST: *Lt. Lance Caldwell,* ROCK HUDSON; *Revere Muldoon,* BARBARA HALE; *Osceola,* ANTHONY QUINN; *Major Harlan Degan,* Richard Carlson; *Kajeck,* Hugh O'Brian; *Lt. Hamilton,* Russell Johnson; *Sgt. Magruder,* Lee Marvin; *Kulak,* Ralph Moody; *Zachary Taylor,* Fay Roope; *Corporal Gerad,* James Best; *Captain Streller,* Don Gibson; *Scott,* John Day; *Corporal Smiley,* Howard Erskine; *Trooper,* Frank Chase; *Hendricks,* Duane Thorsen; *Trader Taft,* Robert Dane; *Major Lawrence,* John Phillips; *Mattie Sue Thomas,* Soledad Jimenez; *Captain Sibley,* Bob Bray.

CREDITS: *Director,* Budd Boetticher; *producer,* Howard Christie; *screenplay,* Charles K. Peck Jr.; *music director,* Joseph Gershenson; *art directors,* Alexander Golitzen and Emrich Nicholson; *camera,* Russell Metty; *editor,* Virgil Vogel. Technicolor. Running time: 86 minutes.

Playing the noble savage character for the final time,

With Rock Hudson

Quinn costarred as a Seminole chief in the second of his Budd Boetticher Technicolor adventure movies, called sarcastically by *Time Magazine* "a swampy melodrama." Quinn by now had gained enough marquee status to allow him to compete with star Rock Hudson for the leading lady, but then he *was* playing an Indian, putting two strikes against him. *Seminole* was standard back-lot fodder dealing with a martinet major in the U.S. Army who is determined to wipe out the Indians in Florida, and the entire thing was punctuated by much war-whooping, Indian raids, military attacks—and little else. The affair ends predictably with the chief's getting killed, the major's getting his comeuppance and the lieutenant's getting his girl, following a screenful of energetic performances.

Because of his knowledge of Florida and the Seminoles, West Pointer Lt. Lance Caldwell (Rock Hudson) is assigned to the command of Major Harlan Degan (Richard Carlson), who distrusts the Indians. Shortly after arriving at his new post, Caldwell visits his childhood sweetheart, Revere Muldoon (Barbara Hale), and learns that she is in love with Osceola (Quinn), leader of the Seminoles and Caldwell's boyhood friend. Through Revere, Caldwell arranges for a peace meeting with Osceola, but before it takes place, one of the Seminole chiefs is killed by Degan's scouting party, and the chief's son, Kajeck (Hugh O'Brian), vows revenge. Despite Caldwell's warnings, Degan attempts a surprise attack on the Seminoles and is badly beaten. Infuriated, he uses Caldwell and Revere to bring Osceola to the fort under a flag of truce, then beats the Indian and has him thrown into a detention pit. Caldwell, angered, berates

With Barbara Hale and Rock Hudson

his superior and is placed under arrest. Kajeck meanwhile makes his move to assume leadership of the tribe by sneaking into the fort, overpowering the sentry and murdering Osceola. Degan charges Caldwell with the murder and orders him before a firing squad. Kajeck and his warriors stage a sudden attack on the fort before Degan's command can be executed, and the Indians demand Osceola's body, exonerate Caldwell and charge Degan with deceit. Caldwell arranges a peace treaty with Kajeck and assures the chief that Degan will be brought to trial.

With Rock Hudson

With Robert Taylor

# Ride, Vaquero!

Metro-Goldwyn-Mayer / 1953

CAST: *Rio*, ROBERT TAYLOR; *Cordelia Cameron*, AVA GARDNER; *King Cameron*, HOWARD KEEL; *Jose Esqueda*, Anthony Quinn; *Father Antonio*, Kurt Kasznar; *Sheriff Parker*, Ted DeCorsia; *Singer*, Charlita; *Barton*, Jack Elam; *Adam Smith*, Walter Baldwin; *Vicente*, Joe Dominguez; *Pete*, Frank McGrath; *Vaquero*, Charles Stevens; *Deputy*, Rex Lease; *Deputy*, Tom Greenway; *Valero*, Paul Fierro; *Storekeeper*, Percy Helton; *Dentist*, Norman Leavitt; *Hussy*, Movita Castenada; *Woman*, Almira Sessions; *Bartender*, Monte Blue; *Dealer*, Philip Van Zandt; *General Sheridan*, Stanley Andrews; *Specialty Dancer*, Italia De Nubila.

CREDITS: *Director*, John Farrow; *producer*, Stephen Ames; *screenplay*, Frank Fenton; *music*, Bronislau Kaper; *assistant director*, Jerry Thorpe; *art directors*, Cedric Gibbons and Arthur Lonergan; *camera*, Robert Surtees; *editor*, Harold F. Kress. Ansco Color. Running time: 89 minutes.

With Ava Gardner, Howard Keel, Robert Taylor, Jack Elam, Ted DeCorsia

Anthony Quinn's vivid performance as a ruthless Mexican bandit in his second Western for director John Farrow made MGM's initial wide-screen production the sterling little gem it has come to be regarded. Out-acting the three stars billed above him, he is top-notch as the roistering, murderous braggart who uses vino as a gargle and is not above sadistically shooting men to death piecemeal. As Jose Esqueda, thought *Time* magazine, "he provides the only glimpses of distinction, and, at moments, he is so good that he seems to have ridden into the scene out of some other movie." And Howard Thompson, reviewing the film in *The New York Times,* felt the whole thing "a pretentious, generally rhetorical horse opera, seasoned with Freud and a modicum of horse sense," but found that "Anthony Quinn's vigorous, colorful portrait of the chief culprit, at any rate, is a pleasure to watch." One of the production's curious twists was the offbeat casting of Robert Taylor, who was given the role not only of a vicious killer, but also as Quinn's lieutenant!

Following the Civil War, the influx of ranchers to the frontier threatens Jose Esqueda's stranglehold on the territory. With his chief henchman and foster brother, Rio (Taylor), Esqueda oversees the attack on the ranch of newly arrived King Cameron (Howard Keel) and his bride Cordelia (Ava Gardner). The bandit burns the ranch to the ground, as a warning not only to Cameron but to other settlers. Undaunted, Cameron rebuilds, and noting that Sheriff Parker (Ted deCorsia) is unable or unwilling to stop Esqueda, Cameron calls the townspeople together to draw up plans to protect their ranches, but Esqueda and his men break up the meet-

As Jose Esqueda

ing. Deciding to take Esqueda on alone, Cameron turns his ranch house into a fortress. When the bandit dispatches Rio and his men to burn it down again, Cameron and Cordelia, with the help of Father Antonio

With Ava Gardner and Robert Taylor

With Jack Elam, Terry Wilson, Frank McGrath, Robert Taylor, Joe Dominguez

(Kurt Kasznar), the town priest, beat off the attack and capture Rio. Rather than turn Rio over to the sheriff, Cameron convinces the outlaw to stay and help work the ranch. Rio soon finds himself attracted to Cordelia, and she to him. Esqueda is infuriated when he learns that Rio has thrown in with Cameron, but secretly believes that his lieutenant will soon return. Cordelia persuades Rio to take her to Esqueda's hideout, where she hopes to convince the bandit to let her and her husband live in peace. Esqueda laughs off her pleas and starts a quarrel between her and Rio.

Feeling that Rio has gone soft, Esqueda decides to stage an attack on the town, where he kills the sheriff and takes control, setting up headquarters in the saloon. During his wait for Rio, Esqueda encourages his men to pillage the place and kill indiscriminately. When Cameron fearlessly enters the saloon, Esqueda challenges him to draw and shoots the rancher down, wounding him over and over again. As he is about to finish off Cameron, he is interrupted by Rio, and the two draw against each other and die together as the troops of the nearby outpost scatter the gang.

With Robert Taylor and Howard Keel

[ 136 ]

With Jeff Chandler

# East of Sumatra

Universal–International / 1953

CAST: *Duke Mullane,* JEFF CHANDLER; *Lory Hale,* MARILYN MAXWELL; *Kiang,* ANTHONY QUINN; *Minyora,* SUZAN BALL; *Daniel Catlin,* John Sutton; *Macleod,* Jay C. Flippen; *Baltimore,* Scat Man Crothers; *Paulo,* Eugene Iglesias; *Cowboy,* Peter Graves; *Atib,* Aram Katcher; *Cupid,* Earl Holliman; *Clyde,* Antony Eustrel; *Drake,* James Craven; *Keith,* John Warburton; *Co-Pilot,* Michael Dale; *Mr. Vickers,* Gilchrist Stuart; *Corcoran,* Charles Horvath.

CREDITS: *Director,* Budd Boetticher; *producer,* Albert J. Cohen; *screenplay,* Frank Gill Jr.; *story,* Jack Natteford and Louis L'Amour; *music director,* Joseph Gershenson; *art directors,* Bernard Herzbrun and Robert Boyle; *camera,* Clifford Stine; *editor,* Virgil Vogel. Technicolor. Running time: 82 minutes.

Anthony Quinn's stock native warrior characterization, again for director Budd Boetticher, seemed to illustrate the actor's growing frustration with the caliber of roles

he was being assigned—Best Supporting Actor award notwithstanding. The waste of his acknowledged talents in progressively more insipid stories and parts was never more clearly on view than in this Grade-C jungle effort which only he and Color by Technicolor dignified. Jeff Chandler and lots of stock Universal faces as well as stock Universal footage were employed to act as adhesive agents to hold this slapdash production together, with nobody bothering to even cover over the very visible seams.

As chief engineer for a mining firm in the Far East, Duke Mullane (Chandler) is assigned to survey the Island of Tungga, off Sumatra's east coast, where vast deposits of tin are thought to be located. Mullane's boss, Daniel Catlin (John Sutton), who is engaged to Mullane's ex-girlfriend Lory Hale (Marilyn Maxwell), distrusts his engineer and ignores his requests for food and supplies, sending in only mining equipment. The food had been promised to the island's chief, Kiang (Quinn), with whom Mullane had become friends, hoping to get the natives' cooperation. Catlin shows up with Lory, accuses Mullane of being too soft with the natives and provokes Kiang, telling the chief Mullane has been exceedingly friendly with the half-caste princess Minyora (Suzan Ball), whom Kiang is planning to marry.

When the natives' rice supply is destroyed, Kiang blames Mullane and demolishes the mine crew's plane and supplies. With Minyora's help, Mullane and his men try to escape to the mainland, but are trapped in a native temple by Kiang and his warriors. There Mullane engages Kiang in hand-to-hand combat, killing the chief, and Minyora then leads her people back to their village. Mullane and his men are given free passage, and the engineer leaves for another assignment—with Lory.

With Suzan Ball

With Jeff Chandler

As Kiang

# Blowing Wild

United States Pictures–Warner Bros. / 1953

CAST: *Jeff Dawson*, GARY COOPER; *Marina Conway*, BARBARA STANWYCK; *Sal Donnelly*, RUTH ROMAN; *Ward "Paco" Conway*, ANTHONY QUINN; *Dutch Peterson*, Ward Bond; *Jackson*, Ian MacDonald; *Henderson*, Richard Karlan; *El Gavilan*, Juan Garcia.

CREDITS: *Director*, Hugo Fregonese; *producer*, Milton Sperling; *screenplay*, Philip Yordan; *music director*, Ray Heindorf; *musical score*, Dimitri Tiomkin; *title song*, Dimitri Tiomkin and Paul Francis Webster; *art director*, Al Ybarra; *camera*, Sid Hickox; *editor*, Alan Crosland Jr. Running time: 90 minutes.

With his characterization of Paco Conway, the virile, wealthy oilman with an unscrupulous, oversexed wife in this all-star potboiler, Quinn offers one of the bright spots amid the sluggishness of both story and direction. Otis L. Guernsey, Jr., best summed up the plot in his review in the *New York Herald Tribune* calling it simply "a story about strong men fighting bandits in the Mexican oil fields, with Barbara Stanwyck climbing all over Gary Cooper in a dime-novel version of grand passion." Quinn bravely held his own, knowing that even the audience is aware that he doesn't stand a chance with his wife as soon as Gary Cooper comes looking for work. The ultimate disgrace, however, was being unceremoniously dumped down his own oil well by his wife and beaten to death by the pump. And this after a line like "That's the way it's going to be, baby. Just you and me and the pump." *Blowing Wild,* one of the last small-screen pictures released by Warner Bros., was unsalvageable, it is generally agreed, because director Hugo Fregonese seemingly did not know which road to travel in search of a satisfying conclusion, and the story simply

With Gary Cooper and Ruth Roman

wavered from reel to reel, as did Gary Cooper's pivotal role.

Run off their oil lease by bandits led by El Gavilan (Juan Garcia), Jeff Dawson (Cooper) and Dutch Peterson (Ward Bond) make their way to a small Mexican town to find work, and run into a stranded American girl, Sal Donnelly (Ruth Roman), looking for a meal ticket back to the States. Dawson calls on an old friend, Paco Conway (Quinn), who has become a rich oil man and married Dawson's former girlfriend, Marina (Barbara Stanwyck). Dawson, however, declines Paco's offer of a job and instead hires himself and Dutch out to Jackson (Ian MacDonald) to deliver a load of nitroglycerin to an out-of-town rig. En route, they are attacked by El Gavilan's men but manage to complete their delivery, only to have Jackson renege on his deal. Dawson beats him up to get the money owed, but the police force him to return it to Jackson. Paco then persuades Dawson to accept his original job offer as his field supervisor.

Marina begins making advances toward Dawson, who rebuffs her, telling her he's in love with Sal, now a blackjack dealer in town. Angered, Marina contrives a story about an affair between Dawson and herself to make Paco jealous, but her husband has other worries besides her flirtations: El Gavilan has threatened to blow up Paco's wells unless he is paid $50,000. Determined finally to put a stop to Marina's amorous activities with Dawson, Paco has a violent quarrel with her, and she pushes him down one of his wells. Dawson believes the death to be accidental until Marina, again spurned, blurts out the truth. Horrified, Dawson nearly strangles her, but is interrupted by El Gavilan's marauding bandits. In the battle, Dawson kills El Gavilan and routs his men as a dynamite blast destroys Paco's wells and the unscrupulous Marina.

With Barbara Stanwyck

With Silvana Mangano

# Ulysses

Lux Films  /  1953

CAST: *Ulysses*, KIRK DOUGLAS; *Penelope/Circe*, SILVANA MANGANO; *Antinous*, ANTHONY QUINN; *Nausicca*, Rossana Podesta; *Euriclea*, Sylvie; *Eurylocus*, Daniel Ivernel; *Telemachus*, Franco Interlenghi; *Alcinous*, Jacques Dumesnil; *Cassandra*, Elena Zareschi; and Evi Maltagliati, Ludmilla Dudarova, Tania Weber, Piero Lulli, Ferruccio Stagni, Alessandro Ferson, Oscar Andriani, Umberto Silvestri, Gualtiero Tumiati, Teresa Pellati, Mario Feliciani, Michele Riccardini.

CREDITS: *Director*, Mario Camerini; *producers*, Dino De Laurentiis and Carlo Ponti; *associate producer*, William W. Schorr; *screenplay*, Franco Brusati, Mario Camerini, Ennio de Concini, Hugh Gray, Ben Hecht, Ivo Berilli and Irwin Shaw; based on Homer's *Odyssey; music director*, Franco Ferrara; *original score*, Alessandro Cicognini; *art director*, Flavio Mogherini; *camera*, Harold Rosson; *editor*, Leo Cattozzo. Technicolor. Running time: 104 minutes.

Released in the United States in 1955 by Paramount Pictures.

With Silvana Mangano

As Antinous

It is only by courtesy that Signores De Laurentiis and Ponti's weighty spectacular can be referred to in relationship to Homer's *Odyssey,* and Anthony Quinn's minuscule role in it marked a low-profile beginning to what has come to be known as the actor's Italian period. Quinn is Antinous, the most persistent of Penelope's suitors, hanging around the palace while Ulysses is off fighting the Trojans and taking an exceptionally long way home. In the title role, Kirk Douglas (with whom Quinn made two more films) gives a tour de force performance to the limits of the ludicrous script patched together by Ben Hecht, Irwin Shaw and five others, who translated to the screen various episodes of Ulysses' ten-year adventure.

In the royal palace at Ithaca, Penelope (Silvano Mangano) has vowed to remain loyal to her missing husband, the king, who has not yet returned from the Trojan Wars. A group of vicious noblemen, including Antinous (Quinn), have taken control and are trying to persuade her that Ulysses is dead and that she should choose one of them as her next husband. During this prolonged intrigue, Ulysses is found on the beach at the Isle of Phaeacia, following the sacking of Troy. Shipwrecked, his men gone, his memory lost, he is nursed back to health by the lovely princess Nausicca (Rossana Podesta), who immediately falls in love with him. Despite his physical well-being, however—he defeats the champion wrestler of Phaeacia in a public exhibition—he remains distant, trying to recall the past. He spends days on the beach peering out to sea, and slowly he has visions of the great storm that destroyed his ship; of slaying the one-eyed Polyphemus; of defying the call of the Sirens; of rebuffing Circe the Enchantress (also Mangano), who held him captive and turned his crew into swine.

As his mind clears, he identifies himself to Nausicca and regrets that he must return home. His hosts provide him with a ship and he sails for Ithaca, where, dressed as a beggar, he enters his palace and finds it full of suitors. Dropping his disguise, Ulysses slaughters the men and returns to his faithful wife.

As Alfio

# Cavalleria Rusticana

Excelsa Films / 1953

CAST: *Alfio,* ANTHONY QUINN; *Lola,* KERIMA; *Santuzza,* MAY BRITT; *Turiddu,* Ettore Manni; *Uncle Brasi,* Umberto Spadaro; *Aunt Camilla,* Grazia Spadaro; *Mamma Lucia,* Virginia Balistreri; and the voice of Tito Gobbi.

CREDITS: *Director,* Carmine Gallone; *producer,* Carlo Ponti; *screenplay,* Mario Monicelli, Basilio Franchina, Francesco De Feo, Art Cohn and Carmine Gallone; based on the *novel* by Giovanni Verga and the *opera* by Pietro Mascagni; *music conductor,* Oliviero De Fabritiis; *art director,* Gastone Medin; *camera,* Karl Struss and Riccardo Pallottini; *editor,* Rolando Benedetti. Ferraniacolor and 3-D. Running time: 80 minutes.

Anthony Quinn enacts the role of Alfio in the dramatic *(i.e.,* nonmusical), 3-D version of *Cavalleria Rusticana.* Although one brief aria is included in the film—sung by Tito Gobbi—and the score contains the Mascagni music, this was a wide-screen, color remake of Amleto Palermi's similarly nonmusical production of the mid-1940s (it premiered in the United States in December 1947), rather than updating the several filmings of the opera itself. Quinn has said that he sang in this version, but no hint of this, nor much of anything else, is on view in the emasculated, black-and-white print which first played in this country in 1963 under the title *Fatal Desire.*

Closely adhering to the Giovanni Verga novel, the story deals with love, deceit, adultery and revenge in a small Sicilian village. Alfio, the village carrier, has married Lola (Kerima), whose former sweetheart, Turiddu (Ettore Manni), has just returned from five years in the army. The greatly distressed Turiddu finds solace with Santuzza (May Britt) and gradually they seem to fall in love. But Turiddu is unable to forget Lola, who is already tiring of Alfio, and one night, while Alfio is working, Turiddu sneaks into Lola's house, unaware that he has been spotted by the jealous Santuzza. The following day, Easter Sunday, she blurts out to Alfio the truth about the trysts between Lola and Turiddu, and Alfio swears a vendetta, challenging Turiddu to a duel with Sicilian knives and killing his rival to avenge his wife's honor.

---

Released in a black and white version by Ultra Pictures in the United States in 1963 as *Fatal Desire.*

On the set

[ 142 ]

With Valentina Cortesa

# Donne Proibite
## (Forbidden Women)

Excelsio/Supra / 1953

CAST: *Lola Baldi,* LINDA DARNELL; *Vally,* VALENTINA CORTESA; *Franca,* LEA PADOVANI; *Rosita,* GIULIETTA MASINA; *Francesco Caserto,* ANTHONY QUINN; *Tamara,* Lilla Brignone; *Bruno,* Roberto Risso; *The Young Girl,* Maria Pia Casilio; *Vittorio,* Carlo Dapporto; and Alberto Farnese, Rossella Falk, Mino Doro, Lola Braccini, Alberto Talegalli, Checco Durante.

CREDITS: *Producer - director,* Giuseppe Amato; *screenplay,* Giuseppe Mangione, Cesare Zavattini, Gigliola Falluto, Giuseppe Amato and Bruno Paolinelli; based on the *novel* "New Life" by Bruno Paolinelli; *music,* Renzo Rossellini; *art director,* Virgilio Marchi; *camera,* Anchise Brizzi; *editor,* Gabriele Varriale. Running time: 90 minutes.

The only things, in the United States at least, that this feeble little Italian drama had going for it were its two American stars, Anthony Quinn and Linda Darnell, who had worked together in the 1940s in *Blood and Sand* and *Buffalo Bill* when she was an important 20th Century-Fox fixture. Anna Magnani was originally to have acted in this film, but without her, the entire pro-

duction was scaled down and, in the view of *The New York Times,* "patched together out of the files of a cheap romance magazine." As it was, it dealt with three dispossessed prostitutes evicted from a bordello, and received melodramatic treatment as a grim character study of each. Quinn is the sucker who wants to run off to Venezuela with one of them, Valentina Cortesa, who subsequently appeared in several films with Quinn. Another of the actresses appearing in *Donne Proibite* was Giulietta Masina, who became friendly with Quinn during the filming, introduced him to her husband, Federico Fellini, and got him the role of Zampano in *La Strada,* which was made almost simultaneously.

When their house is torn down to make way for a new project, the whores become involved in a series of personal events. Tamara (Lilla Brignone) is seriously injured in an accident and joins a convent; Franca (Lea Padovani) devotes herself to becoming acquainted with her small daughter; Lola (Linda Darnell) tries returning to her elderly mother, but faces the hostility of the townsfolk and reluctantly decides she can never go back; and Vally (Valentina Cortesa) is shattered when her past life is uncovered at the moment of her marriage to Francisco (Quinn). Heartbroken, she dashes from his house and is killed by a passing car. As *The New York Times'* Milton Esterow ungallantly put it, "All we see are three ladies put together more artistically than the script."

---

Released in the United States in 1956 as *Angels of Darkness.*

With Giulietta Masina

# La Strada

Ponti–DeLaurentiis / 1954*

CAST: *Zampano,* ANTHONY QUINN; *Gelsomina,* GIULIETTA MASINA;** *Matto (The Fool),* RICHARD BASEHART; *Colombiani,* Aldo Silvani; *La Vedova,* Marcella Rovere; *La Suorina,* Livia Venturini.

CREDITS: *Director,* Federico Fellini; *producers,* Carlo Ponti and Dino DeLaurentiis; *screenplay,* Federico Fellini and Tullio Pinelli; *music director,* Franco Ferrara; *original score,* Nino Rota; *art directors,* Mario Ravasco and E. Cervelli; *camera,* Otello Martelli; *editors,* Leo Cattozo and Lina Caterini. Running time: 115 minutes.

Then for Anthony Quinn came *La Strada,* together with overnight stardom after seventeen years in films and sixty-two motion pictures. In Zampano, the brutish, street-fair strongman, Quinn found at last a role worthy

---

*Released in the United States by Trans-Lux Films in 1956. Awards: Grand Prize, Venice Film Festival 1954; Academy Award, Best Foreign-Language Film 1956; New York Film Critics, Best Foreign Film 1956; David O. Selznick Golden Laurel, Edinburgh Film Festival, 1957.

**In the English-language version, Giulietta Masina's part was dubbed by Geraldine Brooks.

of his considerable skills and established an international audience which rapidly became cognizant of his seldom-appreciated acting abilities. Similarly, of course, director Federico Fellini, as the long-time scriptwriter for Roberto Rossellini, one of the pioneers in the neo-realism movement in the postwar Italian cinema, gained worldwide acclaim with his extraordinary film about every man's loneliness and search for the way of his life, as capsulized by three people: a simpleminded waif, her brute of a master, and a philosophical clown. As unadorned drama, *La Strada,* as written by Fellini and Tullio Pinelli, is seemingly formless, progressing like life itself along the winding road of the title, marked by sad and comic turns.

*La Strada's* well-deserved reputation preceded it to America in the nearly three years before its release, and Quinn, Giulietta Masina (Signora Fellini) and Richard Basehart shared the critics' lavish praise. *The New Yorker,* welcoming Quinn "home" in its review, felt "Anthony Quinn has acted for years in Hollywood without ever giving the performance he gives as the strong man under Fellini." "Superb" was the key word in the majority of critical appraisals of Quinn's portrayal of Zampano.

As the itinerant strongman who travels Italy's backroads on a motorcycle attached to a three-wheeled

As Zampano

cruelty, the loutish Zampano trains the girl as he would train a dog, and Gelsomina, anxious to please, learns to blow a trumpet and beat a drum, acting finally as Zampano's daytime slavey and, occasionally, his nighttime consolation. "Happy" in her new life, Gelsomina learns to forgive Zampano nearly everything—except his brutish indifference and his promiscuity.

The pair plays villages, fairs and country weddings, and, to Gelsomina, it is an idyllic existence, until they join a small circus on the outskirts of Rome. Goaded by a clown and high-wire artist known as Il Matto, The Fool (Richard Basehart), Zampano pulls a knife and is tossed into jail. Il Matto invites Gelsomina to join him on the road but then realizes she is devoted to Zampano. "Everyone serves a purpose," Il Matto tells her, "and perhaps you must serve him." He advises her to wait for the strongman to be released.

Later Zampano and Gelsomina come across Il Matto changing a tire by the roadside, and Zampano forces a fight with the clown, accidentally killing him. In a state of depression, Gelsomina mopes around and whimpers like a dog for days, and Zampano, in desperation, deserts her on a mountainside, showing enough concern, however, to leave behind the trumpet which has given her comfort.

Five years later Zampano learns of her death, and, overwhelmed by his loneliness, he returns to the sea and washes in a symbolic baptism, sobbing out his agony "like a dog," as the clown had once said, "a dog that wants to talk to you and only barks." Zampano has at last come to understand the meaning of Gelsomina's love and devotion, and the terror of his solitude he finds unbearable.

house, Zampano decides he needs an added attraction to punch up his act of breaking iron chains with his chest. In a small seaside village, he buys a feebleminded girl, Gelsomina (Giulietta Masina), from her impoverished mother and hits the road with his new acquisition. Treating Gelsomina as his chattel and with thoughtless

With Giulietta Masina

With Charles Coburn

# The Long Wait

Parklane Pictures–United Artists / 1954

CAST: *Johnny McBride,* ANTHONY QUINN; *Gardiner,* Charles Coburn; *Servo,* Gene Evans; *Venus,* Peggie Castle; *Wendy,* Mary Ellen Kay; *Carol,* Shawn Smith; *Troy,* Dolores Donlon; *Tucker,* Barry Kelley; *Lindsay,* James Millican; *Packman,* Bruno Ve Sota; *Bellboy,* Jay Adler; *Logan,* John Damler; *Pop Henderson,* Frank Marlowe.

CREDITS: *Director,* Victor Saville; *producer,* Lesser Samuels; *screenplay,* Alan Green and Lesser Samuels; based on the *novel* by Mickey Spillane; *music director,* Irving Gertz; *music score,* Mario Castelnuovo-Tedesco; song "Okay" by Harold Spina and Bob Russell; *art director,* Boris Leven; *camera,* Franz Planer; *editor,* Ronald Sinclair. Running time: 94 minutes.

In the screen version of Mickey Spillane's sadistic, sex-crammed novel about an amnesiac stumbling around trying to prove himself innocent of a robbery-murder, Quinn is the two-fisted, hard-as-nails hero spending ninety-or-so screen minutes pulverizing mobster Gene Evans with stunning regularity and finding solace with four-count 'em-four ladies. "This bore has a fine actor like Mr. Quinn hogtied and striving mightily," felt *The New York Times,* "and the climax, a mop-up in an empty warehouse, looks like a rehearsal for a cheap

television thriller." Quinn acted properly vicious as a Spillane hero out of the Mike Hammer detective school here in the role of Johnny McBride, dodging the bullets and bedding the dames, while menacing and being menaced by the shifty-eyed opposition. Acting in virtually every frame of this film, Quinn had his best opportunity to demonstrate the type of screen domination which was

With Frank Marlowe

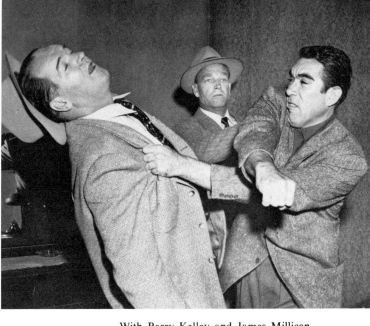

With Dolores Donlon

With Barry Kelley and James Millican

to make him one of the handful of larger-than-life figures of American cinema.

An amnesia victim of a truck accident, Johnny McBride (Quinn) returns to his home town after a two-year absence when he comes across a newspaper photo of himself. There he learns that he had been a teller in the bank owned by Gardiner (Charles Coburn) and a suspect in the robbery of $250,000. Circumstantial evidence also points to him as the murderer of the district attorney. Since the accident which wiped out his memory also burned off his fingerprints, the police have no proof leading to his arrest, but they warn him not to leave town. Checking old clippings, McBride learns that a "Vera West," a secretary at the bank, had disappeared

at the same time he had left town, and his efforts to locate her lead him to Servo (Gene Evans), the town's racket boss. Servo puts out a contract on McBride, who is slowly piecing things together with the aid of four girls, each with a mysterious background indicating she might be the missing "Vera." Keeping a few steps ahead of Servo's henchmen, McBride zeros in on the mystery and unmasks Gardiner himself ·as the mastermind behind the robbery and murder, working in league with Servo. He also discovers that the missing "Vera" is Wendy (Mary Ellen Kay), who had married him before his disappearance and had undergone plastic surgery to alter her appearance before getting close to Servo for information to prove McBride's innocence.

As Johnny McBride

As Attila the Hun

# Attila, Flagello di Dio
## (Attila)

Lux Films / Ponti–DeLaurentiis and
Lux Compagnie Cinematographique de France / 1954

CAST: *Attila the Hun,* ANTHONY QUINN; *Honoria,* SOPHIA LOREN; *Actius,* Henri Vidal; *Grune,* Irene Papas; *Bleda,* Ettore Manni; *Valentinian,* Claude Laydu; *Galla Placidia,* Colette Regis; *Onegesius,* Eduardo Ciannelli; *Ezio,* Christian Marquand; *Roman Consuls,* George Brehat, Guido Celano and Carlo Hinterman; *Hun Chieftans,* Mario Feliciani, Piero Pastore, Aldo Pini and Marco Guglielmi.

CREDITS: *Director,* Pietro Francisci; *producers,* Carlo Ponti and Dino De Laurentiis; *screenplay,* Ennio DeConcini, Primo Zeglio, Claude Andre Pugett, Frank Gervasi and Ivo Perilli; *music director,* Franco Ferrara; *original score,* Enzo Masetti; *art director,* Flavio Mo-

gnerini; *camera,* Aldo Tonti and Karl Struss; *editor,* Leo Catozzo. Technicolor. Running time: 83 minutes.

Anthony Quinn's flamboyant portrayal of the infamous fifth-century barbarian in this early, blood-and-guts Italian spectacular not only helped establish the actor's international reputation but also made him a pioneer (along with Kirk Douglas in *Ulysses*) in the movement bringing American actors to Europe to star in foreign productions, making them more marketable in the United States. About his interpretation of Attila, the majority critical opinion agreed with the *New York Herald Tribune's* Gene Gleason that Quinn plays "with simple, uncomplicated vigor" and with the *Variety* appraisal that "Quinn makes a strong and powerful Attila." Less kind were the words for Pietro Francisci's erratic direction, the talky script and the abominable dubbing of the actors' voices, not too surprising since

Released in the United States as *Attila* in 1958 by Embassy Pictures as A Joseph E. Levine Presentation.

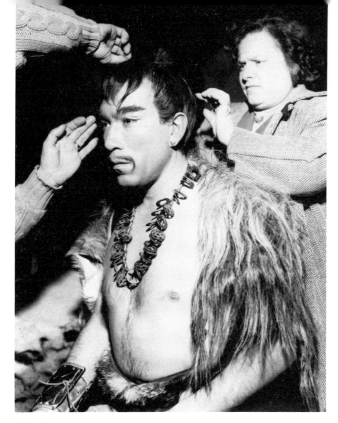

On the set

With Eduardo Ciannelli (third right)

the four "leads" were Mexican-American (Quinn), Italian (Sophia Loren), French (Henri Vidal) and Greek (Irene Papas). Much of the dialogue was suspected to have lost something in the translation, with Attila telling his hordes at one point, "Today Rome, tomorrow the world!" This original platitude virtually summed up the level of this garish, freewheeling view of the Dark Ages, at least in the version which Joseph E. Levine unleashed in the United States in 1958.

The huge, bloody epic purported to be the legend of the Asiatic barbarian who led his mounted hordes to the gates of Rome before he was turned back by Pope Leo I, with the infamous "Scourge of God" halted at last by the Cross. Sophia Loren is the ambitious Honoria, who gives herself in marriage to Attila hoping he'll stop his plans to take Rome by force; Henri Vidal is the Roman commander who negotiates a peace treaty which Attila ultimately ignores; Ettore Manni is Attila's brother, whom the tyrant kills for counseling peace; Claude Laydu is the hysterical, cruel, but weak-kneed Emperor Valentinian, Honoria's brother who grovels under the thumb of their mother Galla Placidia (Colette Regis). A "cast of thousands" of fur-clad extras and assorted spear carriers further peopled this Ponti-de-Laurentiis color spectacular.

As Attila the Hun

As Luis Santos

With Maureen O'Hara

# The Magnificent Matador

20th Century–Fox / 1955

CAST: *Karen Harrison,* MAUREEN O'HARA; *Luis Santos,* ANTHONY QUINN; *Rafael Reyes,* Manuel Rojas; *Don David,* Thomas Gomez; *Mark Russell,* Richard Denning; *Mona Wilton,* Lola Albright; *Jody Wilton,* William Brooks Ching; *Miguel,* Eduardo Noriega; *Sarita Sebastian,* Lorraine Chanel; *Emiliano,* Anthony Caruso; and Jesus Solarzano, Joaquin Rodriguez, Rafael Rodriguez, Antonio Velasquez, Jorge Aguilar, Felix Briones, Nacho Trevino.

CREDITS: *Director,* Budd Boetticher; *producer,* Edward L. Alperson; *associate producer,* Carroll Case; *screenplay,* Charles Lang; *story,* Budd Boetticher; *music director,* Raoul Kraushaar; *camera,* Lucien Ballard; *editor,* Richard Cahoon. CinemaScope and Pathé Color. Running time: 94 minutes.

In Quinn's third bullfight movie (and his fourth film with Maureen O'Hara and under Budd Boetticher), he stars as the graying hero and idol of all Mexico who panics on the day of his greatest fight and mysteriously leaves town with "the fear." The character of Luis Santos, shown brooding rather than fighting, is filled with illogic throughout the film, primarily since the motion picture code still forbade depictions of the bullring actions themselves. The picture, therefore, focused on colorful details of animal husbandry and fanciful melodramatics of the hero's concern, taken for cowardice, for the safety of his protégé who turns out to be his illegitimate son, and of the affair he has with a fiery American lady who takes a fancy to him and puts him up at her country estate. *The New York Times* concluded that "As near as you can make out from this picture, they kill the bulls by running them to death, and, for that matter, Miss O'Hara nigh kills Mr. Quinn the same way."

When he is selected to induct teen-ager Rafael Reyes (Manuel Rojas) as a full-fledged matador, top torero Luis Santos (Quinn) shows an unusual amount of concern, particularly when the youngster draws a vicious bull to fight. Just before the event, Santos interprets a religious sign as an indication that Rafael will be killed

As Luis Santos

With Lola Albright, Richard Denning, William Ching, Maureen O'Hara

in the ring, and he rushes from the arena to the disapproving roar of the crowd. Accepting an invitation from Karen Harrison (O'Hara) to stay at her palatial hacienda, Santos falls in love with the lovely American, while her jealous suitor, Mark Russell (Richard Denning), keeps needling the matador about his cowardice. Santos ultimately reveals to Karen that Rafael is his son, born out of wedlock to a young woman who had died in childbirth before Santos could marry her. Karen persuades him to tell the boy, and Santos is surprised to discover that Rafael had known the secret for some time, thanks to Santos's long-time friend, Don David (Thomas Gomez), in whom Santos has confided. Santos soon realizes the futility of trying to keep his son from following in his footsteps, and, in a triumphant return to the ring, he proudly announces their relationship to the spectators. Together they present a spectacular ring demonstration.

With Manuel Rojas, Maureen O'Hara and Thomas Gomez

With Farley Granger

With Anne Bancroft and Farley Granger

# The Naked Street

United Artists / 1955

CAST: *Nick Bradna*, FARLEY GRANGER; *Phil Regal*, ANTHONY QUINN; *Rosalie Regalzyk*, ANNE BANCROFT; *Joe McFarland*, Peter Graves; *Mrs. Regalzyk*, Else Neft; *Latzi Franks*, Jerry Paris; *Nutsy*, Frank Sully; *Big Eddie*, John Dennis; *Janet*, Angela Stevens; *Margie*, Joy Terry; *Mr. Hough*, G. Pat Collins; *Antonio Cardini*, Mario Siletti; *Attorney Blaker*, Whit Bissell; *Evelyn Shriner*, Jeanne Cooper; *Millie*, Sara Berner; *Attorney Flanders*, James Flavin; *Francie*, Jackie Loughery; *Judge Roder*, Harry Harvey; *Judge Stanley*, Alex Campbell; *Ollie*, Frank Krieg; *Shimmy*, Joe Turkel; *Barricks*, Harry Tyler; *Lennie*, Sammie Weiss.

CREDITS: *Director*, Maxwell Shane; *producer*, Edward Small; *screenplay*, Maxwell Shane and Leo Katcher; *story*, Leo Katcher; *music director*, Emil New-

man; *art director*, Ted Haworth; *camera*, Floyd Crosby; *editor*, Grant Whytock. Running time: 84 minutes.

Anthony Quinn reverted convincingly to his well-established but recently dormant gangster characterization here, with several nuances divorcing him from the stock hood, in this highly improbable crime melodrama distinguished solely by his performance and that of Anne Bancroft, playing his sister. This time Quinn portrays a powerful gangster who takes vengeance on the young punk who seduced his sister. Quinn's consummate skill as an actor enabled him, not so surprisingly, to elicit sympathy and even regret at his final-reel death. With the star and driving force gone, *Variety* felt, "the film does a workmanlike if not particularly inspired job of wrapping up its story and all loose ends in three minutes of footage."

Learning that his sister Rosalie (Anne Bancroft) is

Working titles: *The Brass Ring* and *The Mobster*.

With Angela Stevens

of his death, Bradna arranges a meeting with Regal and threatens to inform reporter Joe McFarland (Peter Graves), Rosalie's childhood sweetheart, of Regal's strong-arm methods. Regal scoffs at the threat that the reporter would write the story exposing him, but McFarland prints the exposé following Bradna's execution. McFarland continues the attacks in print despite beatings by Regal's thugs, and he finally induces one of the racketeer's henchmen to confess to the district attorney that his boss has framed Bradna. As the police close in on Regal, he tries to escape across tenement rooftops but loses his footing and falls to his death. McFarland and Rosalie, brought together through unhappy circumstances, plan to be married.

expecting a child by Nick Bradna (Farley Granger), a two-bit hood condemned to the electric chair for the murder of a shopkeeper, Phil Regal (Anthony Quinn), kingpin racketeer, resorts to bribery, intimidation of witnesses and slick legal tactics to spring Bradna. Regal then forces Bradna to marry Rosalie and warns him to stay out of trouble. Regal looks forward to becoming an uncle, but when the baby is born dead, he vents his rage on Bradna. Angered, Bradna returns to his life of crime and begins cheating on Rosalie. When Regal learns of Bradna's behavior, he decides to frame the hoodlum for murder, and, though innocent, Bradna is once again sentenced to the electric chair. On the eve

With James Flavin

With Peter Graves and Anne Bancroft

With Michael Rennie

# Seven Cities of Gold

20th Century–Fox / 1955

CAST:    *Jose Mendoza*, RICHARD EGAN; *Captain Gaspar de Portola*, ANTHONY QUINN; *Father Junipero Serra*, MICHAEL RENNIE; *Matuwir*, JEFFREY HUNTER; *Ula*, RITA MORENO; *Sergeant*, Eduardo Noriega; *Galvez*, Leslie Bradley; *Juan Coronel*, John Doucette; *Lt. Faces*, Victor Juncos; *Pilot Vila*, Julio Villareal; *Schrichak*, Miguel Inclan; *Dr. Pratt*, Carlos Muzquiz; *Father Vizcaino*, Pedro Galvan; *Captain Rivero*, Angelo de Stiffney; *Blacksmith*, Fernando Wagner; *Pilot Perez*, Ricardo Adalid Black; *Miscomi*, Guillermo Calles; *Indian Boy*, Jaime Gonzalez Quinones; *Father*, Jack Mower; *Mother*, Kathleen Crowley.

CREDITS:    *Producer-director*, Robert D. Webb; *co-producer*, Barbara McLean; *screenplay*, Richard L. Breen and John C. Higgins; based on the *novel* by Isabelle Gibson Ziegler; *music director*, Lionel Newman; *music score*, Hugo Friedhofer; *art directors*, Lyle R. Wheeler and Jack Martin Smith; *special effects*, Ray Kellogg; *camera*, Lucien Ballard; *editor*, High S. Fowler. CinemaScope and DeLuxe Color. Running time: 103 minutes.

Quinn's straightforward performance as the hardened Spanish military explorer settling California in about 1769 provides what spare histrionic excitement there is to this reverent 20th Century-Fox recollection of one of the less celebrated ventures in American history. As the cynical captain seeking new territory for the king, with no particular interest in the salvation of souls, Quinn is properly rugged and tough—and of Latin extraction, which is more than can be said of the film's other "stars." *Time* magazine's critic noted the movie's color, scope and pat excitement as outdoor drama, and then considered: "Best of all is Anthony Quinn, who wears the conquering swagger of Castile like one to that overbearing manner born." The Quinn character of Captain Gaspar de Portola marched out of sight with his troops for several long stretches during the 103 minutes of the proceedings, during which time his lieutenant, Richard Egan, made a boor and a bore of himself, while padre Michael Rennie offered up prayers and tried to convert such savages as Jeffrey Hunter and Rita Moreno. Director Robert D. Webb might well have had his cameraman, Lucien Ballard, follow Quinn and company into

With Michael Rennie

the hostile wilderness in search of the Seven Cities of Cibola, the fabled, but unlocated, site where streets were paved with gold.

In this account of the Spanish expedition's pushing into the region north and west of Old Mexico, its commander, Gaspar de Portola (Quinn), is obliged to take with him Father Junipero Serra (Michael Rennie), the crippled Catholic priest who hopes to establish a string of missions in the new territory. Following many difficulties in the hostile land, the expedition reaches the present site of San Diego, where Portola sets up a garrison, leaving it in the care of lieutenant Jose Mendoza (Richard Egan), before continuing northward in search of the Seven Cities of Cibola. Hostile Indians under the leadership of Matuwir (Jeffrey Hunter) harass the San Diego party, but when Matuwir is wounded and saved by Father Serra, the Indians become friendly. While the padre tries valiantly to convert the savages, Mendoza's roving eye falls meltingly on Ula (Rita Moreno), Matuwir's lovely sister, and the officer seduces the girl.

When Portola returns from his unfulfilled mission and learns of a shortage supply at the garrison, he decides to take the expedition back to Mexico City. Father Serra pleads for just nine more days—the novena—when, he prays, the Spanish supply ships will arrive, and Portola reluctantly agrees. Ula obtains permission from her brother to leave with Mendoza, who unfeelingly rebuffs her marriage proposal. Ashamed, she leaps from a cliff to her death, and Matuwir, furious, demands that Mendoza be turned over to the tribe for punishment. When Father Serra and Portola refuse, the Indians declare war. Realizing that his pride might well kill off the

entire expedition, Mendoza finally surrenders himself to the Indians in order to lift the siege of San Diego, and the war drums stop beating when Matuwir has his revenge.

When the supply ship fails to arrive by the morning of the ninth day, Portola orders the garrison abandoned and the expedition home, but changes his decision when the ship *San Antonio* sails into the bay, making possible the permanent establishment of San Diego.

With Richard Egan

With Kirk Douglas

# Lust for Life

Metro–Goldwyn–Mayer / 1956

CAST: *Vincent Van Gogh*, KIRK DOUGLAS; *Paul Gauguin*, ANTHONY QUINN; *Theo Van Gogh*, James Donald; *Christine*, Pamela Brown; *Dr. Gachet*, Everett Sloane; *Roulin*, Niall MacGinnis; *Anton Mauve*, Noel Purcell; *Theodorus Van Gogh*, Henry Daniell; *Anna Cornelia Van Gogh*, Madge Kennedy; *Willemien*, Jill Bennett; *Dr. Peyron*, Lionel Jeffries; *Dr. Bosman*, Laurence Naismith; *Colbert*, Eric Pohlmann; *Kay*, Jeanette Sterke; *Johanna*, Toni Gerry; *Rev. Stricker*, Wilton Graff; *Mrs. Stricker*, Isobel Elsom; *Rev. Peeters*, David Horne; *Commissioner Van Den Berghe*, Noel Howlett; *Commissioner De Smet*, Ronald Adam; *Ducrucq*, John Ruddock; *Rachel*, Julie Robinson; *Camille Pissarro*, David Leonard; *Emile Bernard*, William Phipps; *Seurat*, David Bond; *Père Tanguy*, Frank Perls; *Waiter*, Jay Adler; *Adeline Ravoux*, Laurence Badie; *Durand-Ruel*, Rex Evans; *Sister Clothilde*, Marion Ross; *Elizabeth*, Mitzi Blake; *Cor*, Anthony Sydes; *Tersteeg*, Antony Eustrel; *Jet*, Ernestine Barrier; *Lautrec*, Jerry Bergen; *Mme. Tanguy*, Belle Mitchell; *Dr. Rey*, Alec Mango; *Cordan*, Fred Johnson; *Pier*, Norman MacGowan; *Jan*, Mickey Maga.

CREDITS: *Director*, Vincente Minnelli; *producer*, John Houseman; *associate producer*, Jud Kinberg; *screenplay*, Norman Corwin; based on the *novel* by Irving Stone; *music director*, Miklos Rozsa; *art directors*, Cedric Gibbons, Hans Peters and Preston Ames; *camera*, F. A. Young and Russell Harlan; *editor*, Adrienne Fazan. CinemaScope and Metrocolor. Running time: 122 minutes.

"The great Vincent would not have learned anything about himself from watching this movie," thought *Commonweal*, "but he would have been awfully pleased at its lush concentration on his world of art." Vincente Minnelli's beautifully mounted production of the biography of Vincent Van Gogh, adapted by Norman Corwin from Irving Stone's 1934 best-seller, strikingly captured the artist's fierce drive as well as the bitter tragedy of the tortured man who completed 800 paintings in his thirty-seven years and sold only two, living instead on handouts from his brother Theo.

For his surprisingly brief but highly visible appearance as the swaggering, contentious Paul Gauguin, Anthony Quinn received the lion's share of the critical acclaim as well as his second Academy Award as Best Supporting Actor. (Kirk Douglas won the New York Film Critics Award as Best Actor for his interpretation of Van Gogh, while losing the Oscar to Yul Brynner.) *Time* called Quinn's Gauguin "splendid," although it felt that "because the Hollywood story builds relentlessly to Van Gogh's ear slicing for its climax, *Lust for Life* falls midway between being a first-rate art film and high-pitched melodrama." Quinn's resemblance to Gauguin, many critics have pointed out, was as uncanny as Kirk Douglas's to Van Gogh, and the film presented him (Gauguin) as deliberate, pipe smoking and unemotional vis-à-vis the nervous, irrational Van Gogh. Quinn, as Gauguin, is given to comment: "If there's one thing I despise, that's emotion in painting," and then he proceeds to tidy up the excitable Van Gogh's palette. And when the friendship between the two artists begins to dissolve, the unemotional Gauguin stares down the frenzied Van Gogh when the latter attempts to attack him with a razor in an alleyway.

The film biography of Van Gogh recounts his tortuous career from his experiences as an evangelist in Le Borinage, a bleak mining district of Belgium, through the turmoil of his love affair with a prostitute (Pamela Brown), who becomes his housekeeper and model, the uncertainty of his life in Paris where he receives encouragement from Theo (James Donald) and is introduced to the great impressionists of the day, and the explosiveness of his residence in Arles with Paul Gauguin where he becomes enormously productive, and finally to his increasing states of agonized depression and ultimate suicide.

As Paul Gauguin

Location filming in Le Borinage, Nuenen, The Hague and Provence was done in the summer of 1955. Quinn's few scenes, in the second of the three films he did with Kirk Douglas, provided him with a brief respite between action roles in *Seven Cities of Gold* and *Man from Del Rio,* both of which offered more footage of Quinn, if not the range of characterization in *Lust for Life.*

With Katy Jurado

# Man from Del Rio

United Artists / 1956

CAST: *Dave Robles,* ANTHONY QUINN; *Estella,* Katy Jurado; *Ed Bannister,* Peter Whitney; *Doc Adams,* Douglas Fowley; *Bill Dawson,* John Larch; *Breezy Morgan,* Whit Bissell; *Jack Tillman,* Douglas Spencer; *Fred Jasper,* Guinn (Big Boy) Williams; *George Dawson,* Marc Hamilton; *Mrs. Tillman,* Adrienne Marden; *Dan Ritchy,* Barry Atwater; *The Kid,* Carl Thayler; *Roy Higgens,* William Erwin; *Tom Jordan,* Otto Waldis; *Mr. Brown,* Paul Harber; *Boy,* Jack Hogan; *Stableman,* Frank Richards; *Woman,* Katherine DeMille.

CREDITS: *Director,* Harry Horner; *producer,* Robert L. Jacks; *associate producer,* Richard Carruth; *screenplay,* Richard Carr; *music,* Frederick Steiner; *art*

Filmed as *The Lonely Gun* on Gene Autry's San Fernando Valley Ranch.

*director,* William Glasgow; *camera,* Stanley Cortez; *editor,* Robert Golden. Running time: 82 minutes.

Quinn is especially fond of his role in this offbeat, trim little Western in which he turned in a top acting job in the character study of a rugged gunman who faces prejudice in a Texas border town when the people decide they want him for sheriff—only for his fast gun. Despite *Times*'s backhanded compliment: "It's a tribute to Quinn's inventiveness that by scratching, bumbling, slobbering and gazing dumbly out of his unshaven face, he manages to make a conventional pasteboard character seem like a real human slob," his performance as Dave Robles, the friendless, uneducated Mexican gunfighter, conveyed an inner spirit and depth of characterization hardly ever found in the "B" Western, which *Man from Del Rio* certainly was.

With Peter Whitney

As Dave Robles

With Peter Whitney and Guinn "Big Boy" Williams (right)

Dave Robles (Quinn), a gunman tormented into killing several gunslingers years before the story begins, comes to the small town of Mesa, where he is immediately challenged by Jasper (Guinn Williams), one of the remaining members of the gang Robles had been forced to wipe out. Impressed by the way Robles had outdrawn Jasper, Ed Bannister (Peter Whitney), an ex-gunman himself, who now operates the town's saloon while plotting to gain control of Mesa, befriends Robles and keeps him in liquor. When several gunmen get into a drinking brawl and begin harassing the town's timid sheriff (Douglas Spencer) before grabbing Estella (Katy Jurado), assistant to the town's doctor (Douglas Fowley), Robles alone comes to the rescue, facing down the marauders. The town's leaders press the job of sheriff on Robles, who proudly accepts, feeling that he at last has been given a degree of dignity.

He decks himself out in the proper clothes befitting his office and turns up at a church social, where he is rebuffed by the townspeople because he is not only inferior, but Mexican. When even Estella shuns him,

Robles goes to Bannister's saloon to get drunk and is goaded into a fistfight with the owner. Staggering back to the jail after whipping Bannister, Robles passes out, awakening the next morning to find Doc Adams bandaging his hand. Estella tells Robles that he has broken his wrist and that his gunfighting days are over. Ignoring Estella's pleas to leave town, even if she promises to accompany him, and trying to keep his injury a secret, Robles goes about his duties. Bannister, however, learns of Robles's broken wrist from the town drunk (Whit Bissell) and decides that the time is right to make his move to take over the town. Bannister orders Robles out of town, but the sheriff, determined to make Estella proud of him, refuses and accepts Bannister's challenge to a gunfight. As the two face each other on the main street of Mesa, Robles begins advancing and inches his broken hand, from which he has removed the bandage, toward his holster. Bannister hesitates and is frightened into believing that the drunk had lied about Robles's injury. Bluffing the saloonkeeper into refusing to draw, Robles shows him to be a coward and sends him packing.

With Peter Whitney and Douglas Spencer

As Big Tom Kupfen

# The Wild Party

Security Pictures–United Artists / 1956

CAST: *Big Tom Kupfen,* ANTHONY QUINN; *Erica London,* Carol Ohmart; *Lt. Arthur Mitchell,* Arthur Franz; *Gage Freeposter,* Jay Robinson; *Honey,* Kathryn Grant; *Kicks Johnson,* Nehemiah Persoff; *Ben Davis,* Paul Stewart; *Sandy,* Barbara Nichols; *Singer,* Jana Mason; *Wino,* William Phipps; *Ellen,* Maureen Stephenson; *Branson,* Nestor Paiva; *Bouncer,* Michael Ross; *Customer,* Carl Milletaire; *Bartender,* James Bronte; *Fat Man,* Joe Greene; *Combo,* The Buddy DeFránco Quartet.

CREDITS: *Director,* Harry Horner; *producer,* Sidney Harmon; *screenplay,* John McPartland; *music,* Buddy Bregman; *art director,* Rudi Feld; *camera,* Sam Leavitt; *editor,* Richard C. Meyer. Running time: 91 minutes.

In this weird, sordid, totally unpleasant little melodrama about a sadistic foursome, Anthony Quinn is the leader—a human dreg who had once been a football hero before degenerating into an animalistic psychopath hanging out

Working title: *Step Down to Terror*

in dark jive cellars. *The Wild Party* is considered one of the pioneer beatnik movies, dealing in this case with robbery, rape, sadism, dope addiction, hard-boiled sex and other endearments, prompting *The New York Times* to conclude that the film is "stuffed with more tasteless sociological dressing than a Christmas goose." (It surprisingly opened in New York during Christmas week!) To a driving, infectious jazz beat, supplied by Buddy Bregman and by The Buddy DeFranco Quartet, Quinn and his hopped-up hangers-on (foppish, knife-wielding Jay Robinson, piano-playing Nehemiah Persoff and groupie Kathryn [Mrs. Bing Crosby!] Grant) turns this crude thriller into a harrowing night of terror as they kidnap and manhandle a young couple.

In its review of the film, calling it "a bloody study of jivenile (sic) delinquency" and noting that "Quinn has nothing to do but knock the hero down and push the heroine over," *Time* magazine made this incisive observation of the actor's career: "Anthony Quinn in twenty years before the camera has seldom been permitted by his employers to create anything more significant than a three days' growth of beard." In *The Wild Party,* that three days' growth is on display.

With Kathryn Grant

In need of money to feed their habits, Big Tom Kupfen (Quinn) and his pals go on the prowl for victims. In a small club, Tom spots a young couple, Erica London (Carol Ohmart) and her fiancé Arthur Mitchell (Arthur Franz), and makes a play for the girl, noting her class and breeding. She in turn is at first drawn by his animal magnetism but is finally repelled by his aggressiveness and uncontrolled passion. With his friends, Gage (Jay Robinson), Honey (Kathryn Grant) and Kicks (Nehemiah Persoff), Tom induces the couple to accept a lift in their car, and then proceeds to abduct them, planning to ransom the two to nightclub operator Ben Davis (Paul Stewart). Unable to extort the ransom from Davis, Tom decides to force Erica to marry him and make her wealthy family pay for her freedom. Sending Honey and Kicks to dispatch a wire to Erica's parents telling of the elopement, Tom gets into a hassle with Gage and dumps him down an air shaft in the abandoned beach amusement house where they are in hiding. Kicks, meanwhile, convinces Honey of Tom's viciousness, but she talks him into driving back to warn Tom and let him escape. When Tom, infuriated by the pair's suggestion, starts to strangle Kicks, Honey runs Tom down with her car and races off with Kicks as the police arrive to free the kidnaped couple.

With Kathryn Grant

With Debra Paget

# The River's Edge

20th Century–Fox / 1957

CAST: *Nardo Denning,* RAY MILLAND; *Ben Cameron,* ANTHONY QUINN; *Meg Cameron,* DEBRA PAGET; *Chet,* Harry Carey, Jr.; *Pop Whiskers,* Chubby Johnson; *Barry,* Byron K. Foulger; *Harry Castleton,* Frank Gerstle; *Customs Officer,* Tom McKee.

CREDITS: *Director,* Allan Dwan; *producer,* Benedict Bogeaus; *screenplay,* Harold Jacob Smith and James Leicester; based on the *story* "The Highest Mountain" by Harold Jacob Smith; *music director,* Louis Forbes; *title song,* James Leicester and Bobby Troup; *art director,* Van Nest Polglase; *camera,* Harold Lipstein; *editor,* James Leicester. CinemaScope and DeLuxe Color. Running time: 87 minutes.

As Ben Cameron, small-time rancher and expert outdoorsman, Anthony Quinn turns in another vivid portrait, returning as so often forced to do, more than what the scenarists had given him to work with. Compassionate, honest, occasionally thoughtless—and the good guy vis-à-vis Ray Milland's unusual casting as the heavy.

With Debra Paget and Ray Milland

In this, the last important film directed by veteran Allan Dwan (who made three minor pictures after it, bringing his career total to more than 400), Quinn is an upstanding rancher forced to guide a fugitive bank robber through the mountains to freedom in Mexico. The twist: the rancher's wife is the fugitive's old girlfriend. Most of the action centers on these three, although neither

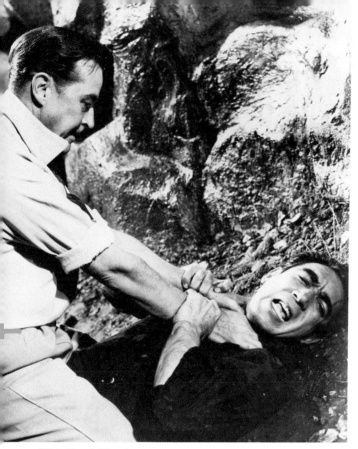

With Ray Milland

mountain passes in search of a guide, Ben Cameron (Quinn), who had married Denning's girlfriend, Meg (Debra Paget). Denning wants to get Meg back and use Cameron to get him across the border with the million dollars he (Denning) has stolen. He arrives at Cameron's ranch as Meg is packing to leave after a violent argument, and he offers to give her a lift into town. On the way, they are stopped by a border patrolman who wants to inspect the car. Denning guns his engine and runs down the officer, while Meg, terrified, tries to run away, with Denning in pursuit. Cameron is in the sheriff's office when the patrolman is brought in, telling what happened just before he dies. Cameron races back to his ranch where he finds Denning and Meg, and is forced to guide them across the border. During their trek into the mountains, Denning accidentally drops his suitcase while scaling a treacherous rockface. The money scatters as an old prospector (Chubby Johnson) happens onto the scene. Denning, forced to kill him, presses home to Cameron and Meg how perilous their own position is.

To save Cameron, Meg convinces Denning they can make it the rest of the way alone, and the two slip off. Cameron follows, however, and with the aid of a rifle he has obtained from a nearby Indian village, gets the drop on Denning. When he tries to convince Denning, though, to use some of the money to start a fire in a cave where they have sought refuge, there is a struggle, interrupted by a rattlesnake, which Meg kills. In another struggle the following day, Cameron injures his leg and Denning sets out by himself. On the dark mountain road, Denning is knocked over a cliff by a crazily careening truck with no lights. Cameron and Meg come across Denning's body as they prepare to take a raft across the river on their way home. In the background, a joyous group of young campers celebrate the discovery of hundreds of soggy bills which they have located in a backwash of the river.

they nor their motivations are credible. *The New York Times'* Howard Thompson turned thumbs-down on the film but found much to praise in Quinn's performance, admitting: "Anthony Quinn is good in anything. No wonder the guy owns two Oscars. At any rate, the bare hands of Mr. Quinn literally hold together this threadbare, unconvincing little melodrama, [although] even Mr. Quinn's talent can't overcome the abrupt foolhardiness of his farmer characterization." In any case, Quinn and Milland make some tough team—even when opposing one another.

Nardo Denning (Milland), a professional killer, con man and bank robber, is driving over treacherous

With Debra Paget

With Lita Milan

# The Ride Back

The Associates and
Aldrich Company–United Artists / 1957

CAST:   *Bob Kallen,* ANTHONY QUINN; *Hamish,*
William Conrad; *Elena,* Lita Milan; *Border Guard,*
George Trevino; *Padre,* Victor Millan; *Child,* Ellen
Hope Monroe; *Luis,* Joe Dominguez; *Boy,* Louis Towers.

CREDITS:   *Director,* Allen H. Miner; *producer,*
William Conrad; *associate producer,* Walter Blake;
*screenplay,* Anthony Ellis; *music,* Frank DeVol; *title song*
sung by Eddie Albert; *art director,* William Glasgow;
*camera,* Joseph Biroc; *editor,* Michael Luciano. Running time: 79 minutes.

Anthony Quinn's performance as the laconic, crafty,
rugged gunman, Bob Kallen, is only one of the distin-
guishing elements about this leathery, psychological
Western which passed virtually unnoticed. Quinn's co-
star, William Conrad, who brings grim authority to his
role as the pursuing lawman, made his debut as a producer on the film; the director, Allen H. Miner, had as
his only previous credit the brilliant documentary, *The
Naked Sea;* the executive producer was Robert Aldrich.

*The Ride Back* delves into the characters of two men
alone in the desert—on the surface, tough and intrac-
table, each acting the role expected of him; underneath,
the tempering qualities, compassion in the fugitive, fear
in the lawman, mutual respect in both as the necessity
for survival engenders a begrudging friendship.

The ride back is a four-day trip across the Mexican
border into Texas for Hamish (William Conrad), a
lonely law officer, and Bob Kallen (Quinn), a fugitive
wanted for murder. Hamish finds Kallen cool and in-
solent, but, despite the insistence of Elena (Lita Milan),
his sweetheart, Kallen chooses to accompany Hamish
back to the States. The trek through rough Apache country becomes a test of wills and authority, with Kallen
constantly challenging Hamish, creating glimmers of uncertainty in the bulldog lawman. When they come upon
the sight of an Indian massacre, they find a single survivor, a small girl, whom they are forced to take with
them. In a second attack, the Indians seriously wound
Hamish just when Kallen had figured that his girlfriend
would be arriving with help to free him from his captor.

With Lita Milan on the set

As Bob Kallen

Kallen seizes the opportunity and abandons Hamish and the child in the desert. During his flight back to Mexico, Kallen begins to feel compassion for the first time and returns to the wounded Hamish and the little girl, helping them find their way back to civilization, while himself voluntarily agreeing to face trial for murder.

Critic Bosley Crowther praised both performers and felt that Conrad acquitted himself with "grand authority, even though the fugitive is played by Anthony Quinn, a highly respectable villain whom very few actors would dare take on." Crowther also considered that "Mr. Conrad has plenty of problems which he handles manfully, even the problem of matching the angular acting of Mr. Quinn."

A curious aspect of *The Ride Back* is its striking plot similarity to a television movie Quinn had starred in several years earlier, *The Long Trail*. In the latter, Quinn is a Texas Ranger who is assigned the task of extraditing a murderer from the new state of Oregon but faces violent opposition from the townsfolk when they learn of his assignment. A later Quinn film, *Last Train from Gun Hill,* also explored similar ground, with staunch sheriff Kirk Douglas determined to take friend Quinn's son back to face a murder charge.

With William Conrad

[ 165 ]

With Gina Lollobrigida

# The Hunchback of Notre Dame

Allied Artists / 1957

CAST: *Esmeralda,* GINA LOLLOBRIGIDA; *Quasimodo,* ANTHONY QUINN; *Captain Phoebus,* Jean Danet; *Claude Frollo,* Alain Cuny; *Clopin Trouillefou,* Philippe Clay; *Fleur de Lys,* Danielle Dumont; *Gringoire,* Robert Hirsch; *Louis XI,* Jean Tissier; *Aloyse de Gondelaurier,* Valentine Tessier; *Charmolue,* Jacques Hilling; *Guillaume Rousseau,* Jacques Dufilho; *Mathias Hungadi,* Roger Blin; *La Falourdel,* Marianne Oswald; *The Dwarf,* Pieral; *The President,* Camille Guerini; *Beggar Woman,* Damia; *Coppenole,* Robert Lombard; *Jupiter,* Albert Remy; *Haraucourt,* Hubert de Lapparent; *The Cardinal,* Boris Vian; *Maître Lecornu,* Paul Bonifas; *Madame Lecornu,* Madeleine Barbulee;

*Night Watchman,* Albert Michel; *Andry Le Rouse,* Daniel Emilfork; *Hoodlum,* Georges Douking.

CREDITS: *Director,* Jean Delannoy; *producers,* Robert and Raymond Hakim; *screenplay,* Jacques Prevert and Jean Aurenche; based on the *novel* by Victor Hugo; *music,* Georges Auric; *songs,* Georges Auric, Francisco Lavagnino and Paul Lafargs; *choreography,* Leonide Massine; *art director,* René Renoux; *camera,* Michel Kelber; *editor,* Henri Taverna. CinemaScope and Technicolor. Running time: 110 minutes.

Quinn's distinctive interpretation of Quasimodo in the sumptuous, wide-screen, full-color version of the Victor Hugo classic about the grotesque bellringer of fifteenth-century Paris allowed him the range to further demonstrate his acting skills as the nonromantic hero, and, as usual, he gave a tour de force exhibition, full of vitality as well as pity. Director Jean Delannoy staged

Shot in April 1956 by Paris Film Productions as *Notre Dame de Paris.* Filmed as *Darling of Paris* in 1917 and as *The Hunchback of Notre Dame* in 1923 with Lon Chaney and in 1939 with Charles Laughton.

As Quasimodo

this third sound adaptation of the famous story more for pageantry than for any significant meaning, and allowed Quinn free rein for the creation of Quasimodo while holding tight on the rest of the international cast. Thus despite the spectacular appearance of Gina Lollobrigida, top-billed as Esmeralda, the gypsy girl, it is Quinn in full monster regalia—misshapen back, broken nose, rheumy eye, cripple's shuffle, apelike visage—who remains in the memory, not many lengths behind Lon Chaney and Charles Laughton (despite those who begrudge Quinn his due and refuse to speak his name in the same breath as the actors who preceded him in the role.)

During the production stages, producers Robert and Raymond Hakim tried mightily but unsuccessfully to obtain from RKO the rights to the title by which the Hugo story is always called. Since RKO, however, refused to relinquish its copyright, the Hakims called their

With Gina Lollobrigida

[ 167 ]

version *The Hunchback of Paris* (and *Notre Dame de Paris* in France) until RKO suddenly reversed its original decision, releasing its grip on the title *The Hunchback of Notre Dame.*

The intertwined stories of Esmeralda and Quasimodo are muddled under Delannoy's static direction, reduced to a series of mass scenes and slow-moving vignettes. The scenarists here have focused on the events leading to Esmeralda's trial for witchcraft and the stabbing of her noble lover, Phoebus (Jean Danet). When the obsessed alchemist-priest, Claude Frollo (Alain Cuny), has her sentenced to death, Quasimodo saves her from the hangman and hides her in his belltower, where he becomes her devoted slave. Much of the rich atmosphere so vividly described in the Hugo tale—the happy Festival of the Fools, the conclave of thieves and beggars in the Court of Miracles, the storming of Notre Dame by the angered Parisians—provide the spectacle filmed at the expense of plot in this French-made recapitulation of the classic. Among the casualties are such integral figures as King Louis XI (Jean Tissier) and the poet Gringoire (Robert Hirsch), both of whom seem only to have been dragged into the proceedings and left stranded.

Critical acclaim for the film itself notwithstanding, Quinn himself received nice notices and entered into stardom of the first magnitude on an international level.

*The Hunchback of Notre Dame,* filmed in the spring of 1956, received saturation booking in the New York area, where it opened on the same day as another Quinn movie, *Wild Is the Wind.*

As Quasimodo

As Quasimodo

With Anna Magnani

# Wild Is the Wind

Paramount / 1957

CAST: *Gioia*, ANNA MAGNANI; *Gino*, AN-THONY QUINN; *Bene*, ANTHONY FRANCIOSA; *Angie*, Dolores Hart; *Alberto*, Joseph Calleia; *Teresa*, Lili Valenty; *Wool Buyer*, James Flavin; *Priest*, Dick Ryan; *Party Guests*, Joseph Vitale, Iphigenie Castiglioni, Ruth Lee and Frances Morris.

---

Shot in Nevada as *Obsession*. Previously filmed in Italy (1947) by Geoffredo Alessandrini with Isa Pola, Rossano Brazzi and Umberto Spadaro. Anna Magnani and Anthony Quinn received Academy Award nominations for their performances. Oscar nominations also went to Dimitri Tiomkin and Ned Washington for their title song.

CREDITS: *Director*, George Cukor; *producer*, Hal B. Wallis; *associate producer*, Paul Nathan; *screenplay*, Arnold Shulman; based on the *novel* "Furia" by Vittorio Nino Novarese; *music*, Dimitri Tiomkin; *title song*, Dimitri Tiomkin and Ned Washington; *songs*, Fernando Albano and Pacifico Vento; *art directors*, Hal Pereira and Tambi Larsen; *camera*, Charles B. Lang Jr.; *editor*, Warren Low. VistaVision. Running time: 114 minutes.

For his full-bodied, robust performance as the Italian-American rancher in George Cukor's *Wild Is the Wind*, Anthony Quinn received his first Academy Award nomination as Best Actor. His rich portrayal of a proud man, both sensitive and earthy, who brings his sister-in-law over from Italy to replace his dead wife, marked the start of his new, introverted, deeply subjective approach to his characterizations. In his role, not unlike that of the crippled grape grower in *They Knew What They Wanted*, Quinn is alternately comical and churlish, cheerful and ugly, insensitive to the feelings of his new wife and enraged when he catches her in the sheep pen with the hired hand after he himself had ignored her desires. Totally confused and constantly asking her

With Anthony Franciosa

"Whassa matter? What'd I do?" and berating her with "Why don't you be like Rosanna?" Quinn matches Anna Magnani, playing the immigrant wife (and also winning an Oscar nomination), in boisterousness, rage, rowdiness and pathos. As in the previous Italian-made version of the film, entitled *Furia*, Cukor's production is loaded with symbolism—snorting animals, galloping stallions, birthing ewes. It is to the credit of the two volatile stars that something more than seething melodrama emerged from the screen.

On the day he is to leave for Italy to take a new wife, Gino (Quinn) stops at the grave of Rosanna, the wife who had died. He turns to his daughter Angie (Dolores Hart), to be reassured that he is doing the right thing marrying Rosanna's sister, Gioia (Anna Magnani), and tells Angie that when he gives gifts to Gioia it will be like giving them to Rosanna. Saying farewell to his brother Alberto (Joseph Calleia), his sister-in-law Teresa (Lili Valenty), and Angie, Gino drives to the airport with Bene (Anthony Franciosa), his hired hand. Several weeks later, Bene greets Gino and his new wife as their plane lands, and on the way home, Gino explains to Gioia that Bene is like his son—a Basque, and a true sheepherder. Gioia meets her new family, who neglect to feed her while trying to compare her to Rosanna. Hurt, she goes outside where Angie finds her and welcomes her properly.

Over the months, as Gioia is learning English under Bene's tutelage, Gino takes her to watch as Bene teaches his dogs to herd. On the range, one day, Gioia spots a herd of horses eating the sheep's grass, but protests when Gino wants to shoot the horses. She notices a black beauty and asks Gino to get it for her. He and Bene

With Anna Magnani

rope the animal from the back of Alberto's truck. Later, while Gino is tending to the ranch, Gioia tries to break the black horse but has to be rescued by Bene, who steals a kiss. Teresa spots Gioia running from the barn, followed closely by Bene.

On Gioia's birthday, Gino throws a party and surprises her with the horse, which he has broken. The disappointed Gioia, noting how the friskiness in the animal has disappeared, says that the horse is now nothing more than a sheep. Not hearing her, Gino proposes a toast—but calls her Rosanna. Gioia locks her husband out of their room and tells him to sleep in the grave with Rosanna. Angrily, Gino goes off for two weeks, and Gioia falls in love with Bene, going to his room one night. The next day Teresa tells Gioia she knows of the affair, but Gioia admits her love for Bene and tells of her plans to run away with him. When Gino returns, he finds his wife on the range with Bene, who confesses his affair but renounces Gioia, unable to betray his friend Gino. Bene leaves and Gioia prepares to return to Italy, changing her mind only at the last minute in response to Gino's pleas for forgiveness and promises that they can still find happiness together.

With Anna Magnani and Anthony Franciosa

With Shirley Booth

# Hot Spell

Paramount / 1958

CAST:    *Alma Duval,* SHIRLEY BOOTH; *Jack Duval,* ANTHONY QUINN; *Virginia Duval,* SHIRLEY MacLAINE; *Buddy Duval,* Earl Holliman; *Fan,* Eileen Heckart; *Billy Duval,* Clint Kimbrough; *Wyatt,* Warren Stevens; *Dora May,* Jody Lawrance; *Harry,* Harlan Warde; *Ruby,* Valerie Allen; *Baggage Man,* Stafford Repp; *Essie Mae,* Irene Tedrow; *Attendant,* Bill Walker; *Colored Woman,* Louise Franklin; *Preacher,* Anthony Jochim; *Colored Man,* Johnny Lee; *Librarian,* Elsie Waller; *Pool Players,* Len Hendry and John Indrisano; *Funeral Car Driver,* Watson H. Downs; *Conductor,* William Duray.

CREDITS:    *Director,* Daniel Mann; *producer,* Hal B. Wallis; *associate producer,* Paul Nathan; *screenplay,* James Poe; based on the *play* "Next of Kin" by Lonnie Coleman; *music,* Alex North; *art directors,* Hal Pereira and Tambi Larsen; *camera,* Loyal Griggs; *editor,* Warren Low. VistaVision. Running time: 86 minutes.

The Quinn image, as developed in the 1950s, was of an actor thriving on challenge. In *Hot Spell,* Shirley Booth provided the challenge and stiff competition. With her blistering exposure of Momism, she made a formidable acting rival. Quinn rose to the occasion by creatively molding an even more dominant figure as the brash, belligerent husband, frustrated by his vapid wife's total

With Shirley Booth

With Warren Stevens, Shirley MacLaine, Earl Holliman, Shirley Booth

ignorance of his needs and desires. The mature script which James Poe had crafted from Lonnie Coleman's unproduced play, *Next of Kin,* allowed Quinn to tackle domestic drama, a departure from his long list of roles in action films, and he turned in a sensitive, complex, even compassionate portrayal of Jack Duval, the husband—and made him sympathetic, besides, despite the fact that he was cruel to his wife, unfeeling toward his children, boorish toward their friends, and an adulterer on the side!

During a New Orleans hot spell, Alma Duval (Shirley Booth), a middle-aged housewife who dreams of returning to an earlier, happier time, thoughtfully buys presents for her three grown children to give to their father at the birthday party she is preparing for him. Realizing for some time that things have been strained between Jack (Quinn) and herself, and aware of rumors

that Jack has been cavorting with a nineteen-year-old girl, Alma hopes that the party will bring him back to her. The dinner starts pleasantly but soon disintegrates under emotional strain as Jack becomes engaged in a violent argument with his older son Buddy (Earl Holliman), who works with his father in the latter's employment agency but wants to go into business for himself. Billy (Clint Kimbrough), the sensitive younger son, becomes upset and rushes from the table.

Preparing to leave the house, Jack finds his daughter Virginia (Shirley MacLaine), on the porch necking with her boyfriend Wyatt (Warren Stevens). Jack embarrasses them both by questioning Wyatt about his intentions. Then Jack takes young Billy with him to the pool hall to teach him the game as well as to have a father-son talk, trying to convince the boy that a man has obligations to fulfill himself while being tied down to a family and job. Unable to communicate with Billy, Jack leaves his son there to keep a "business appointment," but Billy follows and sees his father drive off with Ruby (Valerie Allen). When he sees them together, Billy realizes what his father had meant.

At home, Virginia is heartbroken after learning that Wyatt has no intention of marrying her, and Alma resumes her persistent nagging in hopes of getting Jack to take them back to their old home in New Paris, where Alma and Jack had spent the happy early years of their married life. Frustrated, Jack makes his final break the following day, leaving for Florida with Ruby. En route they are killed in an automobile accident, and Alma takes her husband's body back to New Paris, where she comes to the realization that she must stop living in the past—that everything has so changed that she cannot go back.

With Shirley MacLaine, Warren Stevens and Shirley Booth

With Yul Brynner

# The Buccaneer

Paramount / 1958

CAST: *Jean Lafitte*, YUL BRYNNER; *Andrew Jackson*, CHARLTON HESTON; *Bonnie Brown*, CLAIRE BLOOM; *Dominique Yoú*, CHARLES BOYER; *Annette Claiborne*, INGER STEVENS; *Ezra Peavey*, Henry Hull; *Governor William Claiborne*, E. G. Marshall; *Mercier*, Lorne Greene; *Captain Rumbo*, Ted de Corsia; *Collector of the Port*, Douglass Dumbrille; *Captain Brown*, Robert F. Simon; *Scipio*, Sir Lancelot; *Cariba*, Fran Jeffries; *Deacon*, John Dierkes; *Young Sentry*, Ken Miller; *Pyke*, George Mathews; *Captain McWilliams*, Leslie E. Bradley; *Gramby*, Bruce Gordon; *Commodore Patterson*, Barry Kelley; *Captain Lockyer*, Robert Warwick; *Beluche*, Steven Marlo; *Mr. Whipple*, James Todd; *Miggs*, Jerry Hartleben; *Customs Inspector*, Onslow Stevens; *Marie Claiborne*, Theodora Davitt; *Lt. Shreve*, Wally Richard; *Frowsy Wench*, Iris Adrian; *Creole Militia Officer*, James Seay; *Tripes*, Reginald Sheffield; *Woman*, Julia Faye; *Toro*, Woodrow Strode; *Captain Flint*, Paul Newland; *Madame Hilaire*, Norma Varden; *Dragoon Captain Wilkes*, John Hubbard; and Stephen Chase, Brad Johnson, Eric Alden, Peter Coe, Harry Shannon, Henry Brandon, Kathleen Freeman, Raymond Greenleaf, Fred Kohler, Jr., Jack Kruschen, Mike Mazurki, Jack Pennick, Harlan Warde, Ty Hungerford (Hardin), Lane Chandler.

CREDITS: *Director*, Anthony Quinn; *producer*, Henry Wilcoxon; under the *supervision* of Cecil B. De-Mille; *screenplay*, Jesse L. Lasky Jr. and Berenice Mosk; from the screenplay by Harold Lamb, Edwin Justus Mayer and C. Gardner Sullivan; based on Jeanie Macpherson's adaptation of "Lafitte the Pirate" by Lyle Saxon; *music*, Elmer Bernstein; *art directors*, Hal Pereira, Walter H. Tyler and Albert Nozaki; *camera*,

With Charlton Heston

[ 173 ]

With Inger Stevens

With Claire Bloom

Loyal Griggs; *editor,* Archie Marshek. VistaVision and Technicolor. Running time: 119 minutes.

When Cecil B. DeMille dumped the task of directing the new wide-screen and Technicolor version of *The Buccaneer* into the lap of his son-in-law, he handed Anthony Quinn a complete package: a $6,000,000 production, including $1,200,000 for promotion, plus five stars, fifty-five featured players, 100 bit actors, 12,000 extras, 60,000 props (among them more than a dozen authentic pirogues), $100,000 worth of genuine antique furniture and a couple of boxcar-loads of Spanish moss and cypress trees. In addition, DeMille provided one of the best true adventures in American history. Despite these obvious assets, Quinn was forced to make his directorial debut not only with the old man undoubtedly looking over his shoulder but also with the built-in disadvantage of inevitable critical comparison to DeMille's own version of the film two decades earlier. If that weren't enough, the real deathblow came when the film premiered in New York during Christmas week of 1958—in the midst of a newspaper strike! (Some, though, have argued that the lack of publicity might have prevented *The Buccaneer* remake from being a total disaster.)

Curiously, few critics even mentioned Quinn's name at all in their reviews. *Time,* for one, felt that "What (Henry) Wilcoxon and Quinn have produced is just a half-deflated imitation of the old man at his overblown best." *Newsweek,* without crucifying anybody in particular, simply called the film "two hours of some of the most pretentious nonsense to lay claim to a moviegoer's spending money." Quinn himself prefers to merely shrug the whole thing off with no bitterness, planning some day to again direct when he has complete control of the situation.

The criticism of Quinn's *The Buccaneer* notwithstanding, this version played less loosely with facts than did DeMille's and featured a vivid climactic battle which holds its own against the best of DeMille. Using less than three dozen actors, Quinn staged a stirring sequence with a Scots regiment, pipes skirling, marching out of the fog straight into the muzzles of Andy Jackson's barricaded troops.

Action, though, was not the focal point of the Quinn production. The story of Lafitte's love for the daughter of William Claiborne, first governor of Louisiana, is the sum and substance of the plot this time around. What got in the way, apparently, were the widely varying acting styles and disparate accents. Yul Brynner, appearing somewhat uncomfortable with a full head of hair, played Jean Lafitte in his curiously unidentifiable, too-cultured (for a nineteenth-century freebooter), quasi-Continental accent, while Charles Boyer, as his lieutenant Dominique You, sounded simply too French even to pass for Cajun. Then there was Charlton Heston, speaking in an ersatz-Tennessee drawl, as Andrew Jackson. Claire Bloom, at least, was properly English, though seemingly a bit highborn to play a wench, while Swedish-American Inger Stevens had not yet developed enough of a Swedish accent to interfere with her role as Annette Claiborne.

For the record, among the several actors who appeared in both versions of *The Buccaneer* (none, though, repeating roles), were Douglass Dumbrille, Reginald Sheffield, John Hubbard. In the role of Beluche, which Quinn himself had played originally, was Steven Marlo.

With Yul Brynner (left) and Charles Boyer

With Sophia Loren

# The Black Orchid

Paramount / 1959

CAST: *Rose Bianco,* SOPHIA LOREN;*Frank Valente,* ANTHONY QUINN; *Mary Valente,* Ina Balin; *Ralph Bianco,* Jimmie Baird; *Noble,* Mark Richman; *Giulia Gallo,* Naomi Stevens; *Alma Gallo,* Virginia Vincent; *Joe,* Joe Di Reda; *Henry Gallo,* Frank Puglia; *Luisa,* Majel Barrett; *Paul,* Vito Scotti; *Consuello the Dressmaker,* Zolya Talma; *Tony Bianco,* Jack Washburn; *Mr. Harmon,* Whit Bissell; *Priest,* Robert Carricart.

CREDITS: *Director,* Martin Ritt; *producers,* Carlo Ponti and Marcello Girosi; *screenplay,* Joseph Stefano; based on his television script; *music,* Allessandro Cicognini; *art directors,* Hal Pereira and Roland Anderson; *camera,* Robert Burks; *editor,* Howard Smith. Vista-Vision. Running time: 94 minutes.

*For her performance, Sophia Loren won the Best Actress award at the 1958 Venice Film Festival.

Of Anthony Quinn's growing gallery of outstanding screen portraits, his three-dimensional, rock-solid interpretation of Frank Valente, the loud, amiable, warm-hearted Italian-American widower in *The Black Orchid,* hangs among his least heralded. His clumsy, well-intentioned suitor to the gangster's lovely widow; his fatherly compassion toward a neurotic daughter he fears is drifting toward mental illness as had her mother; his immediate rapport with the widow's disturbed son; his nervous but friendly (and distinctively Quinn) horse-laugh—all these ingredients spiced a memorable characterization, textured by the electric qualities which increasingly were establishing the Quinn image on the screen. "When anyone gives his director what Mr. Quinn gives Martin Ritt," felt Bosley Crowther, "it is certainly too bad that the director hasn't something equally good to give back to him. But unfortunately Joseph Stefano, who wrote the original script, did not put into the hands of the director a script that is up to Mr. Quinn."

Quinn's leading lady, Sophia Loren, gave a dignified, almost too cool performance as the stunning, artificial-flower-making widow (one might have expected better casting and slightly more motivation with a somewhat more volatile Anna Magnani in the role), and for her interpretation, she was selected Best Actress at the 1958 Venice Film Festival.

Mourning the recent death of her husband, a petty gangster, and troubled over the fact that her young son is confined to a state farm for juvenile delinquents, Rose Bianco (Sophia Loren) has chosen a lonely, secluded life. Frank Valente (Quinn), a widower and close friend of her next-door neighbor, becomes attracted to Rose, who insists that she's still in mourning and has no interest in men. Through his persistence, however, Frank breaks down her cold reserve and, with quiet insistence, succeeds in winning her love, especially after noticing the effect his tenderness and sincerity has on her son Ralphie (Jimmy Baird), during the weekend visits Rose makes with Frank to the state farm. Rose sympathizes with Frank's need for companionship and love after he tells her of his own unhappy marriage to a woman who

With Sophia Loren and Ina Balin

With Sophia Loren

had been mentally ill for many years before her death.

Ultimately Rose accepts Frank's marriage proposal and Ralphie, thrilled by his mother's impending wedding, is released from the farm and becomes fast friends with Frank. The wedding plans are shattered, however, when Frank's engaged daughter, Mary (Ina Balin), violently opposes her father's marriage to "that gangster's wife." She insults Rose, quarrels with both her father and her fiancé, Noble (Mark Richman), and locks herself in her room for days on end. Frank begins to fear that she will turn into a mental case like her mother,

and Rose, realizing that her impending marriage is doomed by Mary's bitter attitude, calls the wedding off. Young Ralphie unfairly accuses his mother of ruining his chance for freedom and runs away.

Only when Rose forces Mary to realize that her selfish demands are ruining Frank's life, as Rose's own material cravings had ruined her husband's, does Mary relent and accept her father's remarrying. Ralphie, meanwhile, is located by Frank and Noble; when the men return home, Rose and Mary are preparing breakfast together and all is harmony.

With Sophia Loren and Jimmie Baird

With Henry Fonda

# Warlock

20th Century–Fox / 1959

CAST: *Johnny Gannon*, RICHARD WIDMARK; *Clay Blaisdell*, HENRY FONDA; *Tom Morgan*, ANTHONY QUINN; *Lily Dollar*, DOROTHY MALONE; *Jessie Marlow*, Dolores Michaels; *Judge Holloway*, Wallace Ford; *Abe McQuown*, Tom Drake; *Bacon*, Richard Arlen; *Curley Burne*, De Forrest Kelly; *Skinner*, Regis Toomey; *Richardson*, Vaughn Taylor; *Dr. Wagner*, Don Beddoe; *Mr. Petrix*, Whit Bissell; *Shaw*, J. Anthony Hughes; *Edward Calhoun*, Donald Barry; *Billy Gannon*, Frank Gorshin; *MacDonald*, Ian MacDonald; *Hutchinson*, Stan Kamber; *Luke Friendly*, Paul Comi; *Jiggs*, L. Q. Jones; *Fitzsimmons*, Mickey Simpson; *Professor*, Robert Osterloh; *Cade*, James Philbrook; *Pony Benner*, David Garcia; *Foss*, Robert Adler; *Murch*, Joel Ashley; *Chet Haggin*, Joe Turkel; *Bob Nicholson*, Saul Gorss; *Slavin*, Bartlett Robinson; *Mrs. Richardson*, Ann Doran; *Deputy Thompson*, Walter Coy; *Burbage*, Henry Worth; *Dance Hall Girl*, June Blair; *Barber*, Wally Campo; *Sheriff Keller*, Hugh Sanders.

CREDITS: *Producer-director*, Edward Dmytryk; *screenplay*, Robert Alan Aurthur; based on the *novel* by Oakley Hall; *music director*, Lionel Newman; *original score*, Leigh Harline; *art directors*, Lyle R. Wheeler and Herman A. Blumenthal; *camera*, Joe MacDonald; *editor*, Jack W. Holmes. CinemaScope and DeLuxe Color. Running time: 122 minutes.

Anthony Quinn's curious and different role as the complex, clubfooted gambler-gunman whose relationship with the character played by Henry Fonda, as the cool fast draw, leaned rather strongly toward homosexuality, made Edward Dmytryk's multi-plotted *Warlock* somewhat daring for its time. Its complicated story line, working at various levels, and its shadowy psychological innuendos, turned off critics and audiences alike, and from several corners came concern that director Dmytryk and scenarist Robert Alan Aurthur had carried the "new convention" Western too far too fast. Most, undoubtedly, were expecting to relax with a conventional he-man Western featuring three tough and proven hombres in the persons of Henry Fonda, Richard Widmark and Anthony Quinn, who help (or hinder) the townsfolk regain control of their community from outriders. Instead comes the story of professional hired gun who becomes marshal, his hero-worshipping right hand

and conscience, the ex-killer who challenges his one-man rule, one vindictive old girlfriend and one loving new flame. Quinn, in particular, was singled out for comment in most reviews, with *Variety* feeling that "Quinn's brooding performance is menacing and purposely perplexing, given considerable breadth by this actor's native intelligence." As the cripple who lives in the reflection of Fonda's glory, Quinn (blond for the only time in his career) uses a grin, bordering occasionally on the sinister side, as a coverup for his true feelings and basic insecurity, while watching like a mother hen over Fonda because "he's the only one—man or woman—who looked at me and didn't see a cripple." Quinn's incisive acting made the character told by his friend to leave town alone all the more pitiable—a slightly trembling lip nearly hidden by the familiar grin.

As Tom Morgan

To put an end to the drunken brawling and killing that accompanies the San Pablo cowboys when they ride into town, the citizens of Warlock hire professional marshal Clay Blaisdell (Fonda). He brings with him his gambler-gunman friend, Tom Morgan (Quinn), who worships Clay as the "fastest draw in the West." When the pair routs the San Pablo gang, one of its members, Johnny Gannon (Widmark), stays behind and volunteers to become Blaisdell's deputy.

As an uneasy peace settles onto Warlock, the relationship between Blaisdell and Morgan deteriorates when the marshal finds romance with a local girl, Jessie Marlow (Dolores Michaels). Gannon, meanwhile, becomes involved with Lily Dollar (Dorothy Malone), who at one time had been Morgan's mistress and now hates both Blaisdell and him for killing a man she had hoped to marry. Friction begins to develop between Gannon and Blaisdell over the latter's one-man rule, and when the San Pablo boys ride into town for a final showdown, Morgan forces the marshal at gunpoint to remain in his room so that Gannon will be obliged to face his old gang alone.

With Dolores Michaels and Henry Fonda

The townsfolk, however, finally stand behind law and order and back up Gannon. With his idol no longer the top man, Morgan begins to crack and threatens to kill Gannon himself, but Blaisdell tries to dissuade his friend, telling him that it's better if he (Morgan) leaves. Blaisdell is willing to settle down with Jessie and live peacefully. Morgan provokes Blaisdell into a gunfight and is killed. Gannon then orders the marshal to leave town and, realizing that there is no longer a place for him in Warlock, he says good-bye to Jessie and prepares to leave. Before going, though, he faces Gannon on the deserted main street, twice outdraws his opponent without firing, and then, still top man, throws his guns in the dirt, walks past Gannon and leaves.

With J. Anthony Hughes

With Carolyn Jones

# Last Train from Gun Hill

Paramount / 1959

CAST:  *Matt Morgan,* KIRK DOUGLAS; *Craig Beldon,* ANTHONY QUINN; *Linda,* Carolyn Jones; *Rick Beldon,* Earl Holliman; *Catherine Morgan,* Ziva Rodann; *Beero,* Brad Dexter; *Lee,* Brian Hutton; *Skag,* Bing Russell; *Bartender,* Val Avery; *Sheriff Bartlett,* Walter Sande; *Petey Morgan,* Lars Henderson; *Jake,* Henry Wills; *Salesman at Bar,* John R. Anderson; *Hotel Clerk,* William Newell; *Man in Lobby,* Len Hendry; *Andy,* Dabbs Greer; *Minnie,* Mara Lynn; *Wounded Gunman,* Raymond A. McWalters; *Roomer,* Sid Tomack; *Keno,* Charles Stevens; *Cleaning Man,* Julius Tanner; *Saloon Bouncer,* Glenn Strange; *Charlie,* Jack Lomas; *Pinto,* Tony Russo; *Boy,* Ricky William Kelman; *Conductor,* Walter (Tony) Merrill; *Craig's Men,* Eric Alden, Carl H. Saxe and Frank Hagney; *Storekeeper,* Hank Mann; *Cowboy on Train,* Frank Carter; *Drummer on Train,* Mike Mahoney; *Conductor,* Bob Scott; *Cowboy,* Ty Hardin.

CREDITS:  *Director,* John Sturges; *producer,* Hal B. Wallis; *associate producer,* Paul Nathan, *screenplay,* James Poe; based on the *story* "Showdown" by Les Crutchfield; *music,* Dimitri Tiomkin; *art director,* Walter Tyler; *camera,* Charles B. Lang Jr.; *editor,* Warren Low. VistaVision and Technicolor. Running time: 94 minutes.

Quinn's third film with Kirk Douglas (by now the two actors were of equal stature) was the superior John Sturges Western, packed with action overtones and psychological undertones, well-paced and full of atmosphere—and blessed with two strong leads. Anthony Quinn makes the most of the more interesting role as the complex cattle boss and wealthiest man in Gun Hill who finds that his son is the rapist-killer of his (Quinn's) best friend's wife and is torn between fatherly compas-

Working title: *One Angry Day.*

As Craig Beldon

With Earl Holliman

sion and lawful obligation to allow the boy to be arrested. Quinn is the more tragic figure, for despite the fact that the hero (Douglas) who is out to avenge his wife's murder should be the one pitied, the father—determined, swaggering, self-made—is the one truly alone with his only outlet his love for an undeserving son. Interestingly, director Sturges continually shoots Quinn

from low angles to emphasize his massive power as well as his loneliness, and his death scene, also photographed from a low-angled camera, can be compared to the felling of a stately oak.

*Last Train from Gun Hill* has often been cited as a prime example of the "buddy system" kind of picture-making, *i.e.,* two major actors in the leads, rather than the usual leading man-leading lady combination. Previously, for example, Burt Lancaster and Tony Curtis had starred in *The Sweet Smell of Success,* then it was Lancaster and Gary Cooper in *Vera Cruz,* Lancaster and Clark Gable in *Run Silent, Run Deep,* Lancaster and Douglas in (among others) *Gunfight at the O.K. Corral,* and so forth. The Douglas-Quinn tandem allowed for arresting dual performances by two major actors of virtually equal intensity.

With Kirk Douglas

With Earl Holliman

Shortly after the Indian wife (Ziva Rodann) of marshal Matt Morgan (Douglas) is raped and killed by two drunken ranch hands, his young son returns to his father with a saddle belonging to one of the murderers. Recognizing it as the property of his friend Craig Beldon (Quinn), the vengeful lawman rides into Gun Hill, the town Beldon now rules. After an investigation, Matt discovers that the man he wants is Beldon's weakling son, Rick (Earl Holliman), who committed the crime with his sidekick Lee (Brian Hutton). Despite their long friendship, however, Beldon refuses to let Matt arrest his son, but Matt captures Rick, fights his way to the town's only hotel and holes up in a room to await the next train. The one person who comes to Matt's aid is Linda (Carolyn Jones), Beldon's mistress, who supplies the lawman with a rifle.

Holding the gun under Rick's chin, Matt takes the young killer through the streets to the station. The impetuous Lee tries to rescue his friend but inadvertently kills him and is in turn shot down by Matt. With his son dead, Beldon forces Matt to a showdown. On the platform next to the last train from Gun Hill, the two old friends exchange gunfire and Beldon falls mortally wounded.

With Earl Holliman (on ground)

With Sophia Loren

# Heller in Pink Tights

Paramount / 1960

CAST: *Angela Rossini,* SOPHIA LOREN; *Tom Healy,* ANTHONY QUINN; *Della Southby,* Margaret O'Brien; *Clint Mabry,* Steve Forrest; *Lorna Hathaway,* Eileen Heckart; *Manfred "Doc" Montague,* Edmund Lowe; *De Leon,* Ramon Novarro; *Sam Pierce,* George Mathews; *Theodore,* Frank Cordell; *William,* Cactus McPeters; *Sheriff McClain,* Edward Binns; *Hodges,* Warren Wade; *Santis,* Frank Silvera; *Goober,* Cal Bolder; *McAllister,* Robert Palmer; *Photographer,* Howard McNear; *First Gunslinger,* Taggart Casey; *Second Gunslinger,* Leo V. Matranga; *Madam,* Geraldine Wall; *Maid,* Amanda Randolph; *Achilles,* David Armstrong; *Calchas,* Alfred Tonkel; *Servant,* Robert Darin; *Venus,* Bryn Davis; *Juno,* Cathy Cox; *Indians,* Iron Eyes Cody, Eddie Little Sky, Rodd Redwing, Chief Yowlachie; *Acting Double for Edmund Lowe,* Bernard Nedell.

CREDITS: *Director,* George Cukor; *producers,* Carlo Ponti and Marcello Girosi; *associate producer,* Lewis E. Ciannelli; *screenplay,* Walter Bernstein; *adaptation,* Dudley Nichols from the *novel* "Heller with a Gun" by Louis L'Amour; *music,* Daniele Amfitheatrof; *art directors,* Hal Pereira and Eugene Allen; *choreography,* Val Raset; *camera,* Harold Lipstein; *editor,* Howard Smith. Technicolor. Running time: 100 minutes.

George Cukor's refreshing, unusual, and only Western reunited Anthony Quinn with Sophia Loren, who were

With Eileen Heckart and Sophia Loren

With Eileen Heckart and Margaret O'Brien

promising to become a team, working remarkably well together. Quinn is first-rate with his adroit, sensitive and at times hilarious portrait of the explosive manager of a hard-luck troupe of itinerant players carrying culture west of Cheyenne in the 1880s. In this sadly underrated, stunningly photographed "romantic comedy" (Cukor's term), a lovingly staged, somewhat burlesqued bit of Americana was attempted in order to show, apparently, what it was like when Adah Isaacs Menken brought showbiz to the frontier with plays like *Mazeppa* and *La Belle Hélène.* In *Heller in Pink Tights,* the actress becomes a tempestuous, gold-digging Continental performer, and the time is updated by nearly fifteen years (Miss Menken died in 1868), but the road companies are as sleazy as ever and the hammy acting makes no never-mind to the uneducated gunslingers and whiskey-guzzling townsfolk. The troupe's gaudy wagons of scenery and costumes trundle from town to town as the thespians brave the hazards of hostile Indians, unfriendly sheriffs, dangerous saloonkeepers and unappreciative audiences.

Aside from the wonderful ensemble performance from a top-drawer cast, exceptional Technicolor photography distinguished the proceedings, most strikingly in one scene in which drably costumed Indians, pillaging the show wagon, fling yards of brilliantly tinted cloth across the screen.

Followed by bill collectors, the Healy Dramatic Company arrives in Cheyenne to play the West's grandest theater. Its members include Tom Healy (Quinn), the long-suffering manager; Angela Rossini (Sophia Loren), his magnetic leading lady; Lorna Southby (Eileen Heckart), a lusty character actress; Della (Margaret O'Brien), her ingenue daughter; and "Doc" Montague (Edmund Lowe), a broken-down Shakespearean ham. Theater owner Sam Pierce (George Mathews) welcomes the troupe—especially Angela, who, it turns out, is impressed by amorous gunslinger Mabry (Steve Forrest). Healy wants Angela for himself, but has learned to put up with her roving eye. During a rehearsal of *La Belle Hélène,* Pierce complains that it won't satisfy blood-and-guts Cheyenne, so the company

[ 184 ]

switches to the action-filled *Mazeppa,* in which Angela plays the boy hero who is strapped to a galloping horse.

When an old creditor arrives, Angela collects the night's take from Pierce to pay the show's debts, but instead of handing over the money, she puts it and herself up for collateral in a poker game and loses to Mabry. That night, the penniless troupe sneaks out of town pursued by Mabry, who intends to collect his winnings. He overtakes them just as they are ambushed by Indians. Forced to abandon their wagons and costumes, they make their way to a remote trading post under Mabry's guidance. There the gunslinger learns that his archenemy, De Leon (Ramon Novarro), is planning to kill him rather than paying off an old debt. Mabry gets Angela to go into town and wangle the money from De Leon, but she uses it to buy a new theater. Discovering he had been taken again, Mabry becomes enraged and shows up backstage, where he is cornered by De Leon's men. Healy helps him escape after assuring him that he will be repaid. The theater is a great success, and Healy is able to get Angela to settle down at last and marry him.

With Sophia Loren

With Sophia Loren

[ 185 ]

With Lana Turner

# Portrait in Black

Universal–International / 1960

CAST: *Sheila Cabot*, LANA TURNER; *Dr. David Rivera*, ANTHONY QUINN; *Catherine Cabot*, SANDRA DEE; *Blake Richards*, JOHN SAXON; *Howard Mason*, RICHARD BASEHART; *Matthew Cabot*, LLOYD NOLAN; *Cob O'Brien*, Ray Walston; *Miss Lee*, Virginia Grey; *Tani*, Anna May Wong; *Peter Cabot*, Dennis Kohler; *Detective*, Paul Birch; *Dr. Kessler*, John Wengraf; *Mr. Corbin*, Richard Morris; *1st Detective*, James Nolan; *2nd Detective*, Robert Lieb; *Minister*, John McNamara; *Sid*, Charles Thompson; *Foreman*, George Womack; *Patrolmen*, Harold Goodwin and Jack Bryan; *Chinese Dancer*, Elizabeth Chan; *Chinese Headwaiter*, Henry Quan.

CREDITS: *Director*, Michael Gordon; *producer*, Ross Hunter; *screenplay*, Ivan Goff and Ben Roberts; based on their 1947 play; *music*, Frank Skinner; *art director*, Richard H. Riedel; *camera*, Russell Metty; *editor*, Milton Carruth. Eastman Color. Running time: 112 minutes.

When it got around to reviewing *Portrait in Black*, *Time* magazine mentioned: "Actor Quinn is reliably reported to have said 'You're kidding' when it was suggested that he take the role, his first as a drawing-room matron menace." Sadly miscast in this slickly produced murder melodrama which Ross Hunter was (rightly) convinced that Lana Turner's fans would love, Quinn obviously was uncomfortable as the doctor whom Lana seduces into bumping off her invalid husband Lloyd Nolan. "One wonders," noted *The New York Times*, "why he

even hesitated in choosing between dubious dalliance and a medical career in Switzerland," and *Time* commented, "His speech is oddly strangled and his general acting style is that of a beaten prizefighter routinely protesting a decision he knows to have been fair." Of the film itself, *Variety* found: "[Director] Gordon has restored an outmoded style of stiff, self-consciously awkward posturing that emerges ludicrously crude by contemporary dramatic standards, unintentionally amusing the audience at several vital junctures." Of interest to film buffs, of course, is the sight of Quinn's old friend and acting companion, Anna May Wong, inscrutable as ever playing Lana's mysterious housekeeper. It was one of the Oriental actress's last roles, and marked the fifth time she and Quinn had worked on the same film. And Quinn's opportunity to "kill" Lloyd Nolan (it was their sixth movie together) accounted for a delicious in-joke among cinema enthusiasts.

Dr. David Rivera (Quinn), personal physician to Matthew Cabot (Lloyd Nolan), a tough, bedridden shipping magnate, is having an affair with Cabot's wife Sheila (Lana Turner). Wanting out of the marriage but unable to get a divorce, Sheila induces David to murder her husband by injecting an air bubble into his bloodstream. A short time later, however, Sheila receives an anonymous letter congratulating her on the success of the murder. Deciding that the author is Howard Mason (Richard Basehart), Cabot's business manager who long has had an interest in Sheila, the adulterous murderers are forced to kill again, this time dumping the body in San Francisco Bay. When Mason's body is

With Lana Turner and Ray Walston

With Lana Turner and Lloyd Nolan

found, the police arrest young Blake Richards (John Saxon), a tugboat owner known to have threatened Mason. Blake, it turns out, is the fiancé of Sheila's step-daughter Cathie (Sandra Dee), who also becomes involved.

Haunted by his conscience and troubled by the turn of events, David decides to abandon his practice and go to Switzerland. Suddenly he receives a call from Sheila, who tells him she's gotten a second anonymous letter. In a violent confrontation with David, Sheila breaks down and confesses that it was she who wrote the letters, hoping that they would force David to remain with her. When they discover that Cathie has overheard everything, the frenzied David attempts to kill her, but falls to his death from a window ledge as Sheila is left alone to await the police.

For the record, the stars of the 1947 Broadway production of *Portrait in Black* were Claire Luce, Sidney Blackmer and Donald Cook in the Turner, Nolan and Quinn roles.

With Lana Turner

With Sandra Dee and Lana Turner

With Yoko Tani

# The Savage Innocents

Paramount / 1960

CAST: *Inuk,* ANTHONY QUINN; *Asiak,* YOKO TANI; *Trooper,* Carlo Giustini; *Trooper,* Peter O'Toole; *Powtee,* Marie Yang; *Missionary,* Marco Guglielmi; *Imina,* Kaida Horiuchi; *Itti,* Lee Montague; *Anarvik,* Andy Ho; *Hiko,* Anna May Wong; *Iulik,* Yvonne Shima; *Kidok,* Anthony Chin; *Trading Post Proprietor,* Francis De Wolff; *Undik,* Michael Chow; *Pilot,* Ed Devereau.

CREDITS: *Director,* Nicholas Ray; *producer,* Maleno Malenotti; *screenplay,* Nicholas Ray; based on the *novel* "Top of the World" by Hans Ruesch; *music conductor,* Muir Mathieson; *original score,* Angelo Francesco Lavagnino; *art director,* Don Ashton; *camera,* Aldo Tonti and Peter Hennessy; *editor,* Ralph Kemplen. Technirama and Technicolor. Running time: 110 minutes.

In Nicholas Ray's fascinating, bitter, and strangely un-

Original Italian Title: *Ombre Bianche.* Original French Title: *Les dents du diable.*

even drama about contemporary Eskimo life, Anthony Quinn offers still another remarkable display of his acting skills in his individualistic performance as the primitive hunter Inuk. Despite the hulk and distinctive features which most actors would consider disadvantages unless they were content with careers in character roles, Quinn has distinguished the screen with his unique ability to execute totally believable portrayals of diverse multinational and ethnic types, without resorting (except in extreme cases) to bizarre makeup. His technique appears to be the creative channeling of his innate gift for impersonation, his ear for dialects, his eye for human characteristics, his sensitivity for people, and his flair for the theatrical. Since Quinn alone has enacted an Eskimo in a leading role, his interpretation stands as the one by which any others (and to date there have been none) must be compared.

*The Savage Innocents,* an Italian/French/British co-production filmed in Greenland and Hudson Bay and in "igloos" in Pinewood Studios outside of London, was among the first of Quinn's truly international movies—

With Yoko Tani

With Marie Yang

exemplified by a Japanese leading lady, assorted Italians as mounties and missionaries, Orientals impersonating Eskimos, and a young, voice-dubbed Peter O'Toole seen briefly as a Canadian trooper, appearing in one of his earliest screen roles.

*Variety* was convinced that "Anthony Quinn, mainly talking pidgin English-cum-Eskimo, comes out as an authentic Eskimo," and felt that "the memorable moments are those of Quinn hunting down foxes, bears, seals, walruses, and the majesty of the bleak wastes, the ice, the storms and primitive living conditions. The human elements don't come out of it quite so well mainly because Ray's screenplay contains some pretty naïve lines rubbing shoulders with out-of-character talk."

After years of borrowing other men's wives, a normal custom among his people, Inuk (Quinn), a mighty Eskimo hunter, takes his own bride, Asiak (Yoko Tani). Learning that he can exchange fox skins for a rifle at a trading post hundreds of miles away, Inuk makes the long trek along with Asiak and her aged mother Powtee (Marie Tang). Once there, however, Asiak begs to leave because she doesn't care for the ways of "civilized" people. Inuk then builds an igloo some distance from the post, and when the missionaries visit them, he extends his hospitality by offering them his wife. Their rebuff incenses Inuk who feels that his wife has been insulted, and the Eskimo accidentally kills one of them. Forced to flee into the wilderness, Inuk and Asiak are forced to leave Powtee, a burden on the trip, to die in the snow.

Shortly after the birth of his son, Inuk is arrested by two Canadian troopers (Carlo Giustini and Peter O'Toole) for the murder of the missionary. As they take him south for trial, one of the troopers freezes to death.

With Yoko Tani

Inuk saves the second one from a similar fate by taking him back to his igloo. After recovering, the trooper offers to let Inuk go free, certain that the simple Eskimo would never be forgiven for breaking the white man's law. When Inuk refuses, the trooper insults him, spits at Asiak, and runs off. Baffled by the behavior of white men, Inuk and Asiak return to the safety of their home in the frozen wilderness.

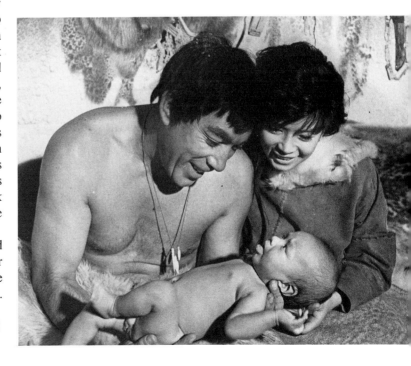

With Yoko Tani

With Gia Scala

# The Guns of Navarone

Columbia Pictures / 1961

CAST: *Capt. Keith Mallory,* GREGORY PECK; *Corporal Miller,* DAVID NIVEN; *Col. Andrea Stravos,* ANTHONY QUINN; *C.P.O. Brown,* Stanley Baker; *Maj. Roy Franklin,* Anthony Quayle; *Maria Pappadimos,* Irene Papas; *Anna,* Gia Scala, *Pvt. Spyros Pappadimos,* James Darren; *Commander Jenson,* James Robertson Justice; *Squadron Leader Barnsby,* Richard Harris; *Cohn,* Bryan Forbes; *Baker,* Allan Cuthbertson; *Weaver,* Michael Trubshawe; *Sgt. Grogan,* Percy Herbert; *Sessler,* George Mikell; *Muesel,* Walter Gotell; *Nikolai,* Tutte Lemkow; *Commandant,* Albert Lieven; *Group Captain,* Norman Wooland; *German Gunnery Officer,* Christopher Rhodes; *Bride,* Cleo Scouloudi; *Patrol Boat Captain;* Nicholas Papakonstantantinou.

CREDITS: *Director,* J. Lee Thompson; *producer,* Carl Foreman; *screenplay,* Carl Foreman; based on the *novel* by Alistair MacLean; *music,* Dimitri Tiomkin; *art director,* Geoffrey Drake; *special effects,* Bill Warrington and Wally Veevers; *assistant director,* Peter Yates; *camera,* Oswald Morris; *editor,* Alan Osbiston. Narrated by James Robertson Justice. A Highroad Presentation. CinemaScope and Eastman Color. Running time: 155 minutes.

Carl Foreman's booming, muscular adventure epic gave Quinn the virile role of the tough old Greek army officer, who, as Bosley Crowther described him, "has the courage of a lion and the simplicity of a goat." As Andrea Stravos, Quinn was able to get more depth of characterization into his role than could either Gregory Peck, as the American mountain-climber pressed into service as the mission's reluctant leader, or David Niven, as the droll, pessimistic British explosives expert and comic relief. Foreman, however, chose to stress action rather than character and DeMillian spectacle rather than credibility, and submerged several recurring Foreman themes—courage, responsibility, survival, moral judgments. Quinn's physical force and vigorous execu-

With Gia Scala, James Darren, David Niven, Stanley Baker, Gregory Peck, Irene Papas

As Andrea Stravos

and sails for the island, efficiently destroying an intercepting German patrol boat en route. The commandos' boat goes down in a storm, but the team manages to get all the gear ashore safely. Franklin is badly injured during the commandos' attempt to scale the almost sheer cliff face, and Mallory takes over the leadership. After crossing the island, they make contact with the local resistance, meeting Maria (Irene Papas), a sturdy partisan, and Anna (Gia Scala), a girl struck dumb following brutal German torture.

The Germans, however, have been alerted to their presence and the entire group is rounded up. Through a trick, the crafty Andrea enables them to overcome the guards, and they manage to escape in German uniforms, leaving Franklin behind filled with false information he

tion of his guerrilla leader role within the limitations of Foreman's script, compensated somewhat for the inability to accept many of the relationships of mistrust and misunderstandings occasionally touched upon in the screenplay, among them Quinn's unexplained and unresolved hatred of and competition with Peck. Implausibilities and stereotypes notwithstanding, *The Guns of Navarone* was a monster box-office smash and remains one of *Variety's* "All-Time Box-office Champs."

Because two giant guns on the Aegean island of Navarone are menacing Allied shipping and preventing pinned down British forces on Kheros, near Turkey, from escaping an imminent German attack, a sabotage team of six is sent to destroy the weapons buried deep in the solid rock of an impregnable cliff. Under the command of Major Franklin (Anthony Quayle) are Mallory (Peck), an expert mountaineer; Miller (Niven), a British corporal who's a genius with explosives; Andrea Stravos (Quinn), a Greek resistance fighter; C.P.O. Brown (Stanley Baker), an able mechanic; and Private Pappadimos (James Darren), a New York-educated killer born on Navarone.

Once assembled, the team dons fishermen's clothes

With Gregory Peck

believes to be true. During their escape, Miller discovers that someone has tinkered with his explosives and unmasks Anna as a traitor. Angered by Mallory's treatment of Franklin, Miller tries to goad him into shooting Anna and assuming the most brutal form of responsibility. While Mallory wavers, Maria shoots Anna. Then, helped by resistance fighters, Andrea and Pappadimos create diversions throughout the city while Mallory and Miller infiltrate the garrison and sabotage the guns. As the British destroyers approach the straits, a giant explosion shatters the cliff, as the surviving members of the team watch from the sea.

As Andrea Stravos

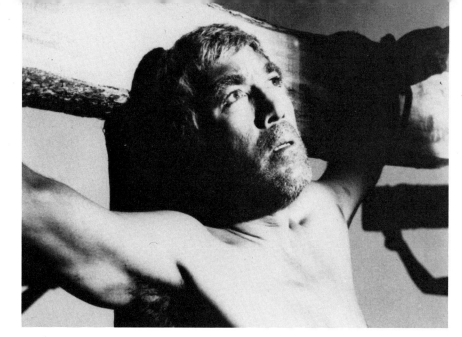

As Barabbas

# Barabbas

Columbia Pictures / 1962

CAST: *Barabbas,* ANTHONY QUINN; *Sahak,* VITTORIO GASSMAN; *Rachel,* SILVANA MANGANO; *Torvald,* JACK PALANCE; *Pontius Pilate,* ARTHUR KENNEDY; *Lucius,* ERNEST BORGNINE; *Sara,* KATY JURADO; *Peter,* Harry Andrews; *Rufio,* Norman Wooland; *Julia,* Valentina Cortese; *Joseph of Arimathea,* Arnoldo Foa; *Lazarus,* Michael Gwynn; *Scorpio,* Guido Celano; *Overseer,* Spartaco Nale; *Commander of Gladiators,* Bobby Hall; *Gladiator,* Joe Robinson; *Emperor,* Ivan Triesault; *Important Gentleman,* Enrico Glori; *Officers,* Carlo Giustini, Frederich Ledebur and Gianni De Benedetto; *Tavern Reveler,* Rina Braido; *Potter,* Douglas Fowley; *Disciple,* Laurence Payne; *Blind Man,* Tullio Tomadoni; *Beggar Woman,* Maria Zanoli; *Christ,* Roy Mangano.

CREDITS: *Director,* Richard Fleischer; *producer,* Dino De Laurentiis; *associate producer,* Luigi Luraschi; *screenplay,* Christopher Fry, Diego Fabbri, Ivo Perilli and Nigel Balchin; based on the *novel* by Pär Lagerkvist; *music director,* Franco Ferrara; *original score,* Mario Nascimbene; *art director,* Mario Chiari; *camera,* Aldo Tonti; *editor,* Alberto Gallitti. Technirama and Technicolor. Running time: 144 minutes.

Previously filmed in Sweden in 1952 by Alf Sjöberg with Ulf Palme in the title role.

With Jack Palance

In his powerful interpretation of the biblical thief and murderer whom the people of Judea chose to pardon in place of the prophet from Nazareth, Anthony Quinn,

With players

With Katy Jurado

With Silvana Mangano

As Barabbas

playing Barabbas as a brute of a man, nearly managed by sheer physical force to save Dino De Laurentiis's superspectacular from collapsing under its own weight. "Mr. Quinn is a sensational sufferer," admired Bosley Crowther. "He grunts and sweats and strains with more credible vengeance and exertion than any actor we can name." Laboring heroically through nearly three hours' worth of melodramatic adventures—stonings, mine collapses, gladiator competitions, death by arrow, lions and cross, Quinn properly towered over a stellar cast (obligatory in biblical screen epics) and offered the kind of sharply edged, finished performance which by now was almost routinely expected of him. As Barabbas, he delivered brilliantly, despite gross nonsupport provided by the script-by-committee with dialogue which, in the view of the *Monthly Film Bulletin,* "alternates between primitive cliché and bald anachronism."

The biblical squalor was there, the panoply of Rome was captured, the stultifying sulphur mines of Sicily were realistically recreated, the savagery of the Roman arena and the great conflagration of Nero's city were vividly portrayed. What was lacking, it has been agreed, were the spiritual subtlety, the simple beauty and the symbolic point of Pär Lagerkvist's fable, and even Quinn's creativity and acknowledged artistry were unable to infuse those elements into this Barabbas. Neither were Vittorio Gassman as his prison chain-mate, Silvana Mangano as his former girlfriend who has turned to follow Christ, Arthur Kennedy as the imperious Pontius Pilate, Katy Jurado as the earthy tavernkeeper in love with Barabbas, Jack Palance as the leader of the arena gladiators, Ernest Borgnine as a Christian who befriends Barabbas, Valentina Cortese as a blood-lusting patrician at the games, Harry Andrews as the Apostle Peter—nor Silvana Mangano's brother (and Dino De Laurentiis's brother-in-law) Roy as Jesus Christ.

With Jackie Gleason

# Requiem for a Heavyweight

Columbia Pictures / 1962

CAST: *Mountain Rivera,* ANTHONY QUINN; *Maish Rennick,* JACKIE GLEASON; *Army,* MICKEY ROONEY; *Grace Miller,* JULIE HARRIS; *Perelli,* Stanley Adams; *Ma Greeny,* Madame Spivy; *Bartender,* Herbie Faye; *Himself,* Jack Dempsey; *Ring Opponent,* Cassius Clay; *Ring Doctor,* Lou Gilbert; *Referee,* Arthur Mercante; *Desk Clerk,* Steve Belloise.

CREDITS: *Director,* Ralph Nelson; *producer,* David Susskind; *associate producer,* Jack Grossberg; *screenplay,* Rod Serling; based on his *television play\*; music,* Laurence Rosenthal; *art director,* Burr Smidt; *camera,* Arthur J. Ornitz; *editor,* Carl Lerner. Running time: 87 minutes.

Few argue that Quinn's memorable portrayal of Mountain Rivera, the washed-up fighter, ranks beside his Zorba of a few years later at the very top of his list of outstanding performances. His striking characterization,

---

\*Emmy Award-winning story telecast on Playhouse 90 (CBS) on October 11, 1956.

right down to the wheezy voice of a man hit too often in the windpipe and the superbly remolded, realistically battered face, captured the pitiful, inarticulate has-been clinging to his dignity while uncomprehending of the circumstances ending seventeen years in the ring. "I won a hundred eleven fights," he rasps haltingly as the doctor tells him he's through. Quinn's matchless artistry in a role up to his considerable talents enables him to bring, with what appears to be total naturalness, all the poignancy, the hopelessness, the bedraggled pride to the screen that Rod Serling had written into the part for his landmark "Playhouse 90" television version in 1956, in which Jack Palance starred as Rivera.

Under the direction of Ralph Nelson, who also had directed the television version and here made his motion picture debut, Quinn created one of the screen's supreme performances and was given outstanding support from Jackie Gleason as his cold, calculating manager; Mickey Rooney as his faithful trainer, doglike in his affection; and Julie Harris as the socially conscious employment counselor who attempts to find him a place in

As Mountain Rivera

life other than in the ring. Quinn and Gleason, who both had worked in *Larceny, Inc.* back at Warner Bros. two decades earlier (but not in the same scenes), apparently had several clashes on the set because of differences in temperaments and acting styles, but none of this is evident in their superb interaction on the screen.

Interestingly, when *Requiem* (the film) later was sold to television, it was discovered to be too short in running time, and several scenes which director Nelson had removed from his final production were reinserted over his objections, causing him to ask that his name be removed from the credits. (It wasn't.)

In 1970, as part of a television show on which Quinn co-starred with Peggy Lee, one of the touching sequences between Mountain Rivera and Grace Miller, the social worker, was re-created, with the same poignancy as the film had.

When Mountain Rivera gets knocked out during a grueling match, he is told that he can never fight again after doctors determine that further punching may blind him. His manager Maish Rennick (Gleason) encourages him to look for other work, and at the state employment bureau, he wins the sympathy of Grace Miller (Julie Harris), who takes a sincere interest in his problem. He responds to her warmth and her effort to help, but is shocked to suddenly discover that Maish, his devoted friend for seventeen years, had bet against him in his last fight. Rivera's long-time trainer Army (Rooney), is heartsick at the treatment at the hands of Maish, who had bet that his boy would go down in the fourth round, and not hang on until the seventh. When Ma Greeny (Madame Spivy), head of a gambling syndicate, warns Maish to come up with the money he owes, the loyal Rivera desperately tries to help his old manager, swallowing his pride and entering the wrestling ring in ludicrous costume, a bigger man than ever, despite the ridicule to which he exposes himself to pay off Maish's losses.

With Jackie Gleason

With Mickey Rooney and Jackie Gleason

With Peter O'Toole

# Lawrence of Arabia

Horizon Pictures/Columbia / 1962

CAST: *Lawrence*, PETER O'TOOLE; *Prince Feisal*, ALEC GUINNESS; *Auda Abu Tayi*, ANTHONY QUINN; *General Allenby*, JACK HAWKINS; *Turkish Bey*, JOSE FERRER; *Colonel Brighton*, Anthony Quayle; *Mr. Dryden*, Claude Rains; *Jackson Bentley*, Arthur Kennedy; *General Murray*, Donald Wolfit; *Sherif Ali Ibn el Kharish*, Omar Sharif; *Gasim*, I. S. Johar; *Majid*, Gamil Ratib; *Farraj*, Michel Ray; *Tafas*, Zia Mohyeddin; *Daud*, John Dimech; *Medical Officer*, Howard Marion Crawford; *Club Secretary*, Jack Gwillim; *R.A.M.C. Colonel*, Hugh Miller; *Cpl. Jenkins*, Norman Rossington.

CREDITS: *Director*, David Lean; *producer*, Sam Spiegel; *screenplay*, Robert Bolt; based on the *writings* of T. E. Lawrence; *music*, Maurice Jarre; performed by Sir Adrian Boult and the London Philharmonic Orchestra; *second-unit directors*, André Smagghe and Noel Howard; *art director*, John Stoll; *camera*, F. A. Young; *editor*, Anne Coates. Super Panavision and Technicolor. Running time: 221 minutes.

---

Winner of seven Academy Awards: Best Picture, Best Direction, Best Photography (color), Best Art Direction (color), Best Musical Score (original), Best Film Editing, Best Sound.

With Peter O'Toole

With Omar Sharif

Anthony Quinn's feisty interpretation of Auda Abu Tayi, the gluttonous, hawk-nosed chief of the maundering, murderous Howeitat tribesmen, who warily allows himself to support Lawrence's assault on Aqaba, is nothing more than an elongated cameo role in David Lean's Super Panavision extravaganza. Quinn being Quinn, however, what might have been a throwaway part emerged as another richly crafted portrayal, realized in surprisingly few scenes. On screen as well as in all advertising, Quinn received second billing after Alec Guinness (who played Prince Feisal), but his vivid acting style and somewhat exaggerated makeup allowed few to forget that he had participated in one of the screen's major epics.

Opening with T. E. Lawrence's death in a motorcycle crash in England in 1935 (there are still those who contend that it may have been a suicide), the story flashes back to British headquarters in Cairo during World War I, when the young Lawrence was attached to the general staff. Requesting to be transferred to Arabia, he is assigned the task of promoting an Arab rebellion against Turkish rule after bringing together various tribal factions. To sustain the independent spirit of the Arab revolt, Lawrence (Peter O'Toole) and one of the tribal leaders, Sherif Ali (Omar Sharif) cross the Nefud Desert with a small force supplied by Auda Abu Tayi (Quinn) and capture the Turkish port of Aqaba. During the trek, however, Lawrence is forced to shoot one of his own men to forestall a bloody tribal quarrel, and his realization that he enjoys the act of killing sends him back to Cairo, after taking Aqaba, filled with remorse and self-doubt.

Lawrence is persuaded by General Allenby (Jack Hawkins) to return and fulfill his mission, and, with arms and money, Lawrence emerses himself in a period of triumphant guerrilla warfare, worshiped by his men

As Auda Abu Tayi

and romanticized internationally by Jackson Bentley (Arthur Kennedy), an American journalist. On a scouting mission with Ali into the Turkish-held town of Deraa, Lawrence is captured and tortured by the bey (Jose Ferrer). Broken, he returns to Allenby to request reassignment, but the general sends him back to the desert, telling Lawrence that his leadership is needed for the impending attack on Damascus. Lawrence's assault on a Turkish column becomes a needlessly brutal massacre, but he leads his force into the city, sets up an Arab council to run it and then sees it collapse under tribal divisions. Leaving Allenby and Feisal to hammer out a settlement, Lawrence the idealist finds his role played out, and he returns to England and anonymity.

With Peter O'Toole

With Horst Buchholz

# La Fabuleuse Aventure de Marco Polo
## (Marco the Magnificent)

(Released by Metro-Goldwyn-Mayer as *Marco the Magnificent* in 1966).

Filmed in 1963–4 by Ittac/S.N.C. (Paris), Prodi Cinematografica (Rome), Avala Film (Belgrade), Mounir Rafia (Cairo), Italaf Kaboul (Kabul).*

CAST: *Marco Polo,* HORST BUCHHOLZ; *Kublai Khan,* ANTHONY QUINN; *Emir Alaou,* OMAR SHARIF; *Ackermann,* ORSON WELLES; *Achmed Abdullah,* Gregoire Aslan; *Prince Nayam,* Robert Hossein; *Girl with the Whip,* Elsa Martinelli; *Old Man of the Mountain,* Akim Tamiroff; *Nicolo Polo,* Massimo Girotti; *Spinello,* Folco Lulli; *Princess Gogatine,* Lee Sue Moon; *Guillaume de Tripolis,* Bruno Cremer; *Nicolo de Vicenza,* Jacques Monod; *Matteo Polo,* Mica Orlovic; *Pope Gregory X,* Guido Alberti; *Taha,* Mansoureh Rihai.

CREDITS: *Directors,* Denys de la Patelliere and Noel Howard; *producer,* Raoul Levy; *screenplay,* Raoul

With Horst Buchholz

*Originally begun in 1962 as *L'Echiquier de Dieu* with Alain Delon as Marco Polo under the direction of Christian-Jaque.

With Lee Sue Moon

Polo movie (with Rory Calhoun) being made about the same time. Episodic in nature with an all-star cast, from an almost unrecognizable Orson Welles as Marco's teacher to Omar Sharif as a ladies'-man sheik to a wonderfully absurd Akim Tamiroff as the golden-masked Old Man of the Mountain, and finally to Quinn. Horst Buchholz as Marco Polo is the rather subdued unifying factor, but is virtually written out of the story during the Quinn sequence, in which Kublai Khan is forced to stave off a palace revolt by his own warrior son, Nayam (Robert Hossein), using gunpowder, heretofore employed only in fireworks, to propel bamboo rockets at the rebels. At battle's end, Marco saunters back into view to tell Kublai Khan that the Mongol emperor's message of peace is being duly dispatched to Pope Gregory X and that he (Marco) plans to stay in China. The narrator notes that Marco's visit lasted for seventeen years before returning to Venice to tell of his adventures, which get him thrown into prison.

Levy, Denys de la Patelliere, Jean-Paul Rappeneau and Jacques Remy; *music,* Georges Garvarentz; *art director,* Jacques Saulnier; *camera,* Armand Thirard; *editors,* Jacqueline Thiedot and Noelle Balenci. Eastman Color. Running time: 115 minutes.

In Raoul Levy's financially trouble-plagued, highly improbable Technicolor curiosity which was meant to detail Marco Polo's adventures during his travels to thirteenth-century China, Anthony Quinn turned up for the final two reels, with shaved head, and gave a dignified interpretation of Kublai Khan, possessed of wisdom and understanding as well as a sincere desire for peace. His curious performance, set against elegant sets filled with sumptuously costumed extras, was so alien to the rest of the patchwork film that it might well have been spliced in from some other abortive production. Unfortunately this was the abortive production, a wildly varying combination of costume melodrama and parody epic which *Variety* called "a not-quite-successful tongue-in-cheek affair with undertones of pontifical seriousness." Producer Levy's original version, before he ran out of money, had Christian-Jaque as director and Alain Delon in the leading role. Abandoned, restarted, new director(s), different cast, bits and pieces (apparently) from various versions, off-screen narration to cover inconsistencies: this was the story of the production finally released.

Filmed quite lavishly in France, Italy, Yugoslavia, Egypt and Afghanistan, among other exotic locales, Levy's production hoped to outdazzle another Marco

With Lee Sue Moon and Robert Hossein

With Gregory Peck

# Behold a Pale Horse

Columbia / 1964

CAST: *Manuel Artiguez,* GREGORY PECK; *Captain Vinolas,* ANTHONY QUINN; *Father Francisco,* OMAR SHARIF; *Pilar,* Mildred Dunnock; *Carlos,* Raymond Pellegrin; *Pedro,* Paolo Stoppa; *Rosanna,* Daniela Rocca; *Lt. Zaganar,* Christian Marquand; *Paco Degas,* Marietto Angeletti; *Maria,* Perette Pradier; *Luis,* Zia Mohyeddin; *Teresa,* Rosalie Crutchley; and Mollie Urquhart, Jean-Paul Molinot, Laurence Badie, Martin Benson, Jean-Claude Berck, Claude Berri, Claude Confortes, Michel Lonsdale, Alain Saury, Jose-Luis Vilallonga, Elisabeth Wiener.

CREDITS: *Producer-director,* Fred Zinnemann; *associate producer,* Alexander Trauner; *screenplay,* JP Miller; based on the *novel* "Killing a Mouse on Sunday" by Emeric Pressburger; *music,* Maurice Jarre; *art director,* Auguste Capelier; *camera,* Jean Badal; *editor,* Walter Thompson. Running time: 118 minutes.

Fred Zinnemann's strikingly photographed, strongly acted screen version of Emeric Pressburger's novel of hate, revenge and reprisal in contemporary Spain, stands as a valiant effort unrealized in its execution, failing ultimately because of its overly somber, dramatically thin premise. Another magnetic performance from the

With Daniela Rocca

comfortably dependable Anthony Quinn, as the haughty, venal, whip-toting captain of the Civil Guard who harbors a deathless grudge against an aging Loyalist hero, is not quite enough to inject the needed spark to energate the J P Miller screenplay which lacks both dramatic substance and emotional urgency. In this story which makes no heroic declaration and creates no hero, Quinn's role is totally without a redeeming aspect—even bravery—while the Gregory Peck character of the Loyalist is equally grim and cruel, lightened only by a basic mother-love. Similarily, Omar Sharif's padre, who becomes the peacemaker between the two, is simply boxed in by the script.

The film's title comes from a biblical quotation: "And I looked and behold a pale horse, and his name that sat on him was Death. And hell followed with him" (Revelations 6:8). The opening montage following the printed quotation was borrowed from *Mourir à Madrid (To Die in Madrid)* and conjures up the Spanish Civil War with a raw immediacy, which unfortunately rapidly dissipates as the drama unfolds. The Pressburger story, incidentally, was based on the last, fatal exploit of Francisco Sabater (the character portrayed by the miscast Peck, who is simply not convincingly Spanish), a Loyalist fighter who became a refugee in France and who, as late as the 1960s, organized and led raids into Spain.

Following the Spanish Civil War, guerrilla leader Manuel Artiguez (Peck) goes into exile in France, but continues his harassing raids into Spain from Pau. Two decades later, Paco (Marietto Angeletti), a youngster whose father has been executed by Captain Vinolas (Quinn), the brutal Spanish police chief, is smuggled into Pau to try to persuade Manuel, who had fought with Paco's father, to return across the border to kill Vinolas. Manuel, apathetic after his long struggle, refuses. Then news is brought by a smuggler, Carlos (Raymond Pellegrin), that Manuel's mother Pilar (Mildred Dunnock) is critically ill in a Spanish hospital and

With Gregory Peck and Omar Sharif on the set

has asked to see her son. Unaware that Carlos is in Vinolas's pay, Manuel is determined to risk a visit, but Pilar, dying and knowing that she is being used as bait, begs Father Francisco (Sharif) to warn Manuel to stay away. The priest, after searching his soul, decides that his duty is to God before the State, and delivers the message while on a pilgrimage to Lourdes.

Manuel is distrustful of all priests, but when Paco recognizes Carlos as a traitor, he realizes that Father Francisco is telling the truth and decides to return to Spain anyway. Briefed by Paco, he sneaks into the hospital and finds both Carlos and Vinolas within range of his gunsight. He chooses to kill Carlos first and is shot down by Vinolas's men. Vinolas's triumph is haunted by the question of why, knowing his mother was dead and he was walking into a trap, Manuel had still chosen to return.

With Omar Sharif and Gregory Peck on the set

With Christian Marquand and Omar Sharif

With Ingrid Bergman

# The Visit

20th Century–Fox / 1964

CAST: *Karla Zachanassian*, INGRID BERGMAN; *Serge Miller*, ANTHONY QUINN; *Anya*, Irina Demick; *The Doctor*, Paolo Stoppa; *Captain Dobrik*, Hans-Christian Blech; *Town Painter*, Romolo Valli; *Mathilda Miller*, Valentina Cortese; *Bardrick*, Claude Dauphin; *The Innkeeper*, Eduardo Ciannelli; *Chesco*, Marco Guglielmi; *First Idler*, Lelio Luttazzi; *Cadek*, Dante Maggio; *The Conductor*, Renzo Palmer; *Darvis*, Fausto Tozzi; *The Teacher*, Richard Munch; *The Mayor*, Ernst Schroeder; *The Priest*, Leonard Steckel; *Fisch*, Jacques Dufilho.

CREDITS: *Director*, Bernhard Wicki; *producers*, Julien Derode and Anthony Quinn; *screenplay*, Ben Barzman; based on Maurice Valency's adaptation of the *play* by Friedrich Duerrenmatt; *music*, Hans-Martin Majewski; *art director*, Leon Barsacq; *camera*, Armando Nannuzzi; *editor*, Sam E. Beetley. CinemaScope. Running time: 100 minutes.

Though somewhat softened for the screen, Friedrich Duerrenmatt's shattering drama focusing on the idea than man and justice can be bought, *The Visit*, co-produced by Anthony Quinn, retains much of the play's electricity, despite the sometimes heavy going for the average viewer. Quinn's Serge Miller, leading merchant and council member of a small Central European village, effectively portrays the overconfident former lover who

ends up a broken man, virtually a trapped animal at bay, when his fellow citizens condemn him to death in order to obtain a benefaction from the woman who had left town years before in disgrace and has returned to make this communal decree the precondition of her gift. Ingrid Bergman, as "the richest woman in the world," is superbly malevolent as the lady with power of life and death, coming back to exact vengeance on the man responsible for her life's being loveless.

The drama's original climax was altered for the screen, with the vengeful woman permitting her former lover to go free to avoid the possibility that the townspeople might think him a martyr, but with the knowledge that conscience will plague both him and the people who convicted him. Various opinions have been put forth trying to explain the film's ultimate failure. Among them: Bernhard Wicki's ponderous direction, Ben Barzman's glum script, Ingrid Bergman's too-strident Karla, Anthony Quinn's too-placid Serge—or the very real possibility that everybody simply talked themselves to death. Kate Cameron was perhaps most apt in her New York *Daily News* review: "In writing of the play, John Chapman said it was cut to fit the personalities of the stars [Alfred Lunt and Lynn Fontanne], but in revamping it to the screen, it was not recut for the talents of either Ingrid Bergman or Anthony Quinn."

In this simple parable, Karla Zachanassian (Ingrid

With Ingrid Bergman

With Ingrid Bergman, Ernst Schroeder and Eduardo Ciannelli

Bergman), returns to her home town of Guellen a fabulously wealthy woman after fleeing twenty years earlier pregnant and branded as promiscuous in court by the man who had seduced her, Serge Miller (Quinn). As Guellen is now in a state of financial decay, she offers a million dollars to the town plus an equal amount to be distributed among the inhabitants if Serge, whom she had once loved, is brought to trial and executed. At first the good citizens are aghast and righteously denounce the woman and her demands. Cleverly, however, she forces them to change their minds by offering new automobiles, television sets and other luxuries on credit. Gradually everybody, from Serge's wife Mathilda (Valentina Cortese) to the mayor (Ernst Schroeder) to

police chief Dobrik (Hans-Christian Blech), is in debt so deeply that Serge's death becomes a civic necessity. After forcing fellow member Serge's resignation, the town council reinstates the death penalty. Serge rejects a suggestion that he commit suicide, so he is tried on the twenty-year-old charge of seducing Karla and bribing friends to denounce her as a prostitute, and is condemned to death. Having achieved her revenge, Karla decides that he shall live, but he must remain in Guellen as a reminder of the town's shame. When she leaves, Karla takes with her Anya (Irina Demick), a girl of about the same age as her dead daughter, who is having an affair with the married police chief, and whose life she fears is likely to be a repeat of her own.

With Ingrid Bergman

With Alan Bates

# Zorba the Greek

20th Century-Fox / 1964

CAST: *Alexis Zorba,* ANTHONY QUINN; *Basil,* ALAN BATES; *The Widow,* IRENE PAPAS; *Madame Hortense,* Lila Kedrova; *Mavrandoni,* George Foundas; *Lola,* Elini Anousaki; *Mimithos,* Sotiris Moustakas; *Pavlo,* George Voyadjis; *Soul,* Anna Kyriakou.

CREDITS: *Producer-director,* Michael Cacoyannis; *screenplay,* Michael Cacoyannis; based on the *novel* by Nikos Kazantzakis; *music,* Mikis Theodorakis; *art director,* Vassilis Photopoulos; *camera,* Walter Lassally; *editor,* Michael Cacoyannis. Running time: 142 minutes.

For Anthony Quinn, the summit was what for many actors would be the once-in-a-lifetime role of Alexis Spaghetti (because he's too tall) California (because he's been to America) Epidemic (because he always messes things up) Zorba, the exuberant, knock-about hedonist of indeterminate years. His powerhouse portrayal, which earned him another Oscar nomination and the Best Actor of the Year award from the National Board of Motion Picture Review, remains the one most closely identified with Quinn, although only few notices bothered to mention that he simply was doing here what he'd been doing for much of his career, but in a more

Originally released by International Classics, a subsidiary of 20th Century-Fox, but reissued under the parent corporation after winning three Academy Awards.

spectacular role. *Commonweal* observed: "It's the same role Quinn has been playing for years, and he plays it magnificently whether he is portraying a revolutionary Mexican, a French painter, an Italian carnival strongman, or Barabbas." And *Newsweek* noted: "Quinn's performance is very strong, beefy and spirited . . . but then Quinn, as a bookkeeper in Fithian, Illinois, would be strong, beefy and spirited."

Few critics failed to hop aboard the bandwagon with their extravagant approval of the Quinn characterization. Bosley Crowther called it "a brilliant performance"; Stanley Kauffmann, writing in *The New Republic,* admitted (somewhat begrudgingly) that Quinn "gives the best performance of his career"; and *Time*

With Eleni Anousaki

magazine, long a Quinn supporter, said of his Zorba: "[He] plays him to hellangone. . . . He is the fire of life itself, a piece of the sun in the shape of a man." Quinn's magnificent acting in the title role was matched by the splendid performance of Lila Kedrova, the French actress, who came dreadfully close to stealing the picture from him—and won the Oscar as Best Supporting Actress.

Landing in Greece to check on the potential of a lignite mine he has inherited, Basil (Alan Bates), a British writer, finds that a gregarious old Greek, Alexis Zorba (Quinn), has attached himself to him. Zorba persuades Basil to take him to Crete where the mine is located, and there they quarter in a tiny hotel owned by Madame Hortense (Lila Kedrova), an aging French cocotte, former cabaret dancer, and ex-mistress of four admirals. Zorba pays court to her, helping her relive a bit of the past, while Basil finds himself drawn to a beautiful widow (Irene Papas), who has made herself unapproachable to the other men in the village.

After surveying the mine with Basil and finding it in need of shoring up, Zorba charms a group of local monks into allowing him to take lumber from their mountaintop forest. Zorba then devises an elaborate cable system to bring the wood down to the mine and leaves for the city to obtain the needed equipment. During Zorba's lengthy absence, Basil reassures Madame Hortense with the news that Zorba has promised to marry her on his return. Then overcoming his own shyness, Basil visits the widow and makes love to her. When he is spotted leaving her house, malicious gossip leads one of her secret admirers to commit suicide. Shortly after Zorba's return, the widow is stoned to death by irate villagers as he and Basil watch helplessly. Later, when Madame Hortense becomes ill, Zorba agrees to marry her out of pity, but soon, while at the mine, he hears that she is dying. He rushes to the hotel where the old soubrette dies in his arms as black-garbed village harridans strip her house clean. The philosophical Zorba assures a shocked Basil that this is the way

As Alexis Spaghetti California Epidemic Zorba

of these people. "Life is trouble," Zorba tells him. "Only dead is not."

When Zorba's overhead cable is completed, the villagers gather to witness its inauguration. The tryout turns to disaster when the lift collapses along with all of Zorba's engineering. Alone Zorba and Basil survey the debris. Basil is depressed and broke, but Zorba is untouched by this failure and is only concerned with the joyful continuation of life and its pleasures. At last Basil realizes that his friend is the Life-Force, touched with a bit of madness, perhaps, but strong and full of energy. "Teach me to dance," Basil inveigles Zorba, and amid the destruction of the mine, the two join in a traditional Greek dance, laughing and leaping with abandon.

With Alan Bates

[ 205 ]

With James Coburn

# A High Wind in Jamaica

20th Century–Fox / 1965

CAST: *Juan Chavez,* ANTHONY QUINN; *Zac,* JAMES COBURN; *Rosa,* Lila Kedrova; *Dutch Captain,* Gert Frobe; *Alberto,* Benito Carruthers; *Margaret Fernandez,* Viviane Ventura; *Frederick Thornton,* Nigel Davenport; *Mrs. Thornton,* Isabel Dean; *Captain Marpole,* Kenneth J. Warren; *Emily Thornton,* Deborah Baxter; *John Thornton,* Martin Amis; *Rachel Thornton,* Roberta Tovey; *Edward Thornton,* Jeffrey Chandler; *Laura Thornton,* Karen Flack; *Harry,* Henry Beltran; *Curtis,* Brian Phelan; *The Big One,* Danc Jackson; *The Dancer,* Trader Faulkner; *The Tallyman,* Charles Lawrence; *Little One,* Charles Hyatt; *The Cook,* Kenji Takaki.

CREDITS: *Director,* Alexander Mackendrick; *producer,* John Croyden; *associate producer,* Clifford Parkes; *screenplay,* Stanley Mann, Ronald Harwood and Denis Cannan; based on the *novel* by Richard Hughes; *music,* Larry Adler; *art directors,* John Howell and John Hoesli; *camera,* Douglas Slocombe; *editor,* Derek Yorke. CinemaScope and DeLuxe Color. Running time: 135 minutes.

Quinn returned to swashbuckling for the first time in more than a dozen years in his fourth pirate film, contributing a colorful, deeply grounded performance as Juan Chavez. This screen version of Richard Hughes's 1929 sea story, which had been adapted previously to the Broadway stage in 1943 as *The Innocent Voyage,* faithfully follows the author's original vision of the conflicts between buccaneers' rough mores and the even tougher amorality of children, captured in the tale of a family of British youngsters inadvertently kidnaped by Caribbean pirates in the 1870s. "As the rough-hewn native pirate captain," said *The New York Times'* A. H. Weiler, "Anthony Quinn, in battered cockade hat and tattered clothes, appears to be attempting to parallel his portrayal of Zorba the Greek. But this is a surface characterization in which his feelings for the kids and others only occasionally touch." Playing the hard-as-nails commander, he does manage over the film's rather lengthy 135 minutes to nicely shade his portrayal, changing his attitude from gruff annoyance on first learning that he and his first mate (James Coburn) are seagoing babysitters to paternal affection and finally to resignation about being hanged because of the incriminating testimony of one of his charges. If the more subtle points and nuances of the Hughes novel have been blurred in the transferral to the screen, *A High Wind in Jamaica* remains grand screen adventure robustly told and acted.

With Deborah Baxter

In 1870, after a hurricane destroys their Jamaican home, Frederick (Nigel Davenport) and Mrs. Thornton (Isabel Dean) decide that their five children must be sent to England for an education, feeling that the youngsters' personalities are being affected by primitive pagan beliefs of the islanders. Together with two Creole children, Margaret (Viviane Ventura) and Harry (Henry Beltran), the Thornton youngsters are entrusted to Captain Marpole (Kenneth J. Warren) who is sailing for England. A few days out of port, Marpole's schooner is attacked by a pirate brigantine under the command of Juan Chavez (Quinn), a morose buccaneer who's trying

With James Coburn and Deborah Baxter

to stay ahead of the new steam-powered warships and merchant vessels, and Zac (James Coburn) his first mate.

The children are taken aboard as part of the booty and rapidly adjust to their bizarre new surroundings and soon take to terrorizing the pirates with their madcap pranks, unaware of the reality of their situation. Reaching Tampico, the pirates consult Rosa (Lila Kedrova), madam of a local brothel, hoping to get rid of the children. While there, however, one of the youngsters is accidentally killed, and Rosa forces the crew to put out to sea with the rest of them. Regarding them as evil demons, the crew becomes restive, while Chavez himself becomes more protective, and when Emily Thornton (Deborah Baxter) is injured and needs medical attention, he refuses to let the crew attack a Dutch steamer. The crew stages a mutiny, locks up Chavez, and attacks under Zac's leadership. The Dutch captain (Gert Frobe), begs Emily to set him free, but terrified and unable to understand, she stabs him to death. Only Chavez witnesses this violence, but he resolves never to tell. He and his men are captured by the British navy and brought to trial. Questioned about what really happened, Emily breaks down after incriminating Chavez, who then refuses to betray the information that would destroy the girl. With his crew, Chavez is led away to the gallows.

As Juan Chavez

With players

With Michele Morgan

# Lost Command

Columbia / 1966

CAST: *Lt. Col. Pierre Raspeguy*, ANTHONY QUINN; *Captain Philippe Esclavier*, ALAIN DELON; *Lt. Ben Mahidi*, GEORGE SEGAL; *Countess de Clairefons*, MICHELE MORGAN; *Captain Boisfeuras*, MAURICE RONET; *Aicha*, CLAUDIA CARDINALE; *Ben Saad*, Gregoire Aslan; *General Melies*, Jean Servais; *Merle*, Maurice Sarfati; *Orsini*, Jean-Claude Bercq; *Verte*, Syl Lamont; *Mayor*, Jacques Marin; *DeGuyot*, Jean Paul Moulinot; *Ahmed*, Andreas Monreal; *Dia*, Gordon Heath; *Sapinsky*, Simono; *Fernand*, Rene Havard; *Administration Officer*, Armand Mestral; *Viet Officer*, Burt Kwouk; *Mugnier*, Al Mulock; *Mother Raspeguy*, Marie Burke; *Ibrahim*, Aldo Sanbrell; *Priest*, Jorge Rigaud; *Manuel*, Roberto Robles; *Father Mahidi*, Emilio Carrer; *Mother Mahidi*, Carmen Tarrazo; *Pilot*, Howard Hagan; *Geoffrin*, Mario De Barros; *M. P. Major*, Walter Kelly; *Yusseff*, Robert Sutton; *Arab Customer*, Simon Benzakein; *Bakhti*, Hector Quiroga; *Aged Speaker*, Felix De Pomes.

CREDITS: *Producer-director*, Mark Robson; *asso-* *ciate producer*, John R. Sloan; *screenplay*, Nelson Gidding; based on the *novel* "The Centurions" by Jean Larteguy; *music*, Franz Waxman; *art director*, John Stoll; *camera*, Robert Surtees; *editor*, Dorothy Spencer. Panavision and Pathé Color. Running time: 129 minutes.

With Alain Delon

With Alain Delon

As the leader of a platoon of French paratroopers who survive their country's humiliation and defeat in Southeast Asia only to be sent to rebellious Algeria, Anthony Quinn essays another forceful, independent military officer, who, as "the most convincing personification of sheer male force on the screen today," concluded *Films in Review*, "vivifies this whole film and even influences and alters the acting styles of [his co-stars]." In the role of Lt. Col. Pierre Raspeguy, Quinn plays the gruff, low-born soldier who has risen to field grade because of the attrition of guerrilla warfare in Indochina which decimated the ranks of the French army. *Variety* felt that "as intolerant of professional incompetence in his subordinates as he is of the mannered politics of his superiors, Quinn lends a proper balance of ruthlessness and sensitivity to his performance." Filmed in Spain, this ambitious, all-star production by Mark Robson, somewhat more politically ambiguous than the Jean Larteguy novel on which it was based, probably means to say something about the French colonial wars. Under Nelson Gidding's script, though, this theme is superceded by the idea of the inner feelings of tough, highly trained professional paratroopers whose only life is soldiering, and who are lost without it.

After leading the defeated survivors of his paratroop unit out of Dienbienphu in 1954, Lt. Col. Raspeguy learns that his regiment has been disbanded and he himself relieved of all command. The Countess de Clairefons (Michele Morgan), widow of a general killed in Indochina, has considerable influence with the military, however, and Raspeguy embarks on an affair with her, angling for her to put in a good word. Given a new command, Raspeguy persuades some of his former officers—notably the sensitive Captain Esclavier (Alain Delon) and the brutal Captain Boisfeuras (Maurice Ronet)—to join him, but he is unable to locate Algerian-born Lt. Mahidi (George Segal), unaware that Mahidi had joined the guerrillas of his own country after finding his sister Aicha (Claudia Cardinale) active in the Algerian freedom movement. Raspeguy and his men, sent to "pacify" the Algerians, become increasingly more repressive as opposition mounts, to the point of smashing even the civilian administration. Mahidi, meanwhile, is now in command of the rebel army, which harasses Raspeguy's men while the terrorists plant bombs in the cities.

Eventually Raspeguy uncovers the underground network in which Aicha plays an important role. Esclavier, who has fallen in love with her, unaware of her guerrilla activities, becomes disillusioned and brutally beats her into revealing Mahidi's whereabouts. He passes the information to Raspeguy after extracting a promise that the rebel leader will be taken alive. In a bloody battle, Mahidi's army is destroyed, and Boisfeuras deliberately kills its leader. Raspeguy and his officers are decorated for their actions, but Esclavier quits the regiment and walks away from the ceremonies disheartened, only to see, just around the corner, an Algerian youngster painting on the wall the defiant word "Independence!"

As Lt. Col. Pierre Raspeguy

With Virna Lisi

# The 25th Hour

Metro–Goldwyn–Mayer / 1967

CAST: *Johann Moritz*, ANTHONY QUINN; *Suzanna*, VIRNA LISI; *Defense Counsel*, Michael Redgrave; *Nicolai Dobresco*, Gregoire Aslan; *Strul*, Marcel Dalio; *Traian*, Serge Reggiani; *Captain Brunner*, Drewe Henley; *Photographer*, Paul Maxwell; *Goldenberg*, George Roderich; *Prosecutor*, Alexander Knox; *Joseph Grenier*, Albert Remy; *Madame Nagy*, Françoise Rosay; *War Minister Aide*, Jean Desailly; *Colonel Müller*, Marius Goring; *Magistrate*, John Le Mesurier; *Father Koruga*, Liam Redmond; *Nora*, Henia Suchar; *Sgt.*

*Apostol Constantin*, Jan Werich; *Dr. Nagy*, Harold Goldblatt; *Abramovici*, Meier Tzelniker; *Furrier*, Jacques Marin; *Mrs. Koruga*, Dala Milozevic; *Hurtig*, Victor Startic; *Rosa*, Olga Schoberova; *Marcou*, Stoian Decermic; *Ghitza Jon*, David Sumner; *Usher*, Raoul Delfosse; *Varga*, Kenneth J. Warren.

CREDITS: *Director*, Henri Verneuil; *producer*, Carlo Ponti; *screenplay*, Henri Verneuil, Françoise Boyer and Wolf Mankowitz; *based on the novel* by C. Virgil

Gheorghiu; *art director,* Robert Clavel; *camera,* Andreas Winding; *editor,* Françoise Verneuil. Franscope and Metrocolor. Running time: 133 minutes.

The ever-towering image of Anthony Quinn was used by French director Henri Verneuil on which to mold the character of Johann Moritz in the screen version of C. Virgil Gheorghiu's 1950 novel which traces the odyssey of a Rumanian peasant caught up in war. The actor, essaying a taxing role, strove heroically in another of his virile portrayals, spicing it with the needed warmth and humility wherever possible, but discovered he couldn't carry the entire production under his own momentum. The lengthy, rambling, episodic film, which director Verneuil had envisaged as a tragicomedy, simply was unworkable, even with the injection of a good deal of humor not found in the book. *The 25th Hour* swung freely from farce to tragedy and back to buffoonery, and was saddled with a polyglot of accents by a massive multinational cast. Critical opinion similarly ranged broadly, from Judith Crist's voice-in-the-wilderness rave about Quinn's "magnificent portrayal" to Bosley Crowther's thumbs-down notice that "Mr. Verneuil has directed (or permitted) Anthony Quinn to play the role with such shiftings of attitude and method that in one scene he may seem to be a tortured image of himself in *La Strada* and in another the simpleton brother of *Zorba*

With Albert Remy

*the Greek."* Following a quick three weeks at Radio City Music Hall—the *only* Quinn film to play there, MGM quickly changed its ad campaign from images of a smiling Quinn performing colorful native dances while a lusty Virna Lisi (his wife in the film) stands, arms akimbo and peasant miniskirt hiked nearly to her thighs, invitingly seductive. Still using its same catch line: "A love story that rises above the tides of battle!" the company had its artists change Quinn's grin to a glower and put a submachine gun in his hands while planes are strafing advancing troops. The switch in approaches failed to save this Carlo Ponti epic which all, no doubt, had hoped would rival *Doctor Zhivago.*

In this depiction of the travail of a noble peasant between 1939 and 1947, Johann Moritz (Quinn), a simpleminded farmer, finds himself branded a Jew by Nicolai Dobresco (Gregoire Aslan), the lecherous village police chief on the make for Moritz's wife Suzanna (Virna Lisi). Moritz is dragged off to forced labor on a canal to be used as a defense against the Russians, while Suzanna vainly tries to get her husband released. Failing in the attempt, she is persuaded by Dobresco to sign a paper requesting a divorce so that her farm will be saved from confiscation by the advancing Germans. In a daring escape from the canal project, Moritz manages to cross into Hungary, where he is captured by the police and put to work for the Nazi war effort as a

With Marius Goring

With Marcus Ohrner

prison camp guard. Colonel Müller (Marius Goring) spots Moritz and sees in him the ideal specimen of the heroic Aryan race, making him a figurehead for the cause and circulating his photo as an example of pure Aryan blood.

Unaware that he is being used, Moritz becomes the perfect propaganda foil, and at war's end, he is taken prisoner once again because of the notoriety he had received as a German and is tried as a minor criminal at Nuremberg. A pathetic letter from his wife, read in court by Moritz's counsel (Michael Redgrave), detailing the horrors she had suffered during her husband's eight years' absence, moves the court to free him. Together he and Suzanna face the future as displaced persons.

As Johann Moritz

With Martha Hyer, James Randolph Kuhl, Robert Walker, George Maharis

# The Happening

Horizon Pictures-Columbia / 1967

CAST: *Roc Delmonico,* ANTHONY QUINN; *Taurus,* GEORGE MAHARIS; *Sureshot,* MICHAEL PARKS; *Herby,* ROBERT WALKER; *Monica Delmonico,* MARTHA HYER; *Sandy,* FAYE DUNAWAY; *Fred,* MILTON BERLE; S*am the Tailor,* Oscar Homolka; *Inspector,* Jack Kruschen; *O'Reilly,* Clifton James; *Arnold,* James Randolph Kuhl; *1st Motorcycle Officer,* Eugene Roche; *2nd Motorcycle Officer,* Luke Askew.

CREDITS: *Director,* Eliot Silverstein; *producer,* Jud Kinberg; *screenplay,* Frank R. Pierson, James D. Buchanan and Ronald Austin; *story,* James D. Buchanan and Ronald Austin; *music,* De Vol; *production design,* Richard Day; *art director,* Al Brenner; *camera,* Philip Lathrop; *editor,* Philip Anderson. Technicolor. Running time: 101 minutes.

On paper, *The Happening* apparently looked like a riot, a wacky comedy incorporating teeny-boppers, melodrama, black humor, suspense, farce, and even a Keystone Kops chase. And to direct, Elliot Silverstein who

had turned out the brilliant *Cat Ballou.* Sam Spiegel was talked into putting up the money, and Anthony Quinn signed on as a reformed racketeer gone legit. On screen, however, *The Happening* didn't happen. Why it failed to work and virtually collapsed under misfired sight gags and dud one-liners cannot be pinned down precisely, but the general consensus was that Silverstein tried too often for the offbeat, in addition to casting the film with unfunny people (*i.e.,* actors whose metier definitely is not comedy), with the sole exception of Milton Berle, who alone captured the movie's spirit. Quinn, for all his scowling and gruff charm, appeared ill-at-ease in his interpretation of the onetime Mafioso, now a respectable hotel owner. Perhaps his gangster characterizations had become so ingrained that he was unable to play them for laughs, that his timing was completely off. Or it might have been that his distinctive acting style failed to mesh with the mod performances of George Maharis, Michael Parks, Robert Walker and Faye Dunaway (in her screen debut). "What *are* you kids?" he asks them at one point—and pointedly, "I try to talk and it's like you're out in space or something."

With George Maharis

As Roc Delmonico

"Sam Spiegel," felt Bosley Crowther, "should go off someplace and hang his head. It isn't as long as *Lawrence of Arabia,* and that's the only good thing to be said for it."

Escaping a police raid on an all-night outdoor party, four young Miami beach bums take off in a stolen launch. Looking for kicks, they decide to create a "happening" and chase a youngster who has taken potshots at them with his army toys. They follow the boy into his home where his father Roc Delmonico (Quinn), a wealthy businessman and former Mafioso, thinks they mean to kidnap his wife, Monica (Martha Hyer), or their son, and offers himself as a hostage. The foursome, somewhat confused at first, decide to go along with the caper, and Delmonico even volunteers the use of his car, if they promise safety to his wife and boy.

After driving around greater Miami while the "kidnapers" compromise on a $3,000,000 ranson demand, Delmonico confidently phones his wife to ask her to raise the money. Astounded when she refuses, he then calls his business partner Fred (Milton Berle), who, it turns out, is having an affair with Monica. Then he tries Mafia boss Sam the Tailor (Oscar Homolka), and finally, in desperation, his own mother, who offers only advice like "This too shall pass, if you put your mouth in a smile and get it in gear." Embittered by the knowledge that nobody wants him back, Delmonico wrests the pistol from Taurus (George Maharis), the group's leader, and undertakes his own kidnaping, with an eye toward revenge.

Showing the foursome how a real abduction is pulled off, he fakes his own murder, blackmails his wife, his partner and the Mafia itself into coming up with the money, and then frames Monica and Fred for his "slaying" after organizing his new "mob" into a professional team capable of outwitting the police as well as the syndicate. Then, in a towering gesture of contempt, Delmonico burns the money and walks out on his young partners in crime.

With George Maharis, Michael Parks and Faye Dunaway

[ 215 ]

With Rosanna Schiaffino

# The Rover

Selmur Productions/Cinerama Releasing / 1967

CAST: *Peyrol,* ANTHONY QUINN; *Arlette,* ROS-ANNA SCHIAFFINO; *Caterina,* RITA HAYWORTH; *Real,* RICHARD JOHNSON; *Scevola,* Ivo Garrani; *Dussard,* Mino Doro; *Michel,* Luciano Rossi; *Jacot,* Mirko Valentin; *Lt. Bolt,* Gianni Di Benedetto; *Captain Vincent,* Anthony Dawson; *Summons,* Franco Giornelli; *Admiral,* Franco Fantasia; *Archives Officer,* Fabrizio Jovine; *Captain of the Port,* John Lane; *French Officer,* Vittorio Venturoli; *Sans-Culotte,* Gustave Gionni; *Fisherman,* Lucio De Santis; *Arlette (as a child),* Raffaela Miceli; *1st Girl,* Paola Bossalino; *2nd Girl,* Rita Klein; *3rd Girl,* Cathy Alexander; *Hoodlum,* Ruggiero Salvadori.

CREDITS: *Director,* Terence Young; *producer,* Alfredo Bini; *executive producer,* Selig J. Seligman; *screenplay,* Luciano Vincenzoni and Jo Eisinger; *based on the novel* by Joseph Conrad; *music,* Ennio Morricone; *art director,* Gianni Polidori; *camera,* Leonida Barboni; *editor,* Peter Thornton. Eastman Color. Running time: 103 minutes.

In bringing to the screen Joseph Conrad's colorful adventure set against the infamous Reign of Terror in eighteenth century France, the producers found themselves shackled by many of the same problems which beset thirteen previous attempts to capture Conrad on film: the inability to get inside his characters or to find the significance inbred in his preoccupation with philosophical and moral issues. Even taken as straight costume drama steeped in murder and intrigue, *The Rover* remained cloaked in dark shadows which even a somber Anthony Quinn and his old *Blood and Sand* dancing partner, Rita Hayworth, were unable to enlighten. In the film version of the 1923 Conrad classic, a study of the ingredients of heroism which can elevate or destroy a man, Quinn is the tough old pirate Peyrol, an adventurer who has spent a lifetime searching for a place to hang his hat. *The Rover* was filmed in and around Rome in late 1966, but received only limited release and remains one of the least-seen Anthony Quinn movies since the actor moved out of Hollywood's "B" units.

Running the English blockade of Toulon, the stronghold of the Republican fleet, Peyrol (Quinn) and his crew sail the *Maria Galante* into the harbor, where they immediately are arrested. Peyrol is interrogated about a shipment of gold bullion and is branded a deserter and accused of piracy. Managing to escape, he makes his way to an isolated spot near the coast, where he rescues

As Peyrol

With Rita Hayworth

With Rita Hayworth

a deranged girl, Arlette (Rosanna Schiaffino), from a mob of bloodthirsty revolutionaries. He accepts her offer to stay at the house she shares with her Aunt Caterina (Rita Hayworth) and soon begins falling in love with Arlette. Venturing out from this base sometime later with Arlette, Peyrol stumbles upon an old, abandoned tartan and, investigating, discovers bloodstains and a broken doll, the sight of which causes Arlette to faint. Unable to learn what is disturbing the girl, Peyrol takes her back to Caterina's house, where a French naval officer, Real (Richard Johnson), is waiting.

Real soon learns that Peyrol is being sought by the police and suggests that he leave as a decoy to draw the British fleet away from Toulon's harbor entrance. Peyrol agrees on the condition that Real also goes along. Arlette, who has fallen in love with Real, insists that she be allowed to accompany them, but Peyrol, finally aware that her interest in him was out of gratitude, uses a ruse to slip off alone with Real's ship. Maneuvering deftly, Peyrol outruns a pursuing English corvette, but is finally apprehended by a man-of-war after breaking the blockade. As the French fleet sails into the harbor, Peyrol takes a volley broadside and, choosing to go down with his ship, emotionally salutes the British who have tried to capture him.

With Rosanna Schiaffino

With Anjanette Comer

# Guns for San Sebastian

Metro–Goldwyn–Mayer / 1968

CAST: *Leon Alastray,* ANTHONY QUINN; *Kinita,* ANJANETTE COMER; *Teclo,* CHARLES BRONSON; *Father Joseph,* Sam Jaffe; *Felicia,* Silvia Pinal; *Cayetano,* Jorge Martinez De Hoyos; *Golden Lance,* Jaime Fernandez; *Agueda,* Rosa Furman; *Pedro,* Jorge Russek; *Vicar General,* Leon Askin; *Antonito,* Jose Chavez; *Colonel Calleja,* Ivan Desny; *Governor,* Fernand Gravey; *Father Lukas,* Pedro Armendariz, Jr.; *Magdalena,* Aurora Clavel; *Diego,* Julio Aldama; *Luis,* Ferrusquilla; *Kino,* Pancho Cordova; *Renaldo,* Enrique Lucero; *Miguel,* Chano Urueta; *Captain Lopez,* Noe Murayama; *Timoteo,* Guillermo Hernandez; *Bishop,* Francisco Reiguera; *Pablo,* Carlos Berriochea; *Pascual,* Armando Acosta; *Villager,* Guy Fox; *Villager,* Rico Lopez.

CREDITS: *Director,* Henri Verneuil; *producer,* Jacques Bar; *screenplay,* James R. Webb; based on the *novel* "A Wall for San Sebastian" by William Barby Flaherty, S.J.; *music,* Ennio Morricone; *art directors,* Robert Clavel and Roberto Silva; *camera,* Armand Thirard; *editor,* Françoise Bonnot. Franscope and Metrocolor. Running time: 111 minutes.

In this apocryphal tale about the legendary eighteenth-century Mexican bandit-patriot, Leon Alastray, Anthony Quinn carries, with single-handed dedication, the forward movement of director Henri Verneuil's lengthy, sporadically exciting, French-Italian-Mexican-made action drama. Bullishly forging onward as an outlaw taken for a priest who rallies an entire village against Spanish invaders, Yaqui Indians and constantly maurauding bandits, the actor demonstrates his creativity with yet another skillful, multi-faceted characterization despite the nonsense occurring around him, and, as *Variety* noted, "the multiplicity of banal dialogue to fit lip movements." (The film, needless to mention, is dubbed.) Quinn's spirited impersonation of Alastray in relation-

With Silvia Pinal and Fernand Gravey

ship to the roster of screen caricatures in *Guns for San Sebastian* affirms the admiration continually being expressed for his always interesting performance, as expected, whatever the merits of the film.

Pursued by government troops in Mexico, 1746, rebel Leon Alastray (Quinn) is given sanctuary by Father Joseph (Sam Jaffe), an old Franciscan priest, whom he finds wounded in his small church. Punished for his obstinacy in refusing to release Alastray, the priest is sent to the remote village of San Sebastian, taking the bandit with him disguised as a monk. After a long journey across the desert, they reach the village which they find empty, following a Yaqui raid. The townspeople are hiding in the hills, and only a girl, Kinita (Anjanette Comer), is there to welcome them. Father Joseph is felled by a sniper's bullet, and Alastray, still wearing the priest's cowl, is mistaken for the new padre by Teclo (Charles Bronson), a half-breed who rides with the Indians, and is strung up from a tree.

When the villagers return, Teclo warns them that the Yaquis will continue to harass them unless they give up their faith. The townspeople, however, free Alastray and welcome him as their spiritual leader; he reluctantly accepts his new role. He begins by supervising the

As Leon Alastray

As Leon Alastray

building of a dam for crop irrigation—a project which the Yaquis immediately sabotage. When the Indians attack, Alastray leaves the village, and through the intercession of his former mistress Felicia (Silvia Pinal), now the wife of the local governor, he secures guns and ammunition for San Sebastian. Returning to the village, he prods the people into rebuilding the dam and adding a defensive wall. (Ed. note: the novel which was the source for this film was entitled *A Wall for San Sebastian.*)

A new Yaqui attack, led by Teclo and Chief Golden Lance (Jaime Fernandez), is repelled and the Indians are overwhelmed when Alastray dynamites the dam. Teclo and Golden Lance are killed and the assault is thwarted. When the bishop arrives for a mass of thanksgiving, he is accompanied by government troops. One of the captains, bragging of his adventures to the good "priest," recognizes him as the rebel and orders his arrest. Through a ruse, Alastray once again outwits the soldiers and, accompanied by Kinita, who had known from the first that he was not a priest, rides away from San Sebastian.

As Leon Alastray

With Laurence Olivier

# The Shoes of the Fisherman

Metro–Goldwyn–Mayer / 1968

CAST: *Kiril Lakota*, ANTHONY QUINN; *Piotr Ilyich Kamenev*, LAURENCE OLIVIER; *Father David Telemond*, OSKAR WERNER; *George Faber*, DAVID JANSSEN; *Cardinal Rinaldi*, Vittorio De Sica; *Cardinal Leone*, Leo McKern; *The Elder Pope*, John Gielgud; *Dr. Ruth Faber*, Barbara Jefford; *Chiara*, Rosemarie Dexter; *Igor Bounin*, Frank Finlay; *Chairman Peng*, Burt Kwouk; *Gelasio*, Arnoldo Foa; *Augustin*, Paul Rogers; *Gorshenin*, George Pravda; *Vucovich*, Clive Revill; *Capuchin Monk*, Niall MacGinnis; *Cardinal Rahamani*, Marne Maitland; *The Marchesa*, Isa Miranda; *Brian*, George Harper; *Dying Man's Friend*, Leopoldo Trieste; *Dominican*, Jean Rougeul; *English Cardinals*, Peter Copley and Arthur Howard.

CREDITS: *Director*, Michael Anderson; *producer*, George Englund; *screenplay*, John Patrick and James Kennaway; based on the *novel* by Morris West; *music*, Alex North; *art directors*, George W. Davis and Edward Carfagno; *camera*, Erwin Hiller; *editor*, Ernest Walter. Panavision and Metrocolor. Running time: 162 minutes.

Of Quinn's later roles, his most famous characterization after Alexis Zorba and Mountain Rivera is Pope Kiril I, the futuristic (1980s) pontiff of Russian extraction who would strip the Roman Catholic Church of its material wealth to forestall a nuclear catastrophe. His superb, human characterization of Kiril at the head of a strong international cast and topical script was blunted, however, by occasionally awkward plot structure, an inane subplot on the level of daytime TV soap opera, and too-leisurely pacing as director Michael Anderson stressed the vast panoramas of St. Peter's Square and lavish reproduction of the Cathedral and the Vatican while his high-priced cast stood in the foreground talking. *Time* magazine spoke of Quinn as "the Pope of Zorbaesque strength, simplicity and rectitude," while applauding his "solid, intelligent performance." Renata Adler, however, considered in her review in *The New York Times* that casting Quinn as pope was "an inspiration comparable to casting Yogi Berra as an Irish Faust, and his accents, like those of many other characters, keep casting doubt on what his national origin is."

The basic premise of Morris West's novel is that a Catholic priest, sentenced to hard labor in Siberia, is suddenly reprieved by a pragmatic Russian premier (played by Laurence Olivier) and dispatched to Rome so that Russia will have a friend in the papal court should China rise against her. The premier does not count on the fact, of course, that the priest will be

As Pope Kiril I

As Pope Kiril I

With Burt Kwouk and Laurence Olivier

With Vittorio De Sica

elected pope and, in the hope of international amity, will pledge the riches of the church to feed the hungry of the world, including China.

Woven throughout these pertinent political and religious considerations are several subplots, one of which includes a romantic triangle with a television reporter (David Janssen), his doctor wife (Barbara Jefford) and the Italian girlfriend (Rosemarie Dexter) who won't let him go. Quinn, as pope, is dragged into this when, sneaking out of the Vatican to mingle anonymously with the citizens *(Time* noted that "it comes straight out of *Roman Holiday,* with Quinn playing the Audrey Hepburn part"), he accidentally encounters the doctor and helps her solve her marital problems while they are both attending a dying Jew.

A second subplot, this one of more dramatic interest, deals with a young heretic (Oskar Werner), whose advanced theological positions and writings come under the investigation of a pontifical commission. Bitterly accepting his gagging by the Church hierarchy, he makes his way to the chambers of his friend, Pope Kiril, in whose arms he dies after being stricken with a cerebral hemorrhage.

The National Board of Review of Motion Pictures chose *The Shoes of the Fisherman* as the best movie of 1968, and Henry Hart, in his critique of it in *Films in Review,* judged that "Anthony Quinn plays the political prisoner who becomes pope and does so without any of the animal vitality that has been his stock-in-trade. He seems in awe of his role, and his mien is unctuous. The effect is devoid of the strong humanity he—of all actors— could have projected had he not adopted the idea of the papacy that prevails in the humbler Roman Catholic parishes."

With Michael Caine

# The Magus

20th Century–Fox / 1968

CAST: *Maurice Conchis,* ANTHONY QUINN; *Nicholas Urfe,* MICHAEL CAINE; *Lily,* CANDICE BERGEN; *Anne,* Anna Karina; *Meli,* Paul Stassino; *Anton,* Julian Glover; *Kapetan,* Takis Emmanuel; *The Priest,* George Pastell; *Soula,* Danielle Noel; *German Officer,* Jerome Willis; *Maria,* Ethel Farrugia; *Goatherd,* Andreas Malandrinos; *Captain Wimmel,* Corin Redgrave; *2nd Partisan,* George Kafkaris; *Party Host,* Anthony Newlands; *3rd Partisan,* Stack Constantino; *Young Conchis,* Roger Lloyd Pack.

CREDITS: *Director,* Guy Green; *producers,* John Kohn and Jud Kinberg; *screenplay,* John Fowles; based on his *novel; music,* John Dankworth; *art director,* William Hutchinson; *camera,* Billy Williams; *editor,* Max Benedict. DeLuxe Color. Running time: 116 minutes.

In the role of Maurice Conchis, Anthony Quinn had an impossible assignment, as did his co-stars, Michael Caine, Candice Bergen and Anna Karina, all of whom were required, it seems, to look simultaneously profound and puzzling while pretending they actually understood what was happening. The screen version of John Fowles's dazzling and enigmatic 1966 best-seller was completely undecipherable, with the characters enmeshed in some weird game of love and death that may or may not be taking place. Visual splendor and ornate settings notwithstanding, this mind-boggling puzzle with no solution must be considered unfilmable.

Quinn, as a balding, white-maned, larger-than-life intellectual wizard, appears at first to be a rich recluse living in an opulent Greek villa. Suddenly he is a psychiatrist, then a creature with psychic powers, then a

With Michael Caine

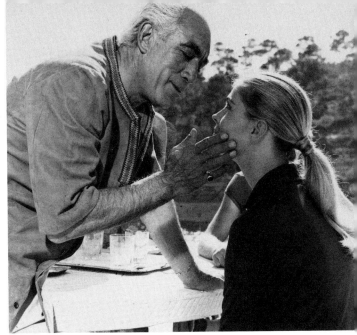

With Candice Bergen

film producer, then the mayor of a Greek village during the Nazi occupation, next a sorcerer—each time with some abstract authority over several people. "As played by Anthony Quinn," said Kathleen Carroll in the New York *Daily News,* "he manages to be about as frightening as a pin prick and only vaguely interesting. It's not Quinn's fault. He tries, but he's still Anthony Quinn, with bronzed face, coal-blacked eyebrows and a Picasso mane."

When Nicholas Urfe (Michael Caine) arrives on the island of Phraxos to teach English at a boys' school, he is still haunted by the memory of Anne (Anna Karina), a lovely airline hostess he had abandoned in London. Soon bored with his lonely life, he begins to explore the desolate island and wanders onto the hilltop estate of wealthy Maurice Conchis (Quinn), something of a magician. Fascinated by the remote retreat, Nicho-

las accepts Conchis's invitation to be his weekend guest and is intrigued by what appears at first to be the ghost of Conchis's girlfriend, Lily (Candice Bergen), who was reported to have died of typhoid during World War I. Subsequent visits to the villa prove, though, that Lily is very much alive, and Conchis revises his explanation— he is actually a psychiatrist and Lily is Julie Holmes, a schizophrenic patient. Lily confirms this, but insists that she is an actress, summoned by Conchis, a film director, to appear in an improvisational movie in which Nicholas evidently also is a participant.

When Anne suddenly turns up on the island between flights, she and Nicholas renew briefly their amorous relationship, but she finds him strangely preoccupied with the elusive Lily and the secretive Conchis. Subsequently Nicholas learns that Anne has committed suicide and tries to blame Conchis. Suddenly the confused teacher finds himself caught up in a conflict between World War II Germans and Greek partisans, and Conchis admits that the villa is a theater designed to help people come to terms with themselves. He then relates a wartime experience when, as the village mayor, he was put in the position of having to execute three hostages personally or let eighty hostages die, and having refused to choose, was left as the only survivor and branded a traitor.

After a final charade which points up his failure as a human being, Nicholas suddenly wakes up in Athens. Returning to Phraxos, he catches a glimpse of Anne, as she disappears in a boat, obviously alive, and slowly realizes he has been the puppet of Conchis, the spiritual hedonist playing God. (The film, at one point in its production, had been entitled *The God Game.)*

With Takis Emanuel (center) and
Jerome Willis

With Anna Magnani

# The Secret of Santa Vittoria

United Artists / 1969

CAST: *Italo Bombolini,* ANTHONY QUINN; *Rosa Bombolini,* ANNA MAGNANI; *Caterina Malatesta,* VIRNA LISI; *Sepp Von Prum,* HARDY KRUGER; *Tufa,* SERGIO FRANCHI; *Babbaluche,* Renato Rascel; *Fabio,* Giancarlo Giannini; *Angela,* Patrizia Valturri; *Gabriella,* Valentina Cortese; *Luigi Lunghetti,* Eduardo Ciannelli; *Vittorini,* Leopoldo Trieste; *Padre Polenta,* Gigi Ballista; *Copa,* Quinto Parmeggiani; *Giovanni Pietrosanto,* Carlo Caprioli; *Francocci,* Francesco Mule; *Sergeant Zopf,* Wolfgang Jansen; *Old Vines,* Aldo De Carellis; *Mazzola,* Marco Tulli; *Corporal Heinsick,* Chris Anders; *Sergeant Traub,* Peter Kuiper; *Hans,* Dieter Wilken; *Otto,* Karl Otto Alberty; *Benedetti,* Gigi Bonos; *Julietta,* Clelia Matania; *Pulci,* Pippo Lauricella; *Capoferro,* Carlo Capannelle; *Bracolini,* Renato Chiantoni; *Dr. Bara,* Pino Ferrara; *Colonel Scheer,* Curt Lowens; *Private Holtzmann,* Tim Donnelly.

CREDITS: *Producer-director,* Stanley Kramer; *associate producer,* George Glass; *screenplay,* William Rose and Ben Maddow; *based on the novel* by Robert Crichton; *music,* Ernest Gold; *art director,* Robert Clatworthy; *camera,* Giuseppe Rotunno; *editor,* William Lyon. Panavision and Technicolor. Running time: 140 minutes.

Anthony Quinn's tireless quest for variety and depth in his roles can be best exemplified simply by placing side by side his characterizations of the humble, esthetic Pope Kiril and the bumbling, drunken Italo Bombolini—pious pontification to pie-in-the-face, pasta-on-the-head burlesque, punctuated by flying chamber pots and well-aimed rolling pins. Indulging himself with gusto, Quinn offered an hilarious, all-stops-out performance opposite his old friend, Anna Magnani, in her first—and last—American-produced movie since *The Fugitive Kind* a decade earlier. His interpretation of the town sot-turned-hero, a variation on the earthy, life-loving characterization for which he is best known, failed to enthuse most critics, who were becoming more vocal in their suggestions that he take out a patent on the role.

Stanley Kramer made the film in the summer of 1968 in the tiny Italian town of Anticoli Corrado and spent about $5,500,000 on it. Some of the reasons for its failure might be summed up in Vincent Canby's *New York Times* critique, in which he called it "a big, square, mechanical film [which] probably won't offend anyone, except perhaps a few movie critics who prefer their Italian films made by Italians, rather than by Americans who can purchase landscapes and faces but not good movies." Overviews of Quinn's work ran the critical gamut. At one end of the scale, for instance, was the *Variety* opinion that "he performs superbly . . . delivering a finely shaded study of a man obsessed with a great and enduring responsibility," and concluding that he gives "one of the top characterizations of his career." On the other hand, *Motion Picture Herald* found his performance "flamboyant and raucous in an outrageously hammy manner heretofore the province on the screen of the late Charles Laughton. There hasn't been so much shoulder-shrugging, eyeball-rolling and hand gesticulating by one actor in one film in years. Whatever his salary, Quinn certainly earned it." Joseph Morgenstern, in *Newsweek,* chided producer-director Kramer for "turning Anthony Quinn into a *boobus Italianus* of stupefying grossness, a Popeye to Anna Magnani's Olive Oyl," and thought that Quinn "plays the part so broadly that he vitiates those few moments in which broadness might have been a genuinely welcome surprise."

News of Mussolini's death is greeted by the villagers of Santa Vittoria as a chance to humiliate the local fascists. When Italo Bombolini (Quinn), the local wine-

As Italo Bombolini

seller, paints out an old fascist slogan which he himself had originally inscribed, the townsfolk's cheers win him the post of mayor. His aspiring son-in-law Fabio (Giancarlo Giannini), however, brings word that the Germans intend to occupy the village and commandeer the wine which constitutes its wealth. The news affects everybody, including the local contessa, Caterina Malatesta (Virna Lisi), and her peasant lover, Tufa (Sergio Franchi), who has deserted the crumbling Italian army and has returned home in despair. Bombolini and his shrewish wife Rosa (Anna Magnani) hit upon an elaborate scheme and enlist the entire town as a bucket brigade to conceal a million bottles of wine in the tunnels of an old cave outside of town. When German commander Sepp von Prum (Hardy Kruger) arrives, it becomes a

With Anna Magnani and Leopoldo Trieste

With Patrizia Valturri

battle of wits for the possession of the wine. Von Prum is distracted in his search by Bombolini's protests of ignorance and by the contessa's obvious charms. Driven to demand hostages, von Prum unwittingly tortures two fascists, released for the purpose by Bombolini. Then the German threatens to shoot Tufa, but the contessa offers to spend the night with von Prum in return for Tufa's life. Beaten, von Prum orders his men out of the village, as the triumphant Bombolini presents him with a bottle of wine.

As Italo Bombolini

With Anna Magnani

With Inger Stevens

# A Dream of Kings

National General / 1969

CAST: *Matsoukas,* ANTHONY QUINN; *Calliope,* IRENE PAPAS; *Anna,* INGER STEVENS; *Cicero,* Sam Levene; *Fatsas,* Val Avery; *Mother-in-Law,* Tamara Daykarhanova; *Falconis,* Peter Mamakos; *Doctor,* James Dobson; *Zenoitis,* Zvee Scooler; *Kampana,* Bill Walker; *Turk,* H. B. Haggerty; *Fig King,* Alan Reed Sr.; *Stavros,* Radames Pera; *Himself,* Theoharis Lemonopoulos; *Falconis's Daughter,* Stasa Damascus; *Mrs. Cournos,* Katherine Theodore; *Tony,* James Fortunes; *Toundas,* Ernest Sarracino; *Mrs. Falconis,* Renata Vanni; *Telecles,* Chris Marks; *Faith,* Sandra Damato; *Hope,* Effie Columbus; *Angelo,* Peter Kogeones.

CREDITS: *Director,* Daniel Mann; *producer,* Jules Schermer; *associate producer,* Harry Mark Petrakis; *screenplay,* Harry Mark Petrakis and Ian Hunter, based on the *novel* by Harry Mark Petrakis; *music,* Alex North; *art director,* Boris Leven; *camera,* Richard H. Kline; *editors,* Walter Hannemann and Ray Daniels. Technicolor. Running time: 107 minutes.

In reviewing *A Dream of Kings,* the critic for *Variety* began his notice: "It stars Anthony Quinn once again portraying super-mensch, the noble ethnic, and it is one of his most powerful and convincing performances." Limning Matsoukas, the robust, expansive rascal who makes a hand-to-mouth living in the Greek sector of Chicago as a small-time gambler, counselor of young boys and uplifter of old men, and, from his shabby office, dispenses "wisdom-inspiration-wrestling instruction," Quinn created another earthy portrait in what is virtually a one-man show. In the moving adaptation of Harry Mark Petrakis's sentimental story of a Greek-American father whose blind obsession is that he can save his only son, suffering from a fatal disease, simply by taking him to the land of his hardy ancestors, Quinn is in just about every scene, demonstrating nearly every facet of the art of acting. The majority of critical opinion was in his corner. Rex Reed, in *Holiday,* called the film "A tour de force by Anthony Quinn. His performance is hypnotic," and William Wolf, critic for *Cue* magazine, raved: "Anthony Quinn at peak talent—he is such a damned effective actor and beautiful man that his performance towers!"

The basic weakness of the film, though, lies in the script by Petrakis and Ian Hunter, who never really allow the audience to know Matsoukas, despite Quinn's electric personality and flamboyant portrayal, after living with the man for every minute of nearly two hours. Nor is there an explanation for the godlike stature his comrades have given him.

Of note: this was Quinn's first American-made movie since *The Happening* and his fourth with Irene Papas. It also marked the final screen appearance of

As Matsoukas

Inger Stevens, who committed suicide shortly thereafter.

Matsoukas, a vital, lusty and extremely improvident member of Chicago's Greek-American community who leads a happy-go-lucky existence, gambles away what little money he earns from his Master Counseling Service in all-night poker sessions, in preparation for the usual bitter invectives and scolding from his harridan wife

With Radames Pera

Calliope (Irene Papas). His lightheartedness ebbs, however, when he has to face his invalid son, Stavros (Radames Pera), whom he deeply loves and promises to take to the mountains of Greece, where fresh air and sunshine will cure the boy's unnamed illness. Learning at last that Stavros has not long to live, Matsoukas is shaken but refuses to accept the idea that the twelve-year-old boy is dying. Matsoukas seeks solace with Anna (Inger Stevens), a ripe young widow who owns a thriving neighborhood bakery shop, and melts the coldness in her heart since her husband's death under his frank advances and passionate seduction.

The following Sunday, Stavros suffers a frightening attack at church, and Matsoukas becomes convinced that the boy must be taken to Greece. That evening, following a christening party, Matsoukas's good friend Cicero (Sam Levene) offers him the money for the trip and insists that he meet him at the bank the next day. The morning finds Matsoukas waiting for Cicero, only to discover that his friend had suffered a heart attack and is dying. Matsoukas then approaches Anna for money, unsuccessfully, and in desperation betrays a lifelong principle and gambles with loaded dice. Discovered and disgraced, he allows himself to be beaten up by the bouncer and returns home shattered. Calliope, however, steals the money from her mother and shoves the roll of bills into her husband's hand. Then, with Stavros in his arms, Matsoukas gives Calliope a last long look and rushes to the airport for the flight to Athens.

With Alan Reed

With Ingrid Bergman

# A Walk in the Spring Rain

Columbia / 1970

CAST: *Will Cade,* ANTHONY QUINN; *Libby Meredith,* INGRID BERGMAN; *Roger Meredith,* Fritz Weaver; *Ellen,* Katherine Crawford; *Boy,* Tom Fielding; *Ann Cade,* Virginia Gregg; *Bucky,* Mitchell Silberman.

CREDITS: *Director,* Guy Green; *producer,* Stirling Silliphant; *screenplay,* Stirling Silliphant; based on the *novella* by Rachel Maddux; *music,* Elmer Bernstein; *title song,* Elmer Bernstein and Don Black; *art director,* Malcolm C. Bert; *camera,* Charles B. Lang; *editor,* Ferris Webster. Panavision and Technicolor. Running time: 98 minutes.

The two major pluses *A Walk in the Spring Rain* had going for it in the face of its afternoon soap opera theme were its two consummate lead performers and the fact that in the wake of the plethora of youth-oriented films of the late 1960s and 1970s, this movie celebrates the right of people over forty to enjoy life.

In spite of his versatility as an actor and acknowledged ability to inject vitality into any role he's handed, Anthony Quinn simply was miscast as a hearty, sweet-tempered Tennessee mountaineer, able to sexually re-awaken a genteel sophisticate from New York. "Quinn, the most passionate lover in his age class in films today," thought the critic for *Motion Picture Herald,* "gives his most restrained performance in ages, and as a result, it is one of his best ever." That critique represented the proverbial voice in the wilderness, with *Time* sniping that "Anthony Quinn's ersatz Tennessee accent makes him seem the subject of the Scopes trial," and *Variety* deciding that the actor is "the only Spanish-descendant, Zorba-like hillbilly you'll see on the screen this year." More to the point was Archer Winsten's feeling in his review in the *New York Post:* "Anthony Quinn and Ingrid Bergman are left out there wrestling with a script they can't quite make human and habitable."

Of passing interest is the billing in this film: Quinn received first billing on the left and Ingrid Bergman was on the right but slightly higher (a fairly recent ploy in the "billing war" which, it turns out, is of more impor-

With Ingrid Bergman and Tom Fielding on the set

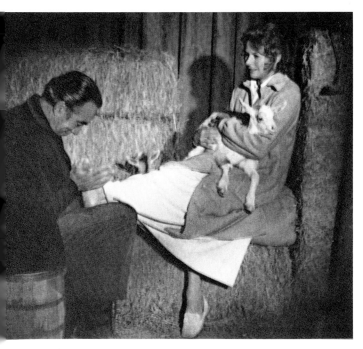

With Ingrid Bergman

tance to actors' managers than to actors). Quinn, incidentally, had taken second billing to Miss Bergman in their previous film together, *The Visit.*

Happily alive to the world around her, Libby Meredith (Ingrid Bergman) slips comfortably into middle age when she and her professor-husband Roger (Fritz Weaver) spend his sabbatical year in the Great Smoky Mountains of Tennessee, where he plans to write a book. Their nearest neighbor, Will Cade (Quinn), with a silent wife (Virginia Gregg) and a son Boy (Tom

Fielding), who envies and hates him, is embarrassingly eager to show his urban friends the pleasures of pastoral life, introducing Libby and Roger to his world of animals, plants and seasons. Will rapidly becomes attracted to Libby and she is surprised to realize after a time that, in her growing loneliness, she finds his attentions welcome.

When her daughter Ellen (Katherine Crawford) asks her to return home to help care for her grandson, the newly awakened Libby bluntly refuses because she is now totally absorbed in the life of the countryside and in her feeling for Will. One day, however, Boy makes a drunken attempt to molest Libby and is knocked down by his father. Boy dies when his head strikes the fender of Will's jeep. Shattered by his son's death, Will turns all the more to Libby, but she is shocked out of her dream and has Roger take her back to New York, where she can care for her little grandson. The lovers are left with their memories, with Libby recalling hers during a walk in the spring rain.

With Tom Fielding and Ingrid Bergman

With Ann-Margret

# R.P.M.*
## (*Revolutions Per Minute)

Columbia / 1970

CAST: *F.W.J. "Paco" Perez,* ANTHONY QUINN; *Rhoda,* ANN-MARGRET; *Rossiter,* GARY LOCKWOOD; *Steve Dempsey,* Paul Winfield; *Henry Thatcher,* Graham Jarvis; *Hewlett,* Alan Hewitt; *Brown,* Ramon Bieri; *Rev. Blauvelt,* John McLiam; *Dean Cooper,* Don Keefer; *Perry Howard,* Donald Moffat; *Coach McCurdy,* Norman Burton; *President Tyler,* John Zaremba; *Estella,* Inez Pedroza; *Students,* Teda Bracci, Linda Meiklejohn, Bruce Fleischer, David Ladd, John David Wilder, Bradjose, Raymond Cavaleri, Henry Brown, Jr., Frank Alesia and Robert Carricart, Jr.

CREDITS: *Producer-director,* Stanley Kramer; *associate producer,* George Glass; *screenplay,* Erich Segal; *music,* Barry DeVorzon and Perry Botkin Jr.; *songs sung by* Melanie; *art director,* Robert Clatworthy; *camera,* Michel Hugo; *editor,* William A. Lyon. Eastman Color. Running time: 90 minutes.

Quinn's second Stanley Kramer movie found him cast as, in *Newsweek*'s words, "a well-known scholar and swinger who owns a motorcycle and a mistress," playing concerned sociology professor Paco Perez, who suddenly finds the college presidency thrust upon him. Shot in Stockton, California, in late 1969, *R.P.M.* marked Kramer's reentry into contemporary sociology, but whatever impact it might have had among the spate of campus crisis movies then popular was completely dissipated in the length of time before it went into release. By then the market had been saturated by similarly themed films, such as *Getting Straight* and *The Strawberry Statement.* Quinn gives it the old college try as the faculty liberal trying to be one of the guys to his students, but finds at crunch time he has to call in the fuzz. The headline to Ann Guarino's review in the New York *Daily News* said it all: "Quinn A Dirty Old Man in College Rebel Movie," while Vincent Canby, in *The New York Times,* noted that the film dealt with "one of the gut questions of our time. Should Ann-Margret continue to sleep with Anthony Quinn, her bleeding-heart

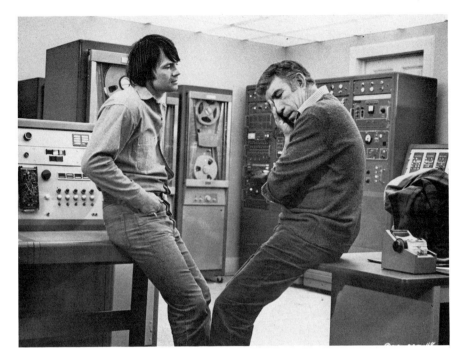

With Gary Lockwood

liberal of a professor, after he becomes acting college president and sends the pigs in to clear out the administration building?"

The film's title, meaning "Revolutions Per Minute," stands in this case for turmoil rather than speed—but only if speed referred to quickness, which *R.P.M.* sorely lacked.

After the administration building of Hudson University is taken over by dissident students led by Rossiter (Gary Lockwood) and Dempsey (Paul Winfield), the college's ineffective president, Chancellor Tyler (John Zaremba), is forced to resign. The trustees call upon Professor F.W.J. "Paco" Perez (Quinn), a fifty-three-year-old professor from Spanish Harlem, to take over and deal with the militants, after first getting him out of the bed he's sharing with one of his graduate students, Rhoda (Ann-Margret). Since the students trust Perez and his nonconformist attitude, he easily gains their confidence in his new role as acting president and, in a meeting with Rossiter, the hard-core revolu-

As "Paco" Perez

With Ann-Margret

tionary, and Dempsey, the black militant leader, he receives a list of twelve demands the demonstrators have drawn up. Perez gets the college board to approve nine, but the last three, giving the students a voice in choosing teachers and curriculum, are rejected.

Rossiter remains adamant, even admitting that when these dozen are accepted there would be more demands, and the militants threaten to destroy a $2,000,000 computer. With the lines drawn, Perez has difficulty holding off the trustees who allow the police chief, Henry Thatcher (Graham Jarvis), to mobilize his forces and prepare for an assault on the building. Perez then raps once more with the militants in a final effort to get them to end their sit-in and abandon their threats of destruction. Feeling that Perez has joined the establishment, Rossiter and his fellow rebels begin taunting him about his sexual prowess, and this turns the tide. Perez merely backs off and allows Thatcher and his men to storm the building. A riot ensues, and Perez, once cheered, is booed as he turns his back on the situation.

With Ann-Margret

With Shelley Winters

# Flap

Warner Bros. / 1970

CAST: *Flapping Eagle,* ANTHONY QUINN; *Lobo Jackson,* Claude Akins; *Eleven Snowflake,* Tony Bill; *Dorothy Bluebell,* Shelley Winters; *Wounded Bear Mr. Smith,* Victor Jory; *Mike Lyons,* Don Collier; *Sergeant Rafferty,* Victor French; *Storekeeper,* Rodolfo Acosta; *Ann Looking Deer,* Susan Miranda; *Silver Dollar,* Anthony Caruso; *Steve Gray,* William Mims; *Larry Standing Elk,* Rudy Diaz; *She'll-Be-Back-Pretty-Soon,* Pedro Regas; *Luke Wolf,* John War Eagle; *Harris,* J. Edward McKinley; *Gus Kirk,* Robert Cleaves.

CREDITS: *Director,* Carol Reed; *producer,* Jerry Adler; *screenplay,* Clair Huffaker; based on his *novel* "Nobody Loves a Drunken Indian"; *music,* Marvin Hamlisch; *art director,* Mort Rabinowitz; *camera,* Fred J. Koenekamp; *editor,* Frank Bracht. Panavision and Technicolor. Running time: 106 minutes.

Playing the title role of Carol Reed's first American film (and a curious choice, working in slapstick comedy), Anthony Quinn conducts and manipulates the proceedings in a performance of sheer bravado. Flapping Eagle, his American Indian who foments a contemporary up-rising to assert the rights of his people, is light-years away from his Northern Cheyenne of *The Plainsman* or even the gentle Charley Eagle of *Black Gold.* Director Reed's lusty, brawling approach to the problems of the modern day red man, combined with his tragicomedy shift into social comment, compromised whatever serious and sympathetic intentions *Flap* might have had, and undoubtedly further wounded the sensibilities of the already super-maligned Indian, whose cause this picture supposedly was promoting.

Quinn's gusto interpretation of Flapping Eagle, certainly undertaken out of personal concern for the cause and admirably executed, divided the mainstream critics more than any of his performances in recent years, and the reviews of the film itself raised questions as to whether the various reviewers saw the same movie. Arthur Knight, writing in *The Saturday Review,* saw it as "an honest attempt to create sympathy for the Indians and certainly deserves far better than the second-class-citizen treatment that Warner Bros. has been giving it." And Howard Thompson, in *The New York Times,* found it "a movie about the bleak plight of to-day's American Indian that is as funny as it is moving,"

With Claude Akins, Victor Jory and Tony Bill

and felt that "it provides Anthony Quinn with his best role in several years." *Variety,* on the other hand, classified the film as "a pointless exercise in sound and fury ... broad, low and artless [in comedy], relieved at times by pretentious cardboard sociology. Of its star, the publication said: "Quinn's part as Flapping Eagle is simply an Indian reprise of his role in *The Secret of Santa Vittoria*—a boozing, wenching nonconformist who rises up against prevailing conditions." And in the *Daily News,* Kathleen Carroll noted in her one-star review that *"Flap* is witless, plodding" and "led by Anthony Quinn, blustering his way through as a one-man up-

rising, [the Indians] are all painted as silly clods." The headline over her review: "Flap Rates One Ugh!"

*Flap* was a $6,000,000 flop, made in early summer of 1969 in and around Albuquerque *(before* Quinn moved on to *R.P.M.),* and sat in Warner Bros.' vaults for nearly eighteen months before going into release.

A roguish Indian of majestic spirit, and something of a tribal revolutionary, Flapping Eagle (Quinn) determines to call attention to the despair and futility in which his people live. Taking time out from his normal pursuits of drinking rotgut with his cronies, whoring it up at the local brothel run by his on-and-off girlfriend, Dorothy Bluebell (Shelley Winters), and maintaining a running battle with the tribe's half-caste police sergeant Rafferty (Victor French), Flap decides that the next great Indian uprising will be a public-relations war to attract notice. In his fight for Red Power, he wrecks a bulldozer which has been disturbing a child and then hijacks a train, which he turns into a long, thin apartment house, justifying each action by old Indian treaties. All of this only involves him in a fight with Rafferty, who lands in the hospital, while Flap, with the police in pursuit, heads for the hills on his malevolent horse H-Bomb. High in the mountains, Flap manages to lasso a police helicopter, bringing it crashing down. Now fully a fugitive, he vows one final, bold move—the Last Great Indian Uprising: a peaceful march on Phoenix, which he claims for the Indian people under an old treaty. As he makes a speech outside City Hall, he is suddenly felled by a bullet from Rafferty's gun and dies in the arms of his friends.

With Pedro Regas and Claude Akins

# The City

Universal / 1971

As Thomas Jefferson Alcala

CAST: *Thomas Jefferson Alcala,* ANTHONY QUINN; *Sheridan Hugotor,* E. G. Marshall; *Sealy Graham,* Robert Reed; *Ira Groom,* Pat Hingle; *Holland Yermo,* John Larch; *Unknown Man,* Kaz Garas; *Sabina Menard,* Skye Aubrey; *Mrs. Lockney,* Peggy McCay; *Detective Loop,* Emanuel Smith; *Detective Kosse,* Paul Lees; *Señora Obregon,* Eulojia Rubio; *Mrs. Cintra,* Pablita Velarde Hardin; *Mrs. Cintra's Granddaughter,* Winona Margery Haury; *Ambulance Attendant,* Jim Smith; *Plainclothesman,* John F. Milholland; *Patrolmen,* Doyle Randall and Ed Pennybacker; *Mr. Fluvanna,* Phil Mead; *Droner,* Robert McCoy; *Motorcycle Policeman,* Thomas Dycus; *Mrs. Laboe,* Felicita C. Jojola; *Frank Nutwood,* Jose Rey Toledo; *Priest,* Ken Dunnagan; *Tram Operator,* Ben J. Abruzzo; *La La Lajilla,* Sue Ann Carpenter; *Bangi Fox,* James L. McConkey; *Virginia Fox,* Marjorie M. Sanford; *Cemetery Caretaker,* Victor A. Sarracino; *Bishop Martin Bremend,* W. Robert Stevens; *Mrs. Mantiguas,* Belle Abeytia; *Commune Hippie,* Scott Britt; and Judson Ford, Manuel J. Gallegos, Howard R. Kirk, James R. Eaton, Bud Conlan, Ross Elder, Syl Lamont, John Van Keuren, Jean Lienau.

CREDITS: *Director,* Daniel Petrie; *producer,* Frank Price; *screenplay,* Howard Rodman; *music,* Billy Goldenberg; *art director,* Howard E. Johnson; *camera,* Jack Marta; *editors,* Robert Watts and Larry Lester. Technicolor. Running time: 110 minutes.

Playing a rumpled, tough mayor of a contemporary southwestern city, fighting off the encroaching elements of technology, Anthony Quinn made a commanding figure of Thomas Jefferson Alcala, the pragmatic politician. The television series, *The Man and the City,* spun off from this feature and marked Quinn's return to the medium as an actor after sixteen years. For his portrayal of Alcala, both in the feature and in the subsequent short-lived series, Quinn received nothing but praise, followed by regrets that the material itself was really not worthy of its star. Of *The City, Variety* said: "Quinn dominated the show, giving his man sufficient depth and compassion beneath a tough-minded exterior

Premiered on ABC Television May 17, 1971.

to suggest that he could capture and sustain viewer interest [in the subsequent series] with his mayor. He is depicted as a man who genuinely cares for his city."

Thomas Alcala, who has been wrestling with the headaches of his ballooning city for sixteen years, is confronted in the upcoming election by a slick, youthful-looking opponent, Sealy Graham (Robert Reed), and is urged by his own campaign manager, Ira Groom (Pat Hingle), to change his rumpled image. Alcala, however, is too involved with more pressing problems than to pay heed to Groom: he's distraught over recent deaths of fellow university trustees and is facing death threats because of a land deal involving the use of university property for industrial parks. Refusing a bodyguard, he brazenly forges ahead, threatening his opponent if the land grant is made a political issue, making the rounds to see the needs of numerous old friends among the Indian community, and speaking to student rallies at the university. There, while waiting for Chancellor Sheridan Hugotor (E. G. Marshall), Alcala meets Sabina Menard (Skye Aubrey), a graduate student, who questions him about his sincerity and needles him into picking out a new suit. At the shopping center where Alcala has agreed to be outfitted by Sabina, a bomb scare clears the area. This threat is followed by a second involving the university's administration building.

Late that night, at City Hall, a lone repairman (Kaz Garas) rigs a bomb to the office elevator Alcala will enter in the morning. But when the mayor arrives, he impatiently bounds up the stairs rather than waiting for the elevator, which explodes when its doors close. The repairman, whose getaway car stalls, is killed, and it is then Alcala, outraged, decides to put up a real fight in the forthcoming elections—but as himself, not in the new image Ira Groom has been hoping to create.

# Across 110th Street

United Artists / 1972

CAST: *Captain Frank Mattelli,* ANTHONY QUINN; *Det. Lt. Pope,* YAPHET KOTTO; *Nick D'Salvio,* ANTHONY FRANCIOSA; *Jim Harris,* Paul Benjamin; *Joe Logart,* Ed Bernard; *Doc Johnson,* Richard Ward; *Gloria Roberts,* Norma Donaldson; *Henry J. Jackson,* Antonio Fargas; *Shevvy,* Gilbert Lewis; *Mrs. Jackson,* Marlene Warfield; *Lt. Reilly,* Nat Polen; *Lt. Hartnett,* Tim O'Connor; *Don Gennaro,* Frank Mascetta; *Chink,* Charles McGregor; *Mr. Jessup,* Joe Attles; *Mrs. Jessup,* Betty Haynes; and Frank Adu, Frank Aldrich, Frank Arno, Tina Beyer, Gerry Black, Samuel Blue, Jr., Alex Brown, Norman Bush, Anthony Cannon, Joe Canutt, Maria Carey, Anthony Charnota, Dick Crockett, Keith Davis, George DiCemzo, Joe Dismas, Brendan Fay, Joe Fields, Clebert Ford, Bernetta Fowler, Andrea Lynn Frierson, George Garro, Joseph George, Steve Gravers, Paul Harris, Dallas Edward Hayes, Jimmy Hayeson, Hilda Haynes, Gloria Hendry, Betty Howard, Pete Hock, Robert Jackson, Phil Kennedy, Nick La Padula, Al Leberfield, Ken Lynch, Ric Mancini, Charlene Mathies, Norman Matlock, Stephen Mendillo, Robert Sacchi, Janet Sarno, Thurman Scott, Eddie Smith, George Strus, Adam Wade, Marvin Walters, Arnold Williams, Mel Winkler, Burt Young.

CREDITS: *Director,* Barry Shear; *producers,* Ralph Serpe and Fouad Said; *executive producers,* Anthony Quinn and Barry Shear; *screenplay,* Luther Davis; based on the *novel* by Wally Ferris; *music,* J. J. Johnson; *songs,* J. J. Johnson and Bobby Womack; *art director,* Perry Watkins; *camera,* Jack Priestley; *editor,* Bryan Brandt. DeLuxe Color. Running time: 102 minutes.

As both executive co-producer and star of *Across 110th Street,* Quinn became involved in his first of the increasingly popular—and financially rewarding—genre of ultra-

With Marlene Warfield
and Yaphet Kotto

violent, profanity-laced, black-oriented gangster films. In an unsympathetic role as an old-line cop, on the take for years and ready to retire, Quinn gives a controlled, nicely shaded performance of a character not clearly defined by screenwriter Luther Davis. His Captain Frank Mattelli actually is part of the film's somewhat irrelevant subplot, dealing with the rivalry between two cops (opposite Yaphet Kotto as the younger, "clean," black lieutenant bucking for Quinn's job), while the police, the Mafia and the black syndicate each tries to track down the gang of hoods which knocked over a Harlem numbers bank. Quinn's fade-out death at the hands of a sniper and in the arms of Kotto seems a

rather convenient way for director Barry Shear to wrap up the proceedings while injecting still one further message with racial overtones. Critical comment on the film found the reviewers in opposite camps. *The New York Times'* Roger Greenspun was appalled that "it manages at once to be unfair to blacks, vicious towards whites, and insulting to anyone who feels that race relations might consist of something better than improvised genocide." Judith Crist, meanwhile, wrote in her *New York Magazine* critique: "You'll find no tougher, more brutal and, sad to realize, truer portrait of the way things are between cops and robbers—organized crime variety."

Disguised as cops, three black hoods, Jim Harris

With Gilbert Lewis, Yaphet Kotto
and Richard Ward

[ 241 ]

With players

(Paul Benjamin), Joe Logart (Ed Bernard) and Henry Jackson (Antonio Fargas), stick up a Harlem numbers bank and make off with $300,000 after killing five syndicate runners and two policemen. The New York City police and the Mafia react with instant concern. Tough police veteran Captain Frank Mattelli (Quinn) resents the intrusion of Lieutenant Pope (Kotto), a black detective, in the case, while Mafia boss Don Gennaro (Frank Mascetta) sends his paranoid son-in-law, Nick D'Salvio (Anthony Franciosa), to reassert control over the Harlem branch and see that the money is recovered. The black syndicate, headed by Doc Johnson (Richard Ward) and his assistant Shevvy (Gilbert Lewis), scorns D'Salvio, while promising only token help, and taunts Mattelli, who has been on the take from Johnson for years.

The robbers, meanwhile, have separated, with Harris leaving his girlfriend Gloria Roberts (Norma Donaldson), and holing up in a slum apartment; Logart returning to his job in a laundry; and Jackson back on the street looking for heroin. D'Salvio's men track Jackson down in a gaudy nightclub, and the sadistic Mafioso has him cut up and castrated. Enraged, Mattelli goes to Doc Johnson with a warning to be passed onto the Mafia, after learning the name of the leader of the crooks. D'Salvio, meanwhile, has grabbed Logart and extracted Harris's name from him under torture before dropping him from the top of a building. D'Salvio's men then follow Gloria as she rushes medicine to Harris, an epileptic, and, after killing the girl, they take off after Harris, who doubles back and guns them down.

Mattelli and Pope arrive at Harris's hideout with reinforcements as the crook retreats to the roof with his $300,000 cache. There, as Pope shoots him, Harris releases the money to the children in the ghetto yards below, as Shevvy, watching from another rooftop, shoots down Mattelli, who is no longer useful to the syndicate.

With Paul Benjamin (on ground)

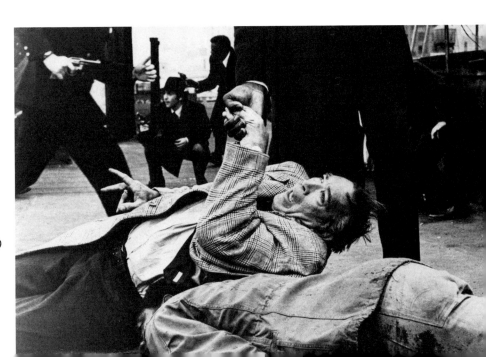

With Franco Nero

# Deaf Smith and Johnny Ears

Metro–Goldwyn–Mayer / 1973

CAST: *Erastus "Deaf" Smith,* ANTHONY QUINN; *Johnny Ears,* FRANCO NERO; *Susie,* PAMELA TIFFIN; *General Morton,* Franco Graziosi; *Hoffman,* Renato Romano; *Hester,* Ira Furstenberg; *Williams,* Adolfo Lastretti; *Senator,* Antonio Faa Di Bruno; *Mrs. Porter,* Francesca Benedetti; *Rosita,* Cristina Airoldi; *Logan,* Romano Puppo; *Bess,* Franca Sciutto; *Barrett,* Enrico Casadei; *James,* Lorenzo Fineschi; *Corey,* Mario Carra; *Moss,* Luciano Rossi; *Von Mittler,* Tom Trentini; *Colonel McDonald,* Renzo Moneta; and Giorgio Dolfin, Margherita Trentini, Fulvio Grimaldi, Paolo Pierani.

CREDITS: *Director,* Paolo Cavara; *producers,* Joseph Janni and Luciano Perugia; *screenplay,* Harry Essex, Oscar Saul, Paola Cavara, Lucia Drudi and Augusto Finocchi; *story,* Harry Essex and Oscar Saul; *music,* Daniele Patucchi; *art director,* Francesco Calabrese; *camera,* Tonino Delli Colli; *editor,* Mario Morra. Technicolor. Running time: 91 minutes.

Anthony Quinn's initial excursion into the "spaghetti Western" genre provided him with the role of a deaf-mute gunfighter who throws rocks at his buddy to capture his attention as they shoot and stumble their way through a mission to prevent a would-be dictator from taking Texas from President Sam Houston in 1834. Whether this ersatz adventure was aimed by director Paolo Cavara and his brigade of writers at emulating or lampooning a class of Italian-style, cowboy epic which Sergio Leone had refined into an art of sorts, the resultant production came close to killing off one of the Italian government's prime sources of motion picture income. The film, made for a mere $1,200,000, failed even to make back its costs, and *Variety* felt: "It's a mostly dull, occasionally ludicrous oater sorely lacking in the excessive violence or marquee voltage that might earn it an action-loving audience." Rex Reed dismissed the epic with this two-sentence notice: "Aside from a vague resemblance to those Marx Brothers comedies when Chico used to clobber Harpo with pie-plates, there is nothing to commend this paella Western. I hope they paid Mr. Quinn lots of money."

To date, Quinn is the foremost American star to participate in one of these on-the-cheap pseudo-Western westerns. (Clint Eastwood, Charles Bronson and various others *became* stars because of their work in these European-made overviews of the American frontier.) His role as the weatherbeaten, saddle-weary Erasmus

[ 243 ]

As Erastus Smith

Smith allowed him to mime a performance for the first time in his career and undoubtedly gave him a quick two-weeks' pay between assignments. In the opinion of the *Monthly Film Bulletin:* "Anthony Quinn wisely underplays a character whose dumbness seems more a contrivance to facilitate dubbing than a dramatic necessity."

Ex-Civil War hero and aging gunfighter, Erasmus (Deaf) Smith (Quinn), and his young saddle-mate, Johnny Ears (Franco Nero), bumming around trying to eke out livings as hired guns, are hired by agents of President Sam Houston to protect the Republic of Texas during its passage into the Union. While investigating the mass murder of the family of his old army commander, Colonel McDonald (Renzo Moneta), Smith identifies the chief political conspirator against the Republic as Morton (Franco Graziosi), a former general who, with German backing, is maintaining a secret fortified garrison from which he plans to assume dictatorship. In Austin, meanwhile, Ears has fallen for one of the local prostitutes, Susie (Pamela Tiffin), and is disinclined to help his friend. Smith infiltrates Morton's garrison alone, but is spotted and pursued while making off with dynamite from the well-stocked arsenal. Ears arrives in time to rescue his mute buddy, and together they succeed in decimating the entire garrison, then leave Texas with Susie in tow. During their first night on the trail Smith decides that his partnership with Ears is ended, and he steals away into the darkness.

With Franco Nero

# The Don Is Dead

Universal / 1973

CAST: *Don Angelo DiMorra,* ANTHONY QUINN; *Tony Fargo,* FREDERIC FORREST; *Frank Regabulto,* ROBERT FORSTER; *Vincent Fargo,* Al Lettieri; *Ruby Dunne,* Angel Tompkins; *Luigi Orlando,* Charles Cioffi; *Marie Orlando,* Jo Anne Meredith; *Don Aggimio Bernardo,* J. Duke Russo; *Mitch DiMorra,* Louis Zorich; *Johnny Tresca,* Anthony Charnota; *Nella Fargo,* Ina Balin; *Joe Lucci,* Joe Santos; *Giunta,* Frank de Kova; *Don Tolusso,* Abe Vigoda; *Augie the Horse,* Victor Orgo; *Pete Lazatti,* Val Bisoglio; *Mike Spada,* Robert Carricart; *Harold Early,* Frank Christi; *The Arab,* Sid Haig; *Corsican,* Maurice Sherbanee; *Vitto Rocobone,* George Skaff; *Ralph Negri,* Vic Tayback; *Mariano Longobardo,* Carlos Romero.

CREDITS: *Director,* Richard Fleischer; *producer,* Hal B. Wallis; *associate producer,* Paul Nathan; *screenplay,* Marvin H. Albert; based on the adaptation by Christopher Trumbo and Michael Philip Butler of the *novel* by Marvin H. Albert; *music,* Jerry Goldsmith; *art director,* Preston Ames; *camera,* Richard H. Kline; *editor,* Edward A. Biery. Technicolor. Running time: 115 minutes.

In his role of Don Angelo DiMorra, the aging Mafioso, Anthony Quinn has come, it seems, full circle. Enmeshed once again in gang warfare, asserting his power over the newcomers, he is updating the type of characterizations being done on the Paramount back-lot thirty-five years earlier. Only then J. Carrol Naish played the part of the crime czar and Quinn was one of the Young Turks. "Quinn," noted A. H. Weiler in his review in *The New York Times,* "is moodily menacing and as polished and relaxed as a professional long familiar with this sort of role." Rex Reed agreed, remarking that "Anthony Quinn, who should have played The Godfather, gets his chance and gnaws a hole through the screen. Right performance, wrong movie." *The Don Is Dead* fell into line of countless imitators of *The Godfather,* filled with action and gore while lacking the

With Robert Forster

With Angel Tompkins

originality, style, craftsmanship and credibility of its trend-setting prototype. Quinn's own low-key, very nearly subsidiary performance, while all around him are striving at top intensity and chewing up the scenery between gun battles, provides (along with the name of producer Hal B. Wallis) the contrived melodrama's sole distinction.

The story, about internecine warfare when Young Turks try to wrest control from the underworld establishment, falls apart when the highly organized syndicate is pictured as unraveling over a pretty nightclub singer, which, if believed, would place the Mafia in more trouble than any federal authorities could cause.

While Frank Regabulto (Robert Forster) and Tony Fargo (Frederic Forrest) are taking delivery of a heroin shipment in a deserted barn, masked hijackers burst in. Tony's brother, Vince (Al Lettieri), hidden in the hayloft as a precaution, guns down the intruders, and Frank bitterly complains of a leak in the operation despite careful planning. Returning to family headquarters, he receives the news that his father, the Don of the syndicate, is dead. At a gathering of the nation's twenty-four crime families, the aging Don Angelo DiMorra (Quinn) is chosen the new Don, but the Fargo brothers announce they'll go their own unaffiliated way. Don Aggimio Bernardo (J. Duke Russo), serving a prison sentence, is represented by his wily accountant, Luigi Orlando (Charles Cioffi), who becomes power-hungry and, with his wife Marie (Jo Anne Meredith), plots to take over the entire syndicate himself.

Using Frank's fiancée, singer Ruby Dunne (Angel

As Don Angelo DiMorra

Tompkins), as a wedge between the hotheaded Frank and the latter's godfather Don Angelo, Orlando creates an intolerable situation by arranging for Ruby to become Don Angelo's mistress while Frank is away on business and then leaking the information to the Don's heir apparent. Open warfare erupts when Frank sides with the independent Fargo brothers against both the DiMorra and Bernardo families.

Despite cool words from Mitch DiMorra (Louis Zorich), speaking as *consigliere* rather than as brother, Don Angelo refuses to believe that he is causing a family breach by turning on Frank because of a woman, but bullets from the various factions begin decimating the syndicate. When Mitch is captured by Tony Fargo, Don Angelo orders an all-out assault on Fargo's construction outfit from his Florida estate, where he's recovering from a heart attack. Word of his brother's death, however, causes Don Angelo to have a paralyzing stroke, and he is forced to watch helplessly as Don Aggimio, recently released from prison, cuts up the territory with Tony Fargo after Frank is killed in Sicily while making a connection, and Orlando is put out of the way by Don Aggimio's men.

With Frederic Forrest and Joe Santos

With Maurice Ronet

# The Destructors

American–International  /  1974

CAST:  *Johnny Deray*, MICHAEL CAINE; *Steve Ventura*, ANTHONY QUINN; *Jacques Brizard*, JAMES MASON; *Lucianne Brizard*, Maureen Kerwin; *Calmet*, Marcel Bozzufi; *Brizard's Mistress*, Catherine Rouvel; *Inspector Briac*, Maurice Ronet; *Rita Matthews*, Alexandra Stewart; *Henri*, Georges Lycan; *Kurt*, Jerry Brouer; *Inspector Marsac*, Van Doude; *Fred Williams*, Pierre Salinger; *Minieri*, Georges Beller; *Wilson*, Pierre Koulak; *Jo Kovakian*, Al Mancini; *Kevin Matthews*, Jonathan Brooks Poole; *Fournier*, Gib Grossac; *The Countess*, Hella Petri; *Lazar*, Vernon Dobtcheff; *Rouget*, Jean Bouchaud; *Matthews*, Robert Rondo; *Fortuit*, J. L. Fortuit; *Wilson*, Pierre Koulak; *Sally*, Barbara Sommers; *Janet*, Martine Kelly; *The Girl*, Danik Zurakowska; *Detective Fargas*, Ed Marcus; *Poker Players*, Alan Rosset, Bill Kearns, James Jones and Gene Moskowitz.

CREDITS:  *Director*, Robert Parrish; *producer*, Judd Bernard; *associate producer*, Patricia Casey; *screenplay*, Judd Bernard from his *story* "What Are Friends For?"; *music*, Roy Budd; *art director*, Willy Holt; *camera*, Douglas Slocombe; *editor*, Willy Kemplen. A Kettledrum Films/P.E.C.F. Production. Panavision and Color by Movielab. Running time: 89 minutes.

Quinn began his thirty-eighth year on the screen playing a tough, no-nonsense narcotics agent, draped in right-side-of-the-law respectability which comes with the

As Steve Ventura

[ 248 ]

superstardom that long before had been just a gleam in the eye of the prison-garbed actor who was knifed in his very first scene. As Steve Ventura, the world-weary undercover man working out of the U.S. Embassy in Paris, he has doggedly pursued an international narcotics ring, determined to bust its pipeline spanning the Atlantic. The job of exposing the chief of the operation, a politically well-guarded man named Brizard (James Mason), has been a flop and has cost the lives of three of Ventura's best agents. And to add to Ventura's frustrations, the Quai d'Orsay has been lodging strong official protests about the harassment by the Americans of Brizard, an important French citizen.

More helpful, however, is Police Inspector Briac (Maurice Ronet), who suggests to Ventura, strictly unofficially, that a man might be located who would be prepared, for a fee, to kill Brizard. The man Briac has in mind is a cool, ruthless, reliable marksman, a loner with an Algerian war background. To Ventura's aston-

With Michael Caine

ishment—and delight—Briac's man turns out to be Deray (Michael Caine), an old friend Ventura has not seen for ten years. There is genuine warmth and affection in their reunion, and Deray eagerly agrees to find and liquidate Brizard. After all, what are friends for?

Provided with false papers and a new name, Deray heads for Marseilles on his hard-kill mission, and there he quickly penetrates Brizard's operation by using his charms on the chief's attractive daughter Lucianne (Catherine Rouvel). Then, to gain Brizard's confidence, Deray cold-bloodedly kills an informer by throwing him from the top of a building. Deray is rewarded with a job inside the Brizard operation. Back in Paris, Ventura, tipped off that Brizard is about to take delivery of a large drug shipment from Turkey, decides he now wants Brizard taken alive so that the French can bust him with the haul. This means Deray must be stopped from carrying out his contract, but since he is working undercover and cannot be contacted, Ventura has Briac call the Marseilles police with orders to arrest Deray on phony bank robbery charges. Brizard, meanwhile, has learned that Deray is wanted and could prove an embarrassment with the narcotics shipment due. Sending Deray off on a decoy mission, Brizard then phones the police, who trap the undercover man near an old, unused Maginot Line bunker. Shooting it out with the police, Deray makes a spectacular getaway and returns to Marseilles as the hunted, rather than the hunter.

The police are now after Deray. So is Brizard, and, for that matter, so is Ventura, who finally reaches his old friend and hired killer. As Brizard and his men close in, Ventura and Deray dig in for the assault, and at the height of the shoot-out, Deray suddenly finds Brizard in his sights. As he is about to fire, he spots one of Brizard's men aiming at Ventura, and, in a split-second decision, Deray kills the sniper as Brizard cuts Deray down. As he dies in Ventura's arms, Deray appears to have a "Well, what are friends for?" look on his face. A grim Ventura, knowing that Brizard is still there, now takes on the hard kill himself, tracking the crime czar to a grand ball and, using a silencer, guns him down unnoticed in the throng of dancers.

With former Presidential press secretary Pierre Salinger and novelist James Jones

Most critical reports of *The Destructors* were decidedly downbeat. George McKinnon, reviewing in *The Boston Globe,* felt: "Three old pros walk disinterestedly—as well they might—through *The Destructors,* (and) the only interest in the film is watching the trio's acting techniques, and they are pretty mechanical, as if the performers knew they had gotten themselves into a piece of trash. Well, we must say, they seem to be trying [with] Quinn for once not overacting . . . [but] they should have saved this one for television." *Variety* labeled the film "a familiar underworld meller of modest commercial potential" and found the screenplay "a predictable, cliché-clotted blueprint that Robert Parrish directs with little style or imagination." The paper's critic decided that "Michael Caine, Anthony Quinn and James Mason supply some marquee luster but little thespic excitement . . . Nevertheless, the three stars are professional, [but] this film will have trouble making filmgoers care whether Quinn and hired killer Caine ever catch up with oily underworld leader Mason."

*The Independent Film Journal* considered it "fairto-middling drug melodrama with lots of action but much too much plot for the average viewer," and concluded that "both Caine and Quinn are clearly depending on their personalities to get them through, but in certain scenes they don't even seem to have the energy enough to turn the charm on."

# Other QUINN Films

## KING: A Filmed Record... Montgomery to Memphis (1970)   182 minutes.

Released by Maron Films Ltd. on behalf of the Martin Luther King Foundation.

*Directors,* Sidney Lumet and Joseph L. Mankiewicz; *producer,* Ely Landau.

Actors participating include Harry Belafonte, Charlton Heston, Paul Newman, Anthony Quinn, Joanne Woodward, James Earl Jones, Sidney Poitier, Burt Lancaster, Ruby Dee, Ben Gazzara and Clarence Williams III.

Academy Award nomination: Best Documentary of the Year.

## Arruza (1971)   73 minutes.

Churubusco Films (Mexico)/Alpha Company (U.S.A.)

*Producer/director/writer,* Budd Boetticher; *camera,* Lucien Ballard and Carlos Carabajal.

Anthony Quinn provided the off-screen narration for this documentary based on the exploits of the Mexican matador-rejoneador Carlos Arruza, filmed over a thirteen-year period (1953-1966).

## The Voice of La Raza (1972)   55 minutes.

Produced for the Equal Employment Opportunity Commission.

*Producer/director,* William Greaves; *writers,* William Greaves and Jose Garcia; *camera,* William Greaves and Jose Garcia; *music,* Vincent Sancedo; *editor,* John Dandre.

Anthony Quinn narrated and appeared as on-screen interviewer in film probing economic and cultural plight of Spanish-speaking people of the United States. Actress Rita Moreno also appeared to relate her childhood experiences in Manhattan's Puerto Rican community. (Filmed in 1970).

(*A Gentleman from Athens*): With Ethel Browning    (*Streetcar Named Desire*): With Peggy Rea and Mary Welch

# ANTHONY QUINN on the Stage

## Clean Beds

A drama in three acts by George S. George (Yovacca G. Satovsky).

*Produced by* Mae West and James Timony in association with Cled, Inc.; *Staged by* Vadim Uraneff.

Henry Hall (*Murrey*); Anthony Quinn (*Worth*); Esther Buckley (*Blowsy Mag*); George Del Rigo (*Kelcy*); Fifi Louise Hall (*Mrs. Murrey*); Pat Gleason (*Jack Letton*); Cash Durrell (*Donald Tabor*); James Welch (*Charlie*); William Hunter (*Callahan*); Gertrude Walker (*Daisy*).

James Timony's Hollytown Theatre, Los Angeles. Opened February 23, 1936.

## The Gentleman from Athens

A comedy in three acts by Emmet Lavery.

*Produced by* Martin Gosch in association with Eunice Healey; *Staged by* Sam Wanamaker.

Watson White (*Cousin Vincent Kilpatrick*); Ethel Browning (*Miss Mary Kilpatrick*); Alan Hewitt (*Morgan Kilpatrick*); Ethel Atwater (*Lee Kilpatrick*); Creighton Thompson (*Daniel*); Gavin Gordon (*Congressman Ed Lawrence*); Anthony Quinn (*Hon. Stephen Socrates Christopher*); Feodor Chaliapin (*Igor Stepanov*); Carleton S. Young (*Newsreel Director*); Lou Polan (*Mike Rykowski*); Leopold Badia (*Congressman Andrews*); Ed Lattimer (*Congressman Brogan*); Arthur Jarrett (*Congressman Harnell*); Elsie Mary Gordon (*Congresswoman Stringley*); Oliver Crawford, Leonard Auerbach (*Newsreel Crew*). enough to turn the charm on."

Mansfield Theatre, New York. December 9, 1947–December 13, 1947. (Opened six days after premiere of "A Streetcar Named Desire.")

Quinn also played the title role at the Ogunquit Playhouse in Maine during the week of August 9, 1948.

# A Streetcar Named Desire

By Tennessee Williams.

*Produced by* Irene Mayer Selznick; *Staged by* Harold Clurman.

Eulabelle Moore (*Negro Woman*); Peggy Rea (*Eunice Hubbel*); Anthony Quinn (*Stanley Kowalski*); Russell Hardie (*Harold Mitchell*); Mary Welch (*Stella Kowalski*); Uta Hagen (*Blanche DuBois*); Harry Kersey (*Steve Hubbel*); Arny Freeman (*Pablo Gonzales*); James Karen (*A Young Collector*); Sidonic Espero (*Mexican Woman*); Angela Jacobs (*A Strange Woman*); Arthur Row (*A Strange Man*).

National Company:

Ethel Barrymore Theatre, New York City, June 28, 1948
  (three weeks) (during summer hiatus of original Broadway company).

  Nixon Theatre, Pittsburgh. September 6, 1948
    (two weeks)
  Harris Theatre, Chicago. September 21, 1948
    (twenty-three weeks)
  Milwaukee, Wisconsin. February 28, 1949 (one week)
  Detroit, Michigan. March 7, 1949 (three weeks)
  Hanna Theatre, Cleveland. March 28, 1949
    (five weeks)
  *St. Paul, Minnesota. May 23, 1949 (one week)
  *Music Hall, Kansas City. June 8–11, 1949
  *Biltmore Theatre, Los Angeles. June 20, 1949
    (six weeks)
  *Geary Theatre, San Francisco. July 26, 1949
    (four weeks)
  Ethel Barrymore Theatre, New York City. August 29, 1949 (fifteen weeks)
  Locust Theatre, Philadelphia. December 26, 1949
    (three weeks)
  Plymouth Theatre, Boston. February 13, 1950
    (four weeks)

## A Streetcar Named Desire

By Tennessee Williams.

*Produced by* Irene Mayer Selznick; *Staged by* Elia Kazan.

---

*Judith Evelyn as Blanche DuBois.

(*Let Me Hear the Melody*): With Cloris Leachman and Melvyn Douglas

Eulabelle Moore (*Negro Woman*); Peggy Rea (*Eunice Hubbel*); Anthony Quinn (*Stanley Kowalski*); George Mathews (*Harold Mitchell*); Jorja Curtwright (*Stella Kowalski*); Uta Hagen (*Blanche DuBois*); Harry Kersey (*Steve Hubbel*); Arny Freeman (*Pablo Gonzales*); Wright King (*A Young Collector*); Edna Thomas (*Mexican Woman*); Angela Jacobs (*A Strange Woman*); Arthur Row (*A Strange Man*).

New York City Center. May 23, 1950–June 11, 1950.

## Borned In Texas*

"A fairy tale" in three acts by Lynn Riggs.

*Produced by the* Festival Theatre (Sam Wanamaker, Terese Hayden and Harriet Ames); *Staged by* Sam Wanamaker.

Frank Tweddell (*Pop Radar*); Clifford Carpenter (*Buzzy Hale*); Marsha Hunt (*Hannie*); Martin Newman (*Red Ike*); Wright King (*Black Ike*); Anthony Quinn (*Texas*); Joseph Boland (*Marshall*); Dudley Sadler (*Neb*); Daniel Reed (*Judge*); Jane Hoffman (*Mrs. Foster*).

Fulton Theatre, New York. August 21, 1950–August 26, 1950.

## Let Me Hear the Melody

A comedy in three acts by S. N. Behrman.

---

*Staged in 1930 as *Roadside*.

*Produced by* Harold Clurman and Walter Fried; *Staged by* Burgess Meredith.

Mary Welch (*Liza*); Melvyn Douglas (*Sayre Nolan*)\*; Cloris Leachman (*Esme Smith*); Evelyn Davis (*Brenda*); Mike Kellin (*Vincent Bendix*); Morris Carnovsky (*Sig Ratchett*); Anthony Quinn (*Alvin Connors*); J. Edward Bromberg (*Manny Korvin*).

Opened Wilmington, Delaware, March 9, 1951; closed Philadelphia, March 24, 1951.

# Becket

A play by Jean Anouilh.

*Translated by* Lucienne Hill; *Produced by* David Merrick; *Staged by* Peter Glenville.

Anthony Quinn (*Henry II, Duke of Normandy and King of England*); Robert Duke (*Henry's Page*); Laurence Olivier (*Thomas Becket*); Sydney Walker (*The Archbishop of Canterbury*); Will Hussung (*The Bishop of Oxford*); Earl Montgomery (*Gilbert Folliot, Bishop of London*); Victor Thorley (*The Bishop of York*); Robert Weil (*A Saxon Peasant*); Hilary Beckett (*His Daughter*); Tom Leith (*His Son*); Dran Seitz (*Gwendolen*); Louis Zorich (*1st English Baron*); Ronald Weyand (*2nd English Baron*); Mel Berger (*3rd English*

_____

\*Replaced Franchot Tone.

(*Becket*): With Laurence Olivier

*Baron*); Ferdi Hoffman (*4th English Baron*); Madeline Morgan (*A French Girl*); Claude Woolman (*A Soldier*); Brian Crowe (*A Young Monk*); Victor Thorley (*The Provost Marshall*); Dino Terranova (*A French Priest*); Will Hussung (*William of Corbeil*); Peter De Firis (*A Servant*); Julian Miller (*2nd Servant*); Marie Powers (*The Queen Mother*); Margaret Hall (*The Queen, Wife to Henry*); Dennis Rosa (*Henry's Elder Son*); Kit Culkin (*Henry's Younger Son*); Tom Leith (*A Monk, Secretary to Becket*); Mel Berger (*1st Monk from Hastings*); Ronald Weyand (*2nd Monk from Hastings*); Robert Eckles (*Louis, King of France*); Will Hussung (*1st French Baron*); Sydney Walker (*2nd French Baron*); Claude Woolman (*The Duke of Arundel*); Edward Atienza (*The Pope*); Dino Terranova (*Cardinal Zambelli*); Louis Zorich (*An Old Footsoldier*); Julian Miller (*A Young Footsoldier*); Sydney Walker (*A Priest*).

St. James Theatre, New York. October 5, 1960–March 25, 1961.

# Tchin-Tchin

*A play by* Sidney Michaels; *Based on a play by* François Billetdoux; *Produced by* David Merrick; *Staged by* Peter Glenville.

Margaret Leighton (*Pamela Pew-Pickett*); Anthony Quinn (*Caesario Grimaldi*); Charles Gordon (*Robert Pickett*); Jean Barker, Sandy Baron (*A Multitude of People*).

Plymouth Theatre, New York. October 25, 1962– April 21, 1963\*.

_____

\*Leighton and Quinn replaced by Arlene Francis and Jack Klugman.

(*Tchin-Tchin*): With Margaret Leighton

[ 253 ]

("*Philco Playhouse*"): In "Pride's Castle" with Catherine McLeod and Louise Allbritton (1949)

# ANTHONY QUINN on Television

PHILCO PLAYHOUSE. NBC, September 11, 1949. "Pride's Castle" with Catherine McLeod, Louise Allbritton, Boyd Crawford, Loring Smith, Clyde Waddell, Bethel Leslie, Jack Lemmon, Patrick Malone. Quinn starred as Pride Dawson in adaptation of Frank Yerby's best-seller.

LIGHTS OUT. NBC, February 5, 1951. "House of Dust" with Nina Foch. Written by A. J. Russell.

FORD THEATER. CBS, April 6, 1951. "Ticket to Oblivion" with Signe Hasso. Wartime thriller with Quinn as an American correspondent who infiltrates the French underground. Franklin Schaffner directed.

DANGER. CBS, April 24, 1951. "Blue Murder" with Coleen Gray. Mystery directed by Yul Brynner (whom Quinn later directed in *The Buccaneer*). Martin Ritt was the producer.

SCHLITZ PLAYHOUSE OF STARS. CBS, December 21, 1951. "Dark Fleece" with Helen Hayes and Carmen Mathews. Drama by Joseph Hergescheimer, produced and directed by William Brown, Jr.

SCHLITZ PLAYHOUSE OF STARS. CBS, November 19, 1954. "The Long Trail" with John Bryant, Robert Armstrong, Maxine Cooper, Hugh Sanders, Steve Darrell. Western drama with Quinn as a Texas Ranger encountering strong community oppositon in at-tempting to extradite a murder suspect from the Oregon Territory. Directed by Jus Addiss.

SCHLITZ PLAYHOUSE OF STARS. CBS, October 7, 1955. "Bandit's Hideout" with Gloria Saunders, Eduard Franz, Kem Dibbs, James Waring. Quinn starred as a gentle Spanish shepherd who resorts to violence when he discovers that his cousin has run off with his (Quinn's) wife and herd. Roy Kellino directed.

PERSON TO PERSON with EDWARD R. MURROW. CBS, May 2, 1958.

THE ED SULLIVAN SHOW. CBS, April 27, 1963.

KRAFT MUSIC HALL PRESENTS MR. ANTHONY QUINN AND MISS PEGGY LEE. NBC, September 23, 1970.

ABC MOVIE OF THE WEEK: THE CITY. ABC, May 17, 1971. (see filmography)

THE MAN AND THE CITY (series). ABC, September 17, 1971–January 5, 1972.

THE DICK CAVETT SHOW: 90 MINUTES WITH ANTHONY QUINN. ABC, October 12, 1971.

THE MERV GRIFFIN SHOW: SALUTE TO STANLEY KRAMER. CBS, October 18, 1971.

THE MIKE DOUGLAS SHOW. As Co-Host. Week of January 22, 1973.

(*"Schlitz"*): In "The Long Trail" (1954)

(*"Schlitz"*): In "Bandit's Hideout" with Eduard Franz (1955)

(*"Person to Person"*): With Katherine DeMille (1958)

(*"Kraft Music Hall"*): With Peggy Lee (1970)

## About the Author

ALVIN H. MARILL is a lifelong cinema student and credit-watcher. In his home town of Brockton, Massachusetts, he had the distinction of attending the closing performances of four of the city's six movie houses and was a spectator when another burned to the ground. A graduate of Boston University, he has been a writer-producer in broadcasting, both in Boston and New York, was an arts critic for the Quincy (Massachusetts) *Patriot-Ledger,* and has reviewed films for Radio New York Worldwide. Now a free-lance writer in New York, he is a frequent contributor to a number of serious cinema publications and is author of *The Cinema of Edward G. Robinson* (with James Robert Parish), *Samuel Goldwyn Presents,* and *Katharine Hepburn* (Pyramid Illustrated History of the Movies). Mr. Marill lives in New Jersey with his wife and two sons.